'I had the doubtful pleasure of being cross-examined by Chester. That experience is rather like having your throat cut: quietly, courteously and swiftly . . .'
Peter Clyne

'The first day in court Chester reminded me of a cheeky, bright-eyed sparrow with eyes and ears everywhere.'
Lindy Chamberlain

'*Walking on Water* is (not just) the kind of good read you should expect from an outstanding senior counsel.'
*Law Society Journal*

'All young persons contemplating a life in the law as a career should read this book.'
*Australian Book Review*

'These memoirs should be a prescribed text for legal studies in schools and police academies. Members of parliament might learn a thing or two as well!'
*The Weekend Australian*

'We should all read *Walking on Water* and be better educated, and no one should embark on litigation before they have done so. By the time they lay the volume down, they will have cooled off, left their solicitor untelephoned, saved themselves a bucket of money and averted a heart attack.'
*Australian Book Review*

'The value of this melange of biography, anecdote and ruminations lies in its rarity . . . Then as now, Porter did not flinch from revelation. We need more books that reveal more about the law and those who practise it.'
*The Sydney Morning Herald*

# CHESTER PORTER

**WALKING ON WATER:**
*A Life in the Law*

RANDOM HOUSE AUSTRALIA

Every effort has been made to identify individual photographers and
copyright holders. The publishers would be pleased to hear from
any copyright holders who have not been acknowledged.

Random House Australia Pty Ltd
20 Alfred Street, Milsons Point, NSW 2061
http://www.randomhouse.com.au

Sydney   New York   Toronto
London   Auckland   Johannesburg

First published by Random House Australia 2003
This paperback edition published by Random House Australia 2004

National Library of Australia
Cataloguing-in-Publication Entry

Porter, Chester, 1926-.
 Walking on water: a life in the law.

  ISBN 1 74051 274 X.

  1. Porter, Chester, 1926- . 2. Lawyers - Australia -
 Biography. I. Title.


 345.940092

Cover design by Darian Causby/Highway 51
Typeset by Midland Typesetters, Maryborough, Victoria
Printed and bound by Griffin Press, Netley, South Australia

10 9 8 7 6 5 4 3 2 1

*To my dear Jean*

# Contents

# Tribute

Chester Porter is sincere in his convictions and has always had a passionate concern for the poor and underprivileged.

His life in the law began in 1948 and he was in practice until June 2000. He learnt much as junior counsel to Mr J.W. Shand KC in the McDermott Royal Commission, which began in 1951.

In 1983 he was badly injured in a motor accident. This had a marked influence on his career because it changed his life. After the accident he was retained to act for two policemen charged with corruption, and in these proceedings he gave one of his best-ever addresses to the jury. Through his own suffering he had discovered a new power and thereafter became a criminal-law specialist.

There are many celebrated trials and inquiries with which he was involved, especially the Roger Rogerson, Judge John Foord and Lindy Chamberlain matters. These cases express the spirit by which Chester Porter approached all of his briefs – with weight and dignity.

Chester analysed every case deeply, isolating the agate point on which the case turned. He methodically kept abreast of legal developments. He became, using Sir Robert Menzies' phrase 'a well-furnished lawyer'.

In *Walking on Water: A Life in the Law* we see Chester Porter's wide-ranging intellect, his resolve and the elevation of his views, which disclose a truly remarkable man. We are fortunate to have the very valuable observations of the practice of law and on human nature from Chester Porter QC because the reflections of leading advocates are rare indeed.

R.W.R. Parker QC
2003

# I

# Before my Admission
# to the Bar

I was born on 15 March 1926. From my first memories I loved animals, and when I was old enough to realise that men had to earn a living I wanted to be a farmer. Such an ambition was beyond my parents' means, and my mother was right in distinguishing my future hobbies from my future profession. My father was a self-made accountant and he had achieved this by very hard work. His father was a small-scale farmer at Marsfield (about where Macquarie University is located now) but it was not a very successful enterprise.

My mother was from a Jewish family by the name of Leefson, although she became an Anglican quite early in her life. She was a very shrewd woman and to her I largely owe the wise choice of a profession. My father had wanted to be a lawyer but circumstances prevented this. My mother fancied that I had the talent to be a barrister, a suggestion I readily adopted when I was about 11 or 12 years of age. I hardly ever swerved from this ambition thereafter. By my final year at school, 1942, I was longing to study law and become a barrister, complete with wig and gown. I had the encouragement and help of both my parents.

I completed my final four years of high school at Shore, three of them on a scholarship – the Open Entrance Scholarship – which by chance in 1938 had few contestants. I was lucky. Shore is a well-known Anglican School which I reached after attending various private schools. Firstly at the age of four-and-a-half I, with quite a number of other little boys, attended Roseville Girls College, a private school, then very small and now quite large. Then, but not now, it accepted boys in the kindergarten. I had no sisters so the experience was quite an adventure. The teaching was excellent and I was reading easily at a very early age.

Next I was a boarder at Mowbray House School, a small private school which closed soon after the Second World War. Subsequently I boarded at Barker College, back then a small Anglican school.

In comparison, Shore was quite large when I enrolled at the beginning of 1939. Seeing schools now I marvel at the halls, gyms and other facilities. My grandchildren seem to be educated in the lap of luxury. Even in private schools there was not much luxury about in the depression and war years when I was at school. I was well taught, but I did not enjoy school life much at any school. It was probably my fault. Free speech got me into quite a lot of trouble. I was in far more fights than most boys, and my opponents were almost invariably bigger and better fighters than me. But I survived. I was captain of Shore's debating team and received much useful coaching in this skill from the masters.

While I was at school in my final year I became a naval bomb spotter. We had a little post (which is still there) at Ball's Point and our job was to take a bearing on any magnetic mine dropped by enemy planes in Sydney Harbour. Other spotters would do the same from different posts on the harbour and the point of intersection of the bearings would be the location of the mine for treatment by the navy. No mines were ever dropped, in fact, but we practised with a plane dropping flares. The particular plane was an American Kittyhawk, and the pilot flew his plane under the Harbour Bridge, one of several occasions when this stunt was performed during the war. This was in 1943 after I left school. It was quite a spectacle.

It is nearly 60 years ago now that I had my first view of a court in action. I was only 16 years of age and was a clerk waiting to be an articled clerk to a solicitor. For this I had to reach the age of 17.

Since it had been my ambition to be a barrister almost since my age reached double figures, I longed to see a court in action. What an anti-climax it turned out to be! Two black-gowned bewigged figures appeared before a judge of the District Court to argue about leave to enforce a mortgage under the Moratorium Act. This was no murder case or even a divorce fight. It was just plain boring to me then. I felt like giving up all my ambitions. However, after a few days I got over it but had to appreciate that court cases had their degrees of interest, particularly for a very young man.

I was lucky when someone decided not to accept their University Exhibition Scholarship (there were 100 of these means-free scholarships available for New South Wales) and I was next in line and obtained it instead.

In those days, I needed a Latin pass to matriculate in law and I had to be 17 years of age to enrol in the Faculty of Law at Sydney University. For some reason Sydney University started its year much later than usual in 1943 and so I reached my 17th birthday on 15 March without the term having started. Thus I saved a year and when I was admitted to practise on 12 March 1948 I was still 21 years of age, and one of the youngest barristers ever admitted.

I enjoyed Sydney University. At first I was in a very small year of about 22 students, most of us under 18 and hence unable to enlist in the Second World War. I remember Neville Wran who, being about six months younger than me, could not start law but was doing an arts degree. Very early in his career he showed that he was a good organiser and produced one of the best university revues ever. I had met him in a school debate when we captained rival teams and his team won. He was a very vigorous debater.

I won the Pitt Cobbett Prize for Constitutional Law in my first year of law. The prize was five pounds, which was a lot to an articled clerk from Dawson Waldron Edwards and Nicholls doing lectures in the early morning and late afternoon, and earning only one pound per week for five days plus half a day on Saturday. (Saturday work was rather a waste of everyone's time, even some years before it went out of fashion. I remember in my first year at the bar in 1948 coming in to join the enthusiastic few who still worked on Saturday mornings. Most of the time was spent in a coffee shop discussing how necessary it was to work on Saturday mornings.)

The articled clerks where I worked were given generous time off to study for their exams at the end of the year. I studied so long and so hard that I found it hard to concentrate in my first exam, which was Contracts. After I had this problem my father encouraged me to have one day off per week, even in stu vac, naturally in those days Sunday, and I confined my study to no more than eight hours per day. As a chartered accountant Dad had a brilliant brain and a quick mind, and could concentrate very efficiently. I inherited at least this last quality and learned from him that one has an efficient working span. Consistently working beyond one's proper span is eventually inefficient. Thereafter I studied accordingly.

The size of our year in the Faculty of Law grew as people returned from the war. One notable addition to the student body was Gough Whitlam, then as now a charming, amiable person of great ability. We were on opposite sides of politics but that did not prevent us having a very friendly relationship. He called me a 'young Tory' and we had quite a few political discussions. He was a genuine person in his politics, not just aiming to get ahead but with fine ideals and a real program for reform. I hope history will be kind to Gough. He was kind to a lot of people, including me.

Eventually I passed all my law exams and, very much to my surprise, I was awarded first-class honours. The year was quite a substantial one by the time we finished in 1946 but nevertheless it seemed to me that awarding eight first-class honours was generous. I was number seven.

After graduating I had to do another year as an articled clerk, but I was an independent person and did not like being an employee. I was very anxious to go to the bar.

I was debating every week in the University Union Night where I was moderately successful. Although I had captained team debating at Shore and had done quite a bit of team debating at university, it did not appeal as much as parliamentary debating at Union Night. I was probably a better adjudicator than debater and for some years after graduation I was on the Inter-Varsity Debates Selection Committee with John Watson (later Dr John Watson) and Betty Archdale, the head of the Women's College (later a famous head of Abbotsleigh Girls School). Betty was an extremely friendly person, and I always got on well with Johnny Watson. We managed to achieve consensus in all our decisions save for Betty's remarkable marking system. Her top mark was around 30 to 40 per cent. She laughed at herself over this. However it was perfectly fair, applicable to all speakers, and her assessments or orders of merit were consistent with ours. It was strange at times when we were on joint adjudication to hear her say, 'That was a very good speech; I'm going to give him 35 per cent.'

By and large my university days were one of the happy periods of my life. I had been too independent to enjoy my final years at school much, but I found the marvellous exchange of ideas at the University of Sydney exhilarating.

I was also fortunate to have a lady friend, Val Step, a fellow student two years ahead of me. We often studied together in the public library, and one of our favourite haunts on a Saturday afternoon was Taronga Park Zoo. Animals have provided an interest different from the law over the years. As a result my wife, Jean, a science teacher, has accompanied me to many zoos overseas – London, Chester, Paris, Amsterdam, Frankfurt, Stockholm, Jersey, Helsinki, Copenhagen, Zurich, New York, San Diego, New Orleans, Jerusalem, Tel Aviv, Haifa, Vienna, Honolulu, Rome. (What Australian has bothered to see Rome Zoo? I have seen it twice, but it was disappointing, although much improved the second time.)

I asked to cut a few weeks off the last year of my five years of articles and my master solicitor, Mr M.W.D. McIntyre, permitted me to do this, despite advising me strongly against it. I went ahead nevertheless and was admitted on 12 March 1948, a few days before my 22nd birthday, to practise as a barrister.

The ceremony involved in being admitted to the bar is a great occasion for those involved. The proposed barrister's name is stated by his mover at the bar table, and the Chief Justice presiding over a court of three judges asks each new barrister, 'Do you move?' ('Move' means to propose some motion or application to the court and the question at admissions is a traditional formality.) The new barrister simply bows. I was never good at ceremonials and I stumbled but I doubt whether Sir Frederick Jordan CJ alias 'Frosty Freddie', noticed anything amiss.

After the ceremony my brother Hal noticed that I had failed to remove the price tag from my gown and it was wobbling around in a prominent position on my back.

My wig was a present from my mother. I had read that this was the gift Sir Isaac Isaacs' mother had given to him when he was admitted, and I thought the story was worth telling to my proud parents.

I went to the bar so early, against the advices of those who knew better and were perhaps right. However I was very anxious to start my career, and I was not happy as an employee. I had been well treated but I did not like being subject to orders.

Looking back, what I did was a somewhat reckless burning of bridges behind me. Had I finished my articles, and I only had a few weeks to go, I could have been admitted as either a solicitor or a barrister. Not having finished my articles I could only be admitted as a barrister. Had I failed as a barrister I could not easily have fallen back to being a solicitor.

As time went by I gradually lost the excuses of youth and inexperience along with the nickname 'young Chester' that clung to me for many years.

I did not fail in the end, but in the first couple of years it was a near thing.

# 2

# Starting at the Bar

Like most barristers, I have read the success stories of other barristers. In no time other barristers were acting in leading cases in the highest courts of the land. Such stories are the exception rather than the rule. The bar is usually a hard life to begin with and young barristers have been referred to as 'the starving army'.

In this profession most of the time someone is trying to prove that your advice is wrong and/or your case should fail. According to the law of averages, settlements apart, failure is likely in 50 per cent of contested cases. Some barristers spread stories of winning 30 or more cases in succession and perhaps some clients, and even solicitors, believe them. No barrister would.

Alan Jenkins, an amiable, able, and older barrister said to me when I started, 'In this game, Chester, there will be times when you walk on the clouds, and there will be others when you walk in deep despair.' Winning or losing a case is not just a question of one's ego. Good barristers have hearts, and many feel the joys and disappointments of their clients. Specialisation tends to make counsel more detached, especially in family law, because their feelings become hardened to the same types of misfortune day after day, but good counsel often feel the stress of their clients, sharing the exhilaration of victory and the disappointment of defeat. Yet to be a good advocate it is necessary to remain detached. One should never lose self control; one should never become blind to the dangers of litigation.

I came up through the police courts, on low fees and for humble clients. I left my admission ceremony to return to my room in the basement of Denman Chambers, which I shared with Trevor Martin (later Judge Martin QC) and Jack Walton, who later left the bar and became a solicitor. Trevor and Jack mainly used the room as a depot rather than for interviews or study. They found it too depressing. Indeed, the room would have been depressing to most people. It was dark and dank; the wall actually leaked and there was dust everywhere. Those were the good old days when barristers chambers were gloomy and Dickensian, when rents were low and overheads were also low, when many of our advices were in longhand, and we could struggle on if briefs failed to arrive.

Gloomy and overcrowded as our chambers were, I was lucky indeed in 1948 to find any chambers at all, because there was a great shortage. My companions in these chambers were good natured and friendly and we were all patient with each other, despite the surroundings.

I had plenty of time and with my brother Hal's help I managed to improve our room in chambers with painting, cleaning and some furniture. In my latter five years in Denman Chambers I had the room done up professionally and shared with Mick Boulter (later Judge Boulter QC). We each had by then busy practices and so holding conferences at the same time and generally fitting in with each other became exercises in patience. We became very good friends, and in fact I cannot remember any real dispute between us despite working in such close proximity over some years. Since he was older and I was probably more irritating, I realise now what a good-natured person he was. Sharing chambers had its compensation in good company, but the bar is a profession that demands privacy. The postwar chamber shortage that required sharing tried sorely all who did so. Even now I have bad dreams of being forced to practise in half a room! Still, it made us all tolerant and self-controlled, and I remained good friends with Trevor Martin and Mick Boulter for the rest of their lives.

I stayed there until 1963, for some years at the end being on my own. When I left my room in chambers my father said, 'Never sneer at a good business in cheap premises'. How right he was!

I remember the first barristers chambers I ever saw, in about 1946 or 1947, those of C.M. Collins, a counsel of some reputation. Piles of papers were everywhere, and clouds of dust frequently rose when the wrong pile was roughly disturbed. But 'Cliff' Collins knew precisely where every paper was, or so it was said, and so it seemed to me.

It was around the late 1950s that barristers started to make their chambers beautiful and expensive. New buildings were constructed and by the time I moved into Selborne Chambers in 1963 where I remained until I retired in July 2000, the last of the old-style rooms were gone. Expensive typists or secretaries were employed; expensive desks, furniture and equipment were obtained; ornaments were everywhere. No longer could a Mr Pickwick seek comfort in the dark room of a Sergeant Snubbin.

I slugged out many a 'backyarder'; that is, a quarrel between neighbours resulting in some minor charge. I also acted for many a fighting husband or wife in the days when everything depended on fault.

This reminds me of a moment in the early 1950s. I was in a hotel after appearing in court for a battling husband in his umpteenth court fight with his equally aggressive wife. They fought in the Manly Petty Sessions Court every few months in order to establish the necessary fault, but they stayed together.

'Why did you marry her?' I asked my client.

'It was the end of the First World War, I took leave in London and I drank all the booze I could get. Next morning I woke up married to her!'

This story seemed to me to have its legal difficulties, but he maintained its truth. Then why no divorce? They apparently believed in a fight to the finish.

But even this type of litigation came very slowly to a youthful beginner at the bar. I had no legal connections to provide me with regular work. The firm where I had served my·articles did not support me because I had gone to the bar contrary to their advice. My father got me a few briefs examining judgment debtors, but by and large I was only briefed when there was no one else around, and my fees were low enough to satisfy the most parsimonious anti-lawyer. On two occasions I went for a whole fortnight without receiving a letter, a visit or a phone call. It was, to say the least, demoralising.

From my final year of articles I was self-supporting in the sense that I paid all my own expenses plus a modest board to my parents for food and accommodation. I only had myself to support until May 1953 when I married Jean.

Coaching fees helped to supplement my very small fees for advocacy. The rent of our basement room was quite nominal and my expenses at work were minimal. My needs were small and the cost of living in those days was relatively low. What was depressing were the occasional long gaps between briefs. I could not help but wonder whether I would ever have another brief, particularly if I had recently lost a case, as I often did. I had to put up with many humiliations, and many depressing periods of inactivity. There were, at times, moments of black despair. But I survived.

During these periods I was often able to do some useful study of the law. I discovered, at last, that a degree only entitles the graduate to go into the workplace and blunder. There was much to be learned after graduation. Only the learning was the hard way, the fool's way, by experience.

Soon after I came to the bar in 1948 I joined a couple of Rostrum clubs. There I learned a lot more about public speaking and made many good friends. A Rostrum meeting comprised people who were quite similar to a typical jury. Through Rostrum I not merely learned to improve my speaking, but I learned much more about how other people think. (Later, I became a Rostrum Critic, a Rostrum Freeman and, in 1986, Rostrum Speaker of the Year. Most important, however, were the many good friends I made in Rostrum and the many interesting ideas I heard.)

This helped me to learn that the secret of persuasive advocacy is to understand how your tribunal is thinking, and to adjust your arguments accordingly.

I built up a very small practice as a third- or fourth-reserve counsel. This meant that if two or three barristers were not available I was called in. This happened because the police courts were overcrowded with work. Then the coal strike of 1949 put lots of people out of work, cases stopped being contested in the police courts, and I had no practice again. It was not pleasant.

Gradually I got together a following. This was largely through coaching students in solicitors' exams and obtaining briefs through my pupils who were articled clerks and able to steer briefs my way. I was quite a good coach and I learned a lot of law myself that way. One of my achievements was to write an explanation of 'Limitations of Real Property under Old System Title' which for a while was used by many students as a short cut to understanding this area of the law. It spread far beyond my pupils. In fact, it was quite a good exposition of a difficult topic that is now substantially obsolete.

I had classes of as many as four pupils at once and we became good friends, then and later. Through coaching I met Jim Deane, Nick Marcells and Nick Cassim, all of whom supported me over many years at the bar. Through Nick Marcells I met Jack Stamell who was a great Australian-Greek solicitor for whom I came to do many big shop-tenancy cases.

Also through coaching I met Sid Hertz, a generous character who became a friend until his death in the 1980s. Through Sid I met Gordon Beard who was a loyal supporter of me and a very able solicitor. Gordon became my personal solicitor. His partner, Tony McDonald, instructed me in the second *Voyager* Royal Commission. Gordon's previous partner, Bill Mowbray, gave me many briefs in the courts at Wollongong.

There were others I coached; one in particular, John North, practised at Dubbo. He was a close friend and through him I had quite a few briefs from the west. John lived a very unselfish life and did a great deal for his clients and his family. He died some years ago. His son, also called John North, became president of the New South Wales Law Society.

My first jury case came as a result of my following the advice of the late Jock McClemens – a vigorous advocate and a shrewd and humane judge – to 'always be there'. I was in chambers at about 6.30 p.m. one evening when Ken Wild of the Public Solicitor's Office was looking for a counsel for the next day. An old lady pensioner had fallen off a Bondi tram, she claimed because it had failed to stop at a prescribed stopping place. Her injuries were painful but not serious. Under the Legal Assistance Act I was only to be paid if I won (all Legal Aid advices by counsel were free then).

The old lady's story was not improbable. There was some substance in the old saying 'shot through like a Bondi tram'. It was her word against the tram driver and the conductor. In these cases the conductor always happened to see the accident and gave evidence that the driver was without fault. However, in this case an independent witness, not in tramways uniform, gave evidence to support both the driver and the conductor.

I had noticed that this witness had not been asked for his occupation as well as his address, which was the usual procedure. I therefore asked him what his occupation was and he reluctantly said 'tram conductor' and of course I addressed the jury with all the enthusiasm of youth – starving youth perhaps – about the deception which I said had been attempted by the defendant to put this man forward as an independent witness. We won and my client received a damages verdict of £250, a large sum for her, being 50 times more than the basic wage then. It was my first real triumph and my client's windfall.

Ken Wild said at the time that I was either clever or lucky, and I received many a brief from him. Some years later he went to the Crown Solicitor's Office where he introduced me to government work, of which, over the years, I did a great deal.

As a result I also gave many free advices to the Public Solicitor's Office. Many of these were handwritten, and most were correct. One I well remember was regarding a young Aboriginal girl who had just got married. In the past the Aboriginal Welfare Board had taken a large part of her wages and kept them in trust for her. The legal problem was that when she married she applied to the board for money to buy furniture and they duly doled it out, but made a book-keeping error and paid her too much – quite a lot too much. Now they wanted the excess back.

It is hard to believe now how badly Aboriginal people were patronised, and supervised, allegedly for their own good. What white girl in her teens would like her wages taken away for her own good? I was enraged.

As a labour of love I combed the law books and finally raised a defence of equitable estoppel, being in effect conduct on the part of the board making it inequitable or unfair for the girl to have to refund the money. In broad terms, she had spent it and would probably have had to sell furniture at a sacrificial price to raise the sum required. I was prepared to fight the case through the courts for nothing, but the board gave in. Perhaps it was not unarguable law, but it was justice.

The attitude to Aborigines in the early 1950s was changing and many young barristers took up the Aboriginal causes in various cases. One in particular was my room-mate Trevor Martin. Pre-war, the well-meaning ideas were that indigenous peoples had to be protected; they could not be allowed to drink alcohol, they should live in reserves that were carefully guarded (especially against agitating white people), and they were unfit to keep their wages, which had to be held for them. They were looked after by an Aboriginal Welfare Board, which treated them like children – as inferior. It was believed that most would die out or merge into the white community, and be indistinguishable from it. This was known as integration. Thus as a boy I was taught at school that the Aborigines were dying out.

I suppose my generation was the first real opposition to the well-meaning but tyrannical welfare policies. I was Bob Askin's campaign director in his local electorate in the 1965 election in which he became New South Wales Premier. The opening meeting at Dee Why was attended by quite a number of Kooris who stood at the walls holding up placards ventilating their grievances but not in any way disturbing the meeting. At the end of the meeting Bob Askin turned to them and thanked them for their excellent conduct before promising to help them. Soon after this, the Aboriginal Welfare Board was abolished, as were other laws prohibiting visitors to reserves.

We young lawyers had no doubt that inequality before the law was fundamentally wrong, and it was not so long before legal equality was achieved. I supported Bill Wentworth when he had a motion carried at the Liberal Party State Council for a referendum giving Commonwealth legislators powers with respect to Aborigines and counting them as ordinary citizens of the Commonwealth. Aborigines are at least now legally equal. They may keep their wages.

This of course was only the first step in a long journey. The second step was that many Aborigines became proud of their ancestry and totally opposed to an integration that would submerge their heritage. At the same time, they had to acquire their own leaders and this inevitably involved quarrels and backbiting between individuals. Large sums of money started to flow into Aboriginal welfare, but with disappointing results owing to bureaucracy and maladministration.

However, although there have been many setbacks, such as petrol- and glue-sniffing and the ever-present alcohol problems, I believe that things are getting better for the Aboriginal community. Not so long ago our indigenous brothers and sisters were legal inferiors, who frequently lost their children to so-called welfare, particularly if they were partly European children. We have come a long way in not so long a time. There is room for hope for great advances in the future.

I have been interested in politics since the time my age reached double figures. By that time indeed I understood that there was a Great Depression with terrible unemployment and widespread poverty. I thought long and hard about possible remedies. As I grew older I quickly appreciated the concepts of socialism and capitalism. I ultimately chose the latter with all its faults because the former seemed to me to be incompatible with individual liberty. However, for most of my school days my sympathies were with the Labor Party.

By the time I went to university I was firmly anti-Labor and pro-Liberal. I also believed in Christianity, so with these two beliefs I enjoyed being in the minority among students. It is much more enjoyable arguing on the unpopular side, or at least so I found it.

I was vice president of the Sydney University Liberal Club which I also helped to found. It was opened in about 1946 by Bob Menzies in a packed Union Hall. There was much opposition and there were few supporters. From the main platform I had a bird's-eye view of the proceedings, and enjoyed Ming dealing with interjectors.

One gem remains in my mind. A loud voice from the back called out 'Didn't you say you admired Mussolini?' Ming stopped and, using an old speaker's trick, called 'Who said that? Who said that?' Of course, this was to give himself time to think up an answer. The interjector was bold and stood up shouting, 'I said that.' Ming replied more in sorrow than in anger, 'You know, I've been searching Australia for years to find out who started that story.'

I heard Bob Menzies speak on numerous occasions. I was rather left-wing Liberal at the time and very vociferously opposed to the banning of the Communist Party, so I was not an uncritical admirer. But, having heard him as a social speaker telling amusing stories of the bar, I can say that not only was he a great political speaker, he was probably one of the greatest of all after-dinner speakers. He had a brilliant, if at times unkind, sense of humour, and he was a genius as a raconteur.

In my first year as a barrister I joined the Liberal Party proper and heard Billy Hughes speak in opposition to the nationalisation of Australian banks. I was one of the many who fought for the banks in 1948 (and now pay extortionate bank fees as my reward). Billy in his eighties was a brilliant speaker. He could not hear his audience, being deaf, but they could hear him, a very funny man with a quite irrepressible sense of humour and a great memory of the Good Book and the Hymnal. I remember him suddenly interrupting his invective against nationalisation with a loud request for a glass of water. It was rushed to him and he gulped quickly and beamed 'As pants the hart for cooling streams.'

When I married Jean on 2 May 1953 we moved to Newport and then in July 1953 to our present home in Mona Vale. I quickly became president of the Mona Vale Branch of the Liberal Party and president of the Collaroy Electoral Conference. This made me Bob Askin's campaign director in his electorate.

It was difficult not to like Bob Askin. He himself liked people, remembering their names, and being genuinely interested in their affairs. He was a kind man. His government brought in many reforms, for Aborigines, National Parks, the Supreme Court Act and many others. I saw nothing of the many faults attributed to Bob Askin. No one dared to state them until he was dead.

It is only fair to remember that his government was a reforming one, and we now take the reforms for granted, and give him no credit for them.

They say that if you have a heart you should start as a socialist but if you have a brain you should become a conservative. I started as a Liberal at the end of my school days. I left the Liberal Party soon after the second *Voyager* Royal Commission in 1967. I was not formally expelled. They simply failed to send me a membership renewal form. By middle age I was apolitical but I am still interested in politics.

# 3

# Battling in the Police Courts

Australia has a court system which commences with what used to be called Courts of Petty Sessions, now known as Local Courts. Originally these were presided over by laymen, a panel of Justices of the Peace, but these days most of the functions of court are conducted by professional magistrates. Registrars, who are Justices of the Peace, conduct some minor functions such as adjourning cases and granting bail. All criminal cases commence before these Local Courts. Most serious cases go on to a higher court but only after the magistrate has held that the strength of the prosecution case (the Crown case) justifies the case continuing. Otherwise the defendant is discharged. Less serious criminal cases, known as summary offences, are tried by the Local Courts.

The Local Courts also deal with important administrative matters such as granting licences to carry on various occupations, usually by way of appeal. They also have a substantial civil jurisdiction for comparatively small sums of money such as debt recoveries and damages for car accidents and so on.

The humblest court in Australia's legal system was the Court of

Petty Sessions when I started at the bar. Usually the fees for counsel in that court were the lowest fees paid. That is where most young counsel without powerful or wealthy connections, as I was, made or broke their careers.

For some years my practice was largely an effort to survive in the Courts of Petty Sessions, known to all then as Police Courts, with good reason.

Back when I started out as a barrister in 1948, police prosecutors conducted prosecutions in these courts. The bad old days are commemorated in stone letters at 'Central Police Court' in Liverpool Street. Policemen acted as court officers. In the country, police usually drove the magistrate from court to court. The same magistrates heard the same police witnesses day after day and with rare exceptions always believed them. Magistrates did not even have to be qualified lawyers until 1955. Previously they merely completed the magistrates' examinations.

When I became a barrister, magistrates were called stipendiary magistrates. Shortly before this some were appointed as police magistrates with the same powers as stipendiary magistrates. At the bar we said, not altogether facetiously, that before a magistrate took office he had to take an oath: 'Every day, in every way, I will believe the police evidence.' Many magistrates behaved as if this were true.

I have criticised the magistrates prior to 1955. Nevertheless some were very good, particularly those dealing with young offenders in the Children's Court at Albion Street. The general standard improved enormously when professional qualifications became a prerequisite of office. Quite a few magistrates coming up through the public service did some time working in the Public Defender's Office. These magistrates acquired a new perspective, which raised standards.

At the same time a number of barristers adopted a new approach to Police Court advocacy, treating the magistrate as an impartial, intelligent person, which in many cases he was. Now the magisterial bench is recruited from the independent profession as well as from the Public Service. Serious prosecutions are conducted by the Director of Public Prosecutions. The court staff are from the Sheriff's Office. The courts are truly independent and well run, although the workload in some outer suburban courts is terrifying.

Sometimes a defendant can choose between a magistrate or a judge and jury to decide his or her guilt or otherwise. Today the choice might often be made in favour of a magistrate. The improvement of the magisterial bench is one of the great success stories of Australian law today. In recent years as a QC I have felt humble in the presence of experienced magistrates, well versed in the law, and shrewd judges of fact.

One magistrate I remember from many years back was Mr Hodgson SM, who was very well versed in landlord and tenant law, and was a real gentleman. I was in a case before him against Gough Whitlam, then a junior barrister of some ability. Gough thought (correctly) that his client was disbelieved by the bench and therefore would lose. To my surprise he tried to crash through, accusing the magistrate of having made up his mind too quickly. His was vigorous, courageous advocacy which rather surprised His Worship, but it did not succeed and I won. I think the magistrate's decision was probably correct but I remember Gough as a bold courageous advocate who did not go down without a great fight.

When Mr Pickwick appeared before the magistrate Mr Nupkins Esq. at Ipswich, the said magistrate was assisted by a clerk, Mr Jinks, who took down the evidence of the witness. What the witnesses deposed to on oath was recorded in their sworn depositions. Mr Jinks made this record in handwriting and so did numerous deposition clerks throughout England in the time of Charles Dickens.

When I first appeared in the Police Courts in 1948 I was surprised to find that deposition clerks recorded on typewriters, rather than in shorthand, the words of the witness as they were spoken. At the conclusion of the evidence of each witness the depositions were read to him or her and then had to be signed. The time wasted was enormous.

Cross-examination under these circumstances was, to say the least, frustrating. Anguished protests from the deposition clerk demanded that you stopped or went slower. This gave the witness time to think his or her way out of trouble. The end result was often enough a wild deposition of frantic typing, which sounded meaningless when read back. But the witness duly signed. Remarkably few witnesses even tried to correct their depositions.

Thereafter, when appearing in some other court, an unhappy witness giving evidence about the same topic might be confounded with the question, 'Didn't you say in your depositions . . .?' The question assumed an accurate record in the depositions, which was a big assumption. But if the witness suggested an inaccurate record, his or her trembling attention would be drawn to the signature at the end of the depositions attesting to them as a true and correct record.

Deposition clerks varied. Some were close to hopeless, most were remarkably good having regard to the difficulty of their task, and a few were positively amazing, typing with great speed and accuracy. Nevertheless, the system was, to say the least, time wasting and inefficient.

The first important reform was permitting the witness to read his or her depositions before signing. This was quicker than reading them aloud, and meanwhile another witness could be giving evidence during the reading.

Then came the great reforms involving shorthand writers and sound recording so that the Police Courts began to proceed at the same speed as other courts. I can remember the enormous improvements in the 1950s as a result of these changes.

There was probably no harder job than that of a deposition clerk. His reward was likely to be promotion to the bench. I say 'his' because there were few, if any, female deposition clerks. I never came across one. There were no female magistrates. There were no female jurors. These reforms were to come much later.

By and large, advocacy in the Police Courts consisted of finding a legal point (the magistrates were afraid of legal points) or else giving the client what Jack Thom, a famous solicitor and a great advocate, called 'a salute of guns'. The magistrate listened, or pretended to listen patiently to a long and impassioned address before finding inevitably in accordance with the police evidence. If there was no police evidence then he found in favour of the party who had started the proceedings. If both parties had started proceedings (for example, in the case of assault and counterassault) the first to start proceedings was almost always the victor. In the humbler suburbs those who frequently litigated knew this, and raced to the local court office in order to be first.

Of course, in these little Police Court battles, the evidence of a policeman, if available, used to decide everything. The idea that a policeman would not tell the truth was beyond most magistrates' contemplation in the early 1950s. This gave the police licence to bash and lie, and in particular to verbal witnesses. No experienced criminal lawyer was very surprised by the revelations in the 1997 Wood Royal Commission. The responsibility for much of what was revealed in that Royal Commission must rest in part with the courts that were so ready to act on police evidence while disregarding the evidence of mere citizens, even if they were of good character.

Police corruption is not new. In 1948 I learned how Scotland Yard detectives, then regarded as snow white, put a bundle of tools into the hands of a well-known burglar whom they had failed to catch in the act. He was charged with having burglary tools in possession and pleaded guilty, receiving a gaol sentence. Had he told the truth as to what had happened he would have received a much longer sentence for daring to make such dreadful attacks on the police. How did I learn this? From an ex-Scotland Yard detective, then a barrister.

All of this was discouraging to a young idealist, such as I was in 1948. Since I had no connections to propel me into the upper courts then, I learned the hard way about the Police Courts. Then, as now with the Local Courts, these courts had an enormous workload, but by and large the magistrates remained calm and polite. In the Police Courts the standard criminal fare was 'drive under the influence of alcohol' (DUI) cases, assaults and insulting words, as well as committal proceedings for serious crimes to decide whether the defendant should stand trial before a judge and jury. The main civil cases were maintenance and tenancy cases.

My first contested case was in the Central Police Court. I was defending a young lady charged with saying in or near a public place (the street) to a neighbour the following 'insulting words': 'Shut your bloody mouth and give your arse a go.'

I never have been too sure what these words (if they were spoken) meant. They were, in any event, insulting. Despite my best endeavours and her denials that she spoke the words, my client was convicted, largely on the unspoken rule that her neighbour would not have prosecuted her if she had not said the words. This may be a useful rule of thumb but it is hardly reliable. Of course, it helps to clear up long lists of cases in lowly courts.

This very first case of mine illustrated a great problem of the law: how to decide who is telling the truth in the typical criminal case involving the word of one witness against that of another. Both my client and the complainant obviously disliked each other intensely to the point where a false accusation could well be used to injure the other. My client might well have insulted the complainant. The complainant might well have falsely said my client did so in order to achieve a victory in court. How to tell?

According to the law, the finding of guilt against my client should only have been made upon proof beyond reasonable doubt. The magistrate might have had his idea as to the probabilities, but could he be sure beyond reasonable doubt?

Neither gave anything away in cross-examination, each stuck to her story, each obviously hated the other, each was moderately attractive in terms of demeanour. One might say that whether a witness is attractive or not has no relevance to his or her credibility. That is obviously so, but the demeanour of an attractive witness may well impress the court more than that of an unattractive witness. How could you tell who was telling the truth? If one was cool, calm and collected and the other carried away with rage that would merely show one had self-control exceeding that of the other. Would that cast any reliable light on who was telling the truth?

Sometimes a witness trips up and says the wrong thing, perhaps contradicting him- or herself. Does that prove the witness is unreliable or even lying? We do that every day in normal conversation. Some people even have a habit of saying, 'Wait a moment, I tell a lie, I remember now that . . .' I used to beg such people not to use such an expression as 'I tell a lie' in court. However, this rather foolish way of speaking casts no reliable light on the veracity of a witness.

Being wrongly convicted of insulting words can be a matter for real grievance, as can being wrongly convicted of assault if you were defending yourself against aggression, or being wrongly convicted of sexual assault or rape. All these things can happen where one person tells his or her story more impressively than another.

Many of our cases in the Police Courts were for DUI. There were no breath tests then, and blood tests were rare. It was difficult for the police to describe the symptoms of alcohol, and most stuck to 'eyes bloodshot, walked unsteadily, breath smelt (strongly) of alcohol'. We cross-examined at length, usually to no avail in the Police Courts (success before a magistrate in such a case was quite a feat), but with more chance of success on appeal. Medical evidence sometimes saved a defendant.

In one such case years ago I came out of court quite elated at having secured an acquittal from the magistrate. I had been particularly successful in cross-examining a police sergeant, the main prosecution witness, about his impressions of my client who had been charged with DUI. In my pride I said to my solicitor, 'I did pretty well in my cross-examination of Sergeant X; I got some good answers.' 'Oh didn't you know he was fixed?' replied my solicitor. I did not. Had I known, I would not have appeared at all because that would be participating in the criminal offence of perverting the course of justice, at least that is my opinion. Not knowing, and thinking I had done a good job, made me feel completely humiliated.

I remember many neighbourly feuds resulting in assault charges in the Police Courts. These do not seem to be as common now fortunately. Various neighbourhood conciliation procedures seem to be having some success.

As I've mentioned, some of the main civil cases in the Police Courts were maintenance cases. Maintenance of wives separated from their husbands in those days depended upon fault. If a husband was not to blame for his wife leaving him, he did not have to pay her maintenance. That seemed quite fair in those days, but the court's rough stab at finding who was to blame tended to favour the wife. In working men's families these cases were often fought vigorously in the Police Courts and the result was accepted by the parties, so the divorce in the Supreme Court went through undefended. Nowadays maintenance does not depend upon fault, but a woman is generally expected to work.

Disputes as to marital fault usually centred around assaults and abuse, or false accusations of adultery. Actually, in most cases in which I acted the accusations of adultery turned out to be true. Wife beating did occur and assaults by wives on husbands were by no means unknown. I once appeared for a strong man who obtained a divorce from his wife on the old ground of repeated assaults and cruel beatings. His wife had a boyfriend. He would knock that boyfriend over and then stand meekly while his wife quite brutally assaulted him. He said that if he had once resisted her, he could not count on restraining himself from seriously injuring her.

Adultery is bad enough, but it was often accompanied by cruel deception. The deceived spouse was told that he or she was insanely suspicious, even mentally ill. Some such spouses were persuaded for years to believe that their suspicions were groundless. Of course, this conduct still goes on today where adultery may not be an offence in law but it is an offence so far as the spouse is concerned.

Maintenance cases were a little different from divorce cases. The parties had just separated, but the marriage was not necessarily beyond repair. My clients in maintenance cases were usually in humble circumstances and divorce would be not merely an emotional crisis, but a financial disaster. The wages of a working man in the 1950s barely supported one household. They could not adequately support two households. We often tried to achieve a reconciliation and sometimes succeeded. If not, we usually managed to settle the question of maintenance. This did not always please everyone.

In one case (not mine) the wife emerged to tell her mother that the case was settled. The mother exploded: 'Settled? Settled? Why did you settle it? Why didn't you drag him through the court, the same as I did to your father?'

Some cases were very sad, others were quite puzzling. I once appeared for a wife who had been married for 10 years and thought she had an ideal marriage and a wonderful husband. He did much of the housework, he drove the children to school, he left the car for my client while he walked to the station in the rain, he professed undying love and gave his wife lovely anniversary cards, presents and flowers. Yet for some years he had secretly hated her, loathed her, and was in a relationship with another woman. The wife could not understand why he had left her, and only found out as he told his story in court. Of course I was able to destroy him in the witness box: to show that he was a liar in the marriage, and a hypocrite. But I could not restore the dreams of a broken-hearted woman.

Should she have seen more? Did she overload him with household duties? Did she presume too much? It was not for me to judge. I could only feel real sorrow for her. Perhaps she had been foolish; more probably she was simply unlucky in love.

Then there were the numerous assault cases to justify the wife leaving and entitle her to maintenance. Sometimes there were bruises to show, but these did not prove much – it was one person's word against another's as to the cause of the bruises. Alcohol was the cause of many assaults on wives. Sometimes assaults were provoked. Sometimes the husband was simply a mean bully. These were depressing cases and I often felt deeply for my clients, even my clients' spouses.

In my later career I was to encounter the same sorts of cases, but they had resulted in death, and the charges were very serious, usually murder, which I was fortunately able to reduce to manslaughter for which the sentences were much less severe.

Finally, as part of my work in the Police Courts, there were the tenancy cases, the main support of the junior bar in the 1950s. At that time there was an enormous shortage of rental premises: dwelling houses and commercial premises also. All were 'protected' throughout the war and for many years afterwards. This was done by pegging the rent to a so-called 'fair rent' that was absurdly low and could only be increased (slightly) by a magistrate in a Fair Rents Court. A landlord could only recover premises on special grounds in the Police Court (Petty Sessions). All this was achieved by special legislation superimposed upon old legislation and all superimposed upon the common law, which is the judge-made law, the original basis of much of our law, especially land law. Disputes between landlords and tenants showed human nature at its worst and thus there was a great deal of litigation for the value of the tenancy, and at times for revenge.

Landlord and tenant law was a legal maze, and we young barristers (if we were to survive) had to become legal wizards on the topic. The unfortunate magistrates were subjected to technicality upon technicality. If they made a mistake in the law there was likely to be an appeal to the Supreme Court. In the city particularly they had to decide very difficult cases involving expensive houses or very expensive offices or shops. By and large they did very well, and they handled the technicalities with some skill. The gentlemanly Mr Hodgson SM was an astute tenancy lawyer. I believe he was never upset on appeal, and many tried his decisions out in the Supreme Court.

Gradually premises were decontrolled; that is, the tenants lost their protection. Once the tenant was evicted, the premises were decontrolled and any rent that the next tenant was willing to pay could be charged. Obtaining possession was therefore a large financial gain for the landlord. Soon it became lawful to pay the tenant to agree to the termination of the lease, first in the case of commercial premises, then for dwelling houses.

Obviously the big tenancy cases involved shops and offices, particularly the former. Landlords had usually bought the premises subject to the tenant's protection. If the tenant was evicted, the value of the premises increased enormously. The cases nearly always involved weekly or monthly tenancies which, being protected, lasted for years and were sometimes sublet or assigned. Now, of course, business premises are usually leased for terms of years. The magistrates and the barristers gradually superimposed on the law the proposition that a landlord should be entitled to possession if he or she paid the tenant reasonable compensation.

As developers obtained possession of old city buildings, the tenants were evicted, usually with compensation. The amount was negotiated, and was based on the value of the tenant's business and perhaps the cost of re-establishing it elsewhere. But what was the value of a business dependent for its existence on a weekly or monthly tenancy? We negotiated on behalf of our clients; mine were usually tenants. If we failed to agree the landlord would proceed before the court, offering his idea of reasonable compensation. If the magistrate thought the tenant was entitled to more he would refuse to evict him or her, but usually would voice his opinion and adjourn the proceedings to give the parties a chance to negotiate again. By and large nearly all commercial cases were eventually settled between the parties because the magistrate had no power himself to fix the compensation figure, although he could suggest it. The sums of money involved were often very large, and the cases sometimes involved Queen's Counsel.

I remember being led by Ted St John QC appearing for a tenant of a shop in King Street, Sydney. Peter Clyne, then a barrister, appeared for the landlord. His advocacy was superb but we persuaded the magistrate that the compensation offered was not enough. The magistrate stood down from the bench while we resumed negotiations. Finally agreement was reached and Peter's client obtained possession. This was a case where the landlord's urgent need for possession persuaded the court to sit in the few business days between Christmas and New Year.

Peter Clyne was a great debater and an even better advocate. His lack of discretion and failure to appreciate fundamental ethical rules led to his disbarment. Subsequently I appeared for him twice in his efforts to be readmitted to the bar but this never eventuated. I also appeared against him in his efforts to maintain a tenancy eviction service (as I shall relate later).

Today as I walk through the centre of Sydney I can remember places, now redeveloped, where I defended the tenants and ensured that they received substantial compensation before the developers moved in. Many of my clients were Greek, since I had coached several Greek-Australians who later became solicitors. Times change. It is a pity that the old Greek restaurants have almost disappeared from the city along with Sargents, Repins and Mockbells, well-known restaurants of the post-war years. They provided good honest service in those days at reasonable prices.

I have one quite wonderful memory of the Police Courts. It

must have been in the late 1950s. My client was a German Jew who spent the war in various forms of imprisonment in Germany, his life preserved because of his skill in optics, vital for the German war effort. As the Allies advanced in 1945 the Gestapo planned to kill him along with any other surviving Jews, but the Americans got there first. He was one of the very few German Jews in Germany when the war broke out who was still alive by VE Day. Now he was in Australia, a very cheerful, surprisingly happy man. His mind seemed concentrated on his survival, not what might have happened to him. Now he was in a free country, a citizen entitled to equality and justice.

A policeman had booked him for not stopping at a stop sign. The man claimed he had stopped and was prepared to pay good money to a junior counsel – me – rather than submit to a false accusation. He had supreme faith in Australian justice, and he was right.

Deciding whether the policeman or the defendant is right in such a case used to give magistrates no trouble at all. The policeman was always telling the truth and the defendant had every reason to lie. So the defendant was always convicted. Never mind that policemen are human and often had to fill a quota of bookings per shift. (Quota bookings are always officially denied, and the inexperienced may even believe the denials.) Sometimes when a driver slows down there may be a bona fide dispute as to whether he or she actually stopped. If the magistrate makes a genuine intelligent effort in such a case to ascertain who is telling the truth the task is not easy. Of course, one may ask why would a guilty driver bother to pay out quite big money in legal fees just to avoid a small fine, especially back in those days when a conviction would not result in penalty points on a driver's licence.

My client encountered one of the early new breed of magistrates, the well-known and well-regarded Jimmy Letts, a barrister, who applied the simple rule: Was the defendant's guilt proven beyond reasonable doubt? As he put it, there was no real reason to prefer the evidence of one witness against that of the other. Therefore there was no proof beyond reasonable doubt. My client left the court a delighted man. This was no Nazi Germany; this was Australia, and he had received Australian justice.

I am happy to say that Jimmy Letts was accompanied by, and followed by numerous other good magistrates who gave the citizen a fair go against the police, and who insisted upon proof beyond reasonable doubt, as the law requires.

I must say that the police I knew in those days may well have indulged in corruption over comparatively soft crime such as driving offences, prostitution and gambling. However, I do not think there was much hard-crime corruption, which only seemed to arise when the big drug dealers in heroin and cannabis started corrupting many police. That corruption was assisted by courts still believing police, but perhaps not to the same extent as in the early 1950s.

I could never quite understand why my fellow barristers whose views as to police evidence were as hostile, or more so, than mine, became such police lovers once appointed to the bench. Perhaps they were swayed by the deferential respect that was shown to them by the police. In my view, defence lawyers often became Crown-favouring judges, whereas Crown prosecutors often became excellent impartial judges. However, by and large, defence lawyers and Crown prosecutors were equally capable of being good or bad judges.

Most policemen then (as they do now) tried to do a good job. Often enough a decent man felt obliged to do the wrong thing because of the police culture of defending one's mates. Sometimes police were wrongly accused of misconduct. Sometimes a good officer was harshly treated for a minor disciplinary matter. Over the years I have acted many times both for and against police officers. The bar has been enriched by the admission of many ex-police officers. My impression, for what it is worth, is that the ordinary police officer at the coalface is likely to be a good man or woman, but his or her superiors at the higher level let their troops down in many ways.

The jurisdiction of magistrates in criminal cases has been substantially enlarged in recent years, but there has been little protest about this. By and large magisterial justice these days is on a high plane. There are many magistrates who would be capable judges, and at least two have been promoted to the District Court.

There are numerous magistrates today, and of course the quality of justice varies with the individuals. However, it is fair to say that the greatest and least appreciated reform in the law since the war has been the standard of summary justice in the Local Courts. They are not called Police Courts so often now. They are independent of the police and on the whole the citizen can count on receiving a fair go.

There are numerous reasons for this reform, including better supervision by the Supreme Court, better selection and training processes, but mainly a philosophy of independence instilled by numerous chief magistrates and senior magistrates, in particular Clarrie Briese, through whose efforts the concept of Local Courts – as opposed to Police Courts, became a reality. Through his efforts magistrates today are as independent as judges.

Now it is remarkable to see how highly complicated issues are efficiently dealt with by simple, comparatively inexpensive procedures in the Local Courts.

Sometimes I wonder whether the Supreme Court, which has procedures that get more complicated and expensive every year, might give a passing thought to the simple procedures of the Local Court.

# 4

# Human Nature at its Worst

The law does not find people at their best; generally it finds them angry and in dispute, or else accused of offences great or small. Over the years I appeared in many criminal cases, great and small, but generally the clients in these cases were not the most unappealing. I found there were three categories of cases where human nature was at its worst.

The first was landlord and tenant cases. After the war, this was bread-and-butter work for young and not-so-young barristers, since both business and residential premises were in short supply, and tenants had extensive and highly technical protection. Both landlords and tenants often behaved abominably, depending upon who was on top at the time. It was commonplace for tenants to demand extortionate amounts of money in return for giving vacant possession, and landlords were often merciless to tenants. For some years the law was very much weighted in favour of tenants and many people – often wealthy people – exploited that position.

Innumerable battles between landlords and tenants took place in the Police Courts (which had exclusive jurisdiction). There were many weird cases. The best was one in which my friend Jack Lindsay appeared. The landlady was proceeding to evict the tenant on the ground of 'nuisance and annoyance'. The parties were in adjoining houses, each with a backyard convenience, flushed by pulling an old-fashioned chain attached to the tank or cistern above. The tenant kept a pet carpet snake, which once went into the landlady's convenience to drink from the tank, its tail hanging down. The landlady enthroned herself, reached up for the chain and pulled down the carpet snake instead. This, the landlady claimed, was a nuisance and annoyance on the part of the tenant. It was, at least, light relief from the litany of alleged noisy parties and arguments that made up many nuisance and annoyance cases.

Some notable and wealthy citizens enjoyed very cheap rents as a result of laws meant to protect much poorer tenants. In one case, a Point Piper flat was occupied by a well-to-do tenant in his eighties. The magistrate in numerous applications for his eviction was moved to refuse the landlord because of the tenant's age. He lived well into his nineties on an absurdly low fixed rent.

In one case where I succeeded in evicting a tenant for a returned serviceman who was given an advantage by the law over a non-returned serviceman tenant, the successful landlord found the grass so high at the back that it completely concealed an old derelict motor car. Few tenants were keen on mowing the landlord's grass, but this was quite absurd.

The gradual demise of wartime protection for tenants took a lot of the bitterness out of landlord and tenant law, but I still find it a strange aspect of human nature that landlords and tenants tend to persecute each other. I remember acting for a tenant of a restaurant in a country town who was compelled by court order to leave the premises. He was a hardworking, respectable businessman yet in his anger he stripped the premises, taking away even the light fittings, leaving naked wires jutting from the ceiling. This was his revenge and for this stupidity he had to pay damages.

In another case I acted for the landlord of premises on Sydney's northern beaches, let for a high Christmas holiday rent. He found the premises very badly damaged, just for the fun of it. In another holiday renting case the tenant lit a barbecue fire in the lounge.

On the other hand, landlords could be tough. In one case a landlord encouraged students leasing a flat to have wild parties into the early hours so as to drive out elderly 'protected' tenants in the flat below.

The second category where I found human nature to be at its worst involved wills and deceased estates. A legacy is a tax-free windfall to the average battler, or, for that matter, to wealthy people also. Pressure is sometimes exerted to persuade people to make most unfair wills, and the law has only limited remedies in such cases. Elderly parents have been persuaded to disinherit deserving sons or daughters by siblings greedy out of self-interest, or pursuing a family feud.

The sons of farmers were particularly vulnerable to unfair wills. They frequently worked hard as boys and men for mere pocket money, expecting to inherit the farm. At times, an elderly parent disinherited such a son seemingly for no valid reason. The law provided a remedy but only if the son was in need of some support. If he had money to secure a reasonable living for himself, apart from the family farm, he might well fail in a Testators Family Maintenance Act application, now a Family Provision Act application. (A near relative may claim for family provision but only if left without adequate provision for education support or advancement in life.) I found these cases very sad, and the family feuds exposed were at times quite horrifying.

Often an unfair will is challenged by a Family Provision application, but I have had cases where the challenge was based on lack of testamentary capacity (usually old age) and even undue influence. These latter cases were particularly difficult.

All contested will cases tend to bring out bitterness and ill feeling. No one likes to miss out on receiving a large sum of money, but it is particularly galling if one loses out to a near relative.

I remember one case where a man with a wife, and with a brother whom he hated, died suddenly. Just before he died he said to his wife, 'I haven't made a will and now that bastard will get a share of my estate.' This was true of the then law of intestacy, but the wife was able to make an application to the court, as this wife did. I acted for the brother who hated the deceased, yet wanted to take an unintended benefit from his estate. He failed. To do myself justice, he contested the case against my advice, as of course was his right.

The third category of litigation where I have observed human nature at its worst is divorce, now coyly called family law.

I made my first appearance in court in the Divorce Court. I first acted under the old State Matrimonial Causes Act, then Sir Garfield Barwick's Commonwealth Matrimonial Causes Act, and finally under Lionel Murphy's Family Law Act. The provisions of all these Acts had two things in common. They permitted the types of people I can only call bastards and bitches to prosper.

I suppose it is impossible to draft divorce laws that will do justice. The Family Law Act accepts this and treats each party as equally to blame for the failure of the marriage. Perhaps in many cases this is more or less true. In other cases the spouse who is much less to blame suffers injustice, sometimes gross injustice. How could I explain to a hard-working man, whose only fault was that he had worked too hard and had made too much money, that it was fair that his adulterous wife should receive a very large slab of his fortune?

The line between love and hatred, extreme hatred, is often a very vague one, so easy to cross. One husband bulldozed the matrimonial home rather than allow his wife to get it. One of my clients crippled his business and deprived himself of any income rather than comply with a Family Court order to pay his wife a quite modest sum of money.

I often came across the story of the wife who worked hard to support her husband so he could do a university course, only to have him leave her for a younger woman when he qualified to be a professional man.

Before Murphy's Family Law Act, a wife who left her husband could not get maintenance from him unless he had forced her to leave by his conduct. In one case in which I acted for the husband, the wife claimed that she was compelled to leave him because of his crazy jealousy resulting in false accusations of adultery. I won, but neither I nor my client knew that at the time his wife gave evidence against him she was in fact pregnant by another man. The later discovery of this made the divorce simple.

Some husbands were very cruel indeed. One wife for whom I acted was viciously flogged with an electric iron cord to such an extent that her husband received a heavy gaol sentence. Her sin was voting Liberal instead of Labor.

Another client's husband threw her pet dog from a second-floor balcony. I could go on, but it is sufficient to say that there is a substantial number of cases where one party to a marriage has been very badly treated, and in many of these cases the Family Court is compelled by its Act to do injustice between the parties.

Of course, in many other cases the parties are more or less equally to blame for the break-up. Under the Family Law Act, in most cases a reasonable, if rough and ready settlement is worked out between the parties and their lawyers and they are able to get on with their lives with a minimum of trauma. In many other cases one party is reasonable and the other is not, but the reasonable one gives in and the unreasonable one prospers. It goes against the grain but it is often the sensible thing for the reasonable party to do.

Then there are the cases where both parties, full of acrimony, fight every inch of the way. These cases take up many hearing days with preliminary arguments, contested evidence and buckets of bitterness and venom. Neither party even considers what is reasonable. Each wants either to make money or save money, enriched with a nice loading of revenge. The legal representatives in such cases are often accused of charging extortionate fees but it is difficult for such critics to understand how the clients insist on interminable conversations with their lawyers, often after-hours or at weekends, and how the clients always insist that money is no object and no expense is to be spared; that is, until the case is over and a bill is presented, and then often disputed. Family-law specialists tend to be detached and unemotional as a protection against such clients.

Many clients are much more reasonable than those just

described, but their affairs are complicated and the ascertainment of a fair settlement can be a long and involved process. So many businesses have complicated tax-avoidance structures, which the proprietor him- or herself may not understand. Often the accountant does not either.

Many years ago a doctor with a series of companies and trusts to avoid tax was caught up in divorce proceedings and it was necessary to ascertain his true expendable income. This was quite a job. His barrister, more as a matter of interest, asked the doctor's accountant just how much tax was avoided by these complicated arrangements. After some hesitation the accountant ventured a figure – about £25,000 per annum – to a most attentive doctor as well as the barrister. 'And what are his accountancy fees for that?' asked the barrister. The client immediately answered, 'I'll tell you that: £25,000 pounds per annum.' This was, I hope, not too typical of tax-avoidance arrangements.

If the Family Court finds evidence of tax evasion; that is, illegal non-payment of tax, the evidence is referred to the Australian Taxation Office. This practice was rarely followed by the old Divorce Court judges, although taxation officers quite frequently sat in to listen to big divorce cases between wealthy people. Fear of the taxation investigator prompted many a settlement then – and now.

Under the Family Law Act, there are no longer big cases as to fault reported, as they used to be in at least one Sunday paper, the now defunct *Truth*. Under the old New South Wales Act sometimes the issue of adultery was decided by a jury, and an unfavourable result could ruin a man's life. Senior police officers were at times dismissed for such conduct. I remember a doctor who was struck off the roll. Sometimes a man had to pay damages to the husband of his adulteress, plus heavy costs as well. Yet it is very doubtful whether these laws did much to reduce the incidence of adultery. After all, only a few unlucky persons were publicly exposed, although quite a few others had to pay undisclosed settlement amounts.

In my early days at the bar, divorce had the three 'C' traps – collusion, condonation and connivance.

In the so-called public interest, and in order to preserve the sanctity of marriage, parties could not agree that a ground for divorce had occurred. It had to be proved to the satisfaction of the court. Any agreement between lawyers as to the occurrence of a matrimonial offence could well be collusion, a serious matter of professional misconduct likely to result in the lawyer being struck off the roll. It was not even safe to discuss or agree on permanent alimony (as maintenance was then called).

The Chief Judge in Divorce, Mr Justice Bonney, was a terrifying figure and young counsel before him had to be very careful. I only appeared before him once, not successfully.

My great confrontation with collusion was before the other Judge in Divorce, Mr Justice Edwards, who was blessed with a good sense of humour. The famous Peter Clyne was then a solicitor and on the day of the hearing briefed me to do an undefended divorce for a country firm, for whom Peter's employers were the city agents. This was a typical last-minute brief that young junior counsel received, in this case delivered to me at the court where I first met the client at about 9.30 a.m. The court would start at 10 a.m. My client was seeking a restitution order on the basis that her husband had left her against her will and she wanted the court to order him to return to her and render her her conjugal rights. If such an order was made but disobeyed she could then petition for immediate divorce on the ground of desertion, without having to wait for three years.

Some said that this procedure was a short cut to consent divorce. Certainly it was the duty of the court to watch such cases carefully. Solicitors who permitted the parties to collude; that is, to go through this procedure insincerely, intending to use it as a short cut to divorce and deceive the court, could be suspended or struck off for professional misconduct. In the good old days of hypocrisy, divorce was a sensitive area in which a lawyer needed to be very careful to ensure that he or she was not personally involved in the client's deception of the court. In fact, sincere petitions for restitution of conjugal rights were rare indeed; that is, the petitioner did not want the respondent to return but did want a short-cut divorce, as for instance in England where Winifred tried to divorce Monty in 'The Forsyte Saga'.

I met Peter Clyne and the client at 9.30 a.m. I asked her if her husband had left her, how that had occurred, and in particular whether there had been any correspondence between them after he left. She said there had been none. The brief, like many such briefs, gave me very little information. So I went into court, put my client in the witness box and proceeded to examine her, proving marriage and domicile as required. I next got her to tell the court how her husband left her. I was going well. I then asked her whether she had had any letters from him. She said, 'Yes, there were a lot of letters.' I turned to Peter who was examining, apparently for the first time, a big file of papers from the lady's country solicitor. To my horror, he then handed me a thick bunch of correspondence I had never seen. At the judge's request I had to read the letters aloud. Very soon His Honour realised I had in fact never seen the correspondence, and proceeded to enjoy himself.

The first letter said the husband was not coming back and wanted a divorce, then suggested that the wife should pretend to want him back and seek a restitution order. Before Mr Justice Bonney, such a letter would have brought the heavens down but Mr Justice Edwards merely remarked that it was a very interesting letter and would I now read the next letters. There were lots of them, each worse than the last and some involving country solicitors who should have known better. With each letter I was trying to read ahead to see what was coming at the same time as reading out loud to the court. It was not a hot day but beads of sweat lined my forehead. Would the solicitors be called up for their fairly obvious sins? Would I be blamed?

At the conclusion of the reading I suggested that the petition for restitution should be dismissed, as of course it had to be, for obvious collusion. His Honour agreed and made no further comment. Mr Justice Edwards was a kind, tolerant judge who was obviously amused by my predicament. At the same time he let me, and everyone else involved, off very lightly. I did not need to be taught about collusion, but this experience rammed home everything I had been taught on the topic.

Condonation, in a nutshell, meant that if the parties had sexual intercourse after a matrimonial offence by one, then that offence could not be the foundation of divorce proceedings. If desertion had commenced before the sexual intercourse then it terminated and the three years (later two years) desertion period would have to start all over again. Obviously the doctrine had qualifications, called reviver, for repeated misconduct but it served as a very real bar to reconciliation.

Connivance was, broadly, consent. If a party consented to adultery by the other, that connivance would prevent reliance on that adultery as a ground for divorce. Unfortunately, since the courts insisted on strict proof of adultery, even in undefended cases, parties had to be shadowed and eavesdropping often took place. In one English case soon after the war when listening devices were primitive, an ingenious husband constructed apparatus to listen into his lounge room from the garage. He heard suspicious noises, rushed up from the garage and saw his wife draw apart from the lodger on the sofa. He had been too quick, but he pretended not to have seen anything and went back to his listening post in the garage. This time he was patient and in due course heard unmistakable sounds. When he came up again he caught his wife and the lodger in manifest adultery. But the court denied him a divorce on the basis of connivance, saying that he had, in effect, consented to his wife's adultery because he had pretended to ignore the signs the first time. How absurd the law could be!

In later years, with listening devices and invasions of houses by private detectives breaking in (sometimes a credit card was used to operate a Yale lock), photographs of adultery in progress were taken which were enough to satisfy the fussiest judge.

Evidence of adultery could be quite ridiculous. On one occasion I heard Mr Maynard, ex police, then private-inquiry agent, give evidence before Mr Justice Chambers as follows:

Mr Maynard: With Mrs X I went to premises at (address) and we looked through a bedroom window where I saw Mr X with Miss Y, the intervener, having sexual intercourse in a bed.
Mr Justice Chambers: Do you mean actually performing the sexual act?
Mr Maynard: Yes.

Mr Justice Chambers: What did you do?

Mr Maynard: I said 'My name is Maynard, your wife is here with me and she intends to commence divorce proceedings against you on the ground of your adultery with Miss Y.'

Mr Justice Chambers: What did they do then?

Mr Maynard: They just kept on having sexual intercourse, Your Honour.

One of my early clients was a woman charged with assault by her husband. Her defence was an alibi. This was all part of a much larger fight over custody of their only child, a boy. My client had been unsuccessful in other court fights with her husband and this was her first fight with me as her counsel. I had time and I took the trouble. Accompanied by her I substantially re-enacted her alibi, checking railway timetables. We won.

I acted for her in a lot of later litigation. We became friends in the sense that she let me know from time to time how she was going. Ultimately, to her great disappointment, having won and maintained custody of the boy, when he was about 14 or 15 years of age he decided of his own accord to go and live with his father. This often occurred in the cases of teenage sons.

This case does illustrate the hatred churned up by parents disputing the custody of a child. Even under the Family Law Act the conduct of the parties is relevant to their fitness to be parents, hence the frequent mud-slinging in such cases.

The divorce law will never be perfect, despite many reforms. One simple reason is that society cannot afford the resources and court time required to sort out the rights and wrongs between the participants in an unhappy marriage. Even when fault was the crucial issue, in the available time the law could only make a rough stab. (Interestingly, the law with regard to business partnership has the same problem. The time necessary to sort out the rights and wrongs between two business partners through litigation is simply not available. In the case of a lengthy business relationship, the court could easily delve into the facts for a year or more and get nowhere. Such cases are almost invariably settled because the parties simply cannot afford to fund weeks of litigation.)

There is a strong argument for the Catholic concept of either no divorce, or rare divorce, only for serious fault. Since my own marriage has been very happy indeed I could hardly accept this concept for others less fortunate than myself. However, the decline in the number of couples who see fit to marry at all, and the fragility of so many recent marriages today, makes me wonder whether the Family Law Act has gone too far. I believe the abolition of rules of matrimonial conduct and easy divorce have undoubtedly increased the number of divorces. Furthermore, the laws have been so altered that de facto partners confer the same rights on their children without any need for an undertaking of perpetual fidelity. Years ago, many people begged me to help them obtain a quick divorce so as to allow them a quick remarriage. Now this is very unusual. There is no stigma regarding children born out of wedlock.

Perhaps the permissive society has lured too many people into easygoing ways which ultimately deny them the deep satisfaction of a happy marriage. I think the carving up of one spouse's means in favour of the other, without any fault involved, and regardless of the conduct of the parties has served to discourage people from getting married at all.

I think the decline of marriage has produced an instability in society that is a real problem, particularly for children.

# 5

# The McDermott Royal
# Commission

On 5 September 1936 (when I was 10 years old), a sharefarmer and storekeeper called William Henry Lavers disappeared. His body was never found. According to the reports of the time, he got up at about 4.45 a.m. to feed his horses on his farm on the Forbes to Grenfell road and was never seen again. Blood was found on a petrol-pump handle outside the store and witnesses at the time reported seeing and hearing a bluey-grey noisy car which apparently stopped at the garage and left 56-inch tracks in the wet dirt near the pump. It was a tourer car.

At about the same time, Frederick McDermott and a man named McKay were travelling between shearing sheds in a 1926 Essex tourer (probably not bluey-grey at all) owned by a shearer named Parker.

Ten years later one Essie May King came forward purporting to have seen McDermott on 4 September 1936 on the road not far from Lavers' store. There was no particular reason why Mrs King, a travelling showwoman, should remember him, let alone identify him, apart from the reward that was available for the unresolved murder, part of which was paid to her.

A couple of bush characters claimed that McDermott round a camp fire one night had admitted killing Lavers. They too would have had the reward in mind.

McDermott was arrested on 10 October 1946 by a Sergeant Danny Calman and other police, and allegedly made some rather ambiguous but nevertheless incriminating admissions in an interview recorded in shorthand. The record said that he admitted to having said that he had killed Lavers. McKay, his travelling companion, was never charged.

After a seven-day trial in February 1947, McDermott, despite his denials of guilt in court, was convicted of murder. The Crown case was that he had murdered Lavers with the petrol-pump handle, just for a few gallons of petrol.

Without criticising anyone, this trial at Dubbo Supreme Court was very short compared to present-day trials, but long enough for those days. McDermott was defended by the Public Defender instructed by Cecil Bourke, Deputy Crown Solicitor. Cec Bourke was convinced that McDermott was innocent and in 1949 asked me to read the evidence, which I did, and I raised a query as to whether Parker's car would have made a 56-inch track. I was assured that the evidence as to Parker's car's track given at the trial was correct.

McDermott died years ago in 1977, more or less a derelict. In 1946 he was a rough shearer with a real weakness for alcohol. His character was not such as to appeal to a country jury. Yet as a prisoner he impressed the prison officers and the Anglican chaplain who also became convinced that he was innocent. In 1951, mainly because of alibi evidence discovered by the chaplain, the case was reopened. I was briefed for McDermott as the junior to Jack Shand KC (father of Alec Shand QC).

I suggested that a Royal Commission would be the best mechanism for inquiring into the conviction. I got the idea from the famous Dean case where Dean had been convicted very early last century of attempting to murder his wife with arsenic. There had also been a Royal Commission to free Arthur Peden, who had been wrongly convicted years before of murdering his wife with a razor.

A Royal Commission, properly conducted, is a very good way

to ascertain the truth. In fact, Winston Churchill when Prime Minister used a judge conducting a secret Royal Commission to decide between rival claims as to a proposed action during the Second World War.

The Royal Commissioner is usually a judge and he or she is assisted by a counsel assisting, whose duties are to find the relevant evidence and present it at the hearing. Other parties are given leave to appear, to cross-examine witnesses, and to address the Commission. In a Royal Commission into a criminal conviction such as that of McDermott, there was a Supreme Court Judge, Mr Justice Kinsella, as the Royal Commissioner. Counsel assisting was Mr Harold Snelling (later Solicitor General). The Crown was given leave to appear by the senior Crown prosecutor at the trial, Mr Tom Crawford KC, and he was assisted by Alfred Goran (later Judge Goran QC). Mr Jack Shand KC, with myself as his junior, was given leave to appear for the prisoner Fred McDermott.

Each witness was called to the witness box by Mr Snelling who led him or her through their evidence, perhaps also cross-examining with leading questions. Then Crown and defence cross-examined and finally Mr Snelling could cross-examine again. I remember one witness as to the colour of Parker's car whose ultimate memory was obtained through cross-examination by Mr Snelling when neither of the interested parties dared to ask a crucial question.

McDermott's alibi that he was at a shearing shed far from the scene of the crime was based on the shearing records of a Mr Whiteman, a shearing contractor in 1936. It was learnt, during the Royal Commission, that Mr Whiteman, probably being temporarily short of cash, had postdated the shearers' cheques and by mistake had postdated the cut-out (the finishing date) in the shearing book by the same one day. This bona fide error in the records was disclosed by the recovery in 1951 of shearers' cheques from 1936 banked many miles away on the dates appearing on the cheques, which clearly demonstrated that they were postdated. These days the cheques would not be preserved fifteen years later. The result was the complete destruction of McDermott's new alibi defence that had prompted the inquiry in the first place.

Fortunately for McDermott, before the hearing of the Royal Commission commenced, I decided to look further into the tyre tracks that had been left outside the garage store in 1936. Would Parker's car have made a 56-inch track? In those early post-war days most of the cars were still pre-war and Essex tourers from the 1920s were common in Art Gallery Road in Sydney's CBD, near where I worked. So I got Hector Moffatt, the Public Solicitor's investigator, to come with me and measure the tyre tracks of Essex tourers of 1926 and 1927. They were all well under 56 inches. We found out later from the Hudson Motor Company that they were made to be 54 and 7/8 inches, whereas 56 inches was the then standard track. On the rough dirt roads common in those days a standard track was desirable, so the Hudson Motor Company did not correct the error in the motor journals, leaving purchasers to believe that its cars had standard tracks. Hence the police gave bona fide evidence at the trial that Parker's car had a standard track of 56 inches and did not realise this was not the case.

If Parker's car could not have left the suspect car's 56-inch track then McDermott could hardly be guilty. As a result of the inquiry he was pardoned and later received a very small monetary compensation for the five years he had spent in prison.

One particular memory of the McDermott case lingers. When I first went with Jack Shand KC and Reg Hawkins, the Public Solicitor, to interview our client at Long Bay Gaol, a prison officer approached Jack Shand and said, 'You must get him out Mr Shand, he should not be here.' Never since then have I heard, or heard of, a prison officer with a strong belief in the innocence of a prisoner. In the period from 1947 to 1951 McDermott had a remarkable ability to convince people, who were far from gullible, that he was innocent. I am sure he was, but innocent people are often dis-believed, particularly if they are rough, drunken types.

I learned numerous lessons from this Royal Commission.

The first was that despite our famed criminal justice system, it is easy for an innocent person to be convicted. This is particularly so if they have been targeted by the police, and the trial is conducted in an atmosphere of how wonderful the police are to have solved this crime after 10 years. Targeting of a suspect is a high road to injustice, since other avenues tend to be ignored and evidence tends to be distorted.

Secondly, I appreciated how skimpy and superficial are the usual investigations before and during a criminal trial. Nowadays trials take longer and more care is taken, but usually only in a Royal Commission are the resources available for a thorough investigation by the defence. In the McDermott case the trial had taken seven days; the Royal Commission took 38 days.

Thirdly, the unreliability of human recollection and memories of events from years before was impressed upon me. By 1951, 15 years after the crime, memories were often dim on such matters as the colour of a car, for example.

Fourthly, I realised how the inducement of a reward can produce dangerously enthusiastic evidence. The camp-fire conversations very probably involved drunken abuse and boasting, which were elevated by the witnesses into a confession of crime. The identification evidence of Mrs King was truly absurd. She had died before the Royal Commission in 1951 but not before collecting a substantial reward.

Fifthly, this case revealed the unreliability of alleged verbal admissions, being the evidence of numerous police officers against one unreliable shearer. McDermott was entirely in their hands as to what the police said were his replies to questioning.

It is good to know now that there have been some useful reforms addressing such problems since 1951 and it is very doubtful whether McDermott could be convicted on the same evidence today. The evidence of McDermott's verbal confession was ambiguous and possibly consistent with innocence since he only agreed that he had said to others that he killed Lavers, but its effect at the trial had no doubt been deadly. There was only McDermott's word as to any other version of the conversation. In those days, accused persons were reluctant to call police liars lest they antagonised the judge. If it was possible to avoid the effect of an alleged admission without attacking the police, that course was usually followed. For example, a criminal arrested at Darlinghurst police station was alleged to have produced a pistol, saying 'Stand back you bastards or I'll let you have it!' He was charged with attempted murder after the gun went off, even though it did not hurt anybody. His defence was that the police were around him searching him. They found the gun and closed in on him. He pulled out the gun and held it out in order to surrender it, saying 'Stand back you bastards, I'll let you have it.' He was acquitted.

Of course, we barristers knew then that police 'admissions' were often concocted, or obtained by trickery or threats. In many cases we took the police on in direct confrontation, accusing them, on our clients' instructions, of lying. When before juries this defence sometimes succeeded, when before magistrates it hardly ever succeeded, and only a few judges would ever accept the word of an accused against a police officer, even to create a reasonable doubt.

Many years after the McDermott case the High Court of Australia recognised the danger of alleged confessions to the police. Legislation followed so that today the verbal answers of McDermott to police questions could not be given in evidence, except in special circumstances, unless on an ERISP (electronic record of interview of a suspected person). An ERISP is done by audio- and videotape that can't be tampered with because the video also records the time by a continuous time-keeping mechanism displayed on the screen.

Of course in 1946 the readily obtainable sophisticated equipment of today was not yet invented. An ERISP interview by McDermott, if it matched his evidence, would not, in my opinion, have contained any possible admission of guilt.

The law has also advanced with regard to evidence of identification. The High Court has insisted on very clear and strong warnings by the trial judge to the jury as to the dangers of identification evidence. However, in the case of Mrs King's identification I believe many judges today would exclude the evidence as too unreliable even to be considered by the jury.

Why was McDermott ever accused? He was a drunken wandering shearer who happened to be in the district and was questioned by the police at the time, like numerous other shearers. His de facto wife, Florrie Hampton, knew this in 1945–6 and, when both were well under the influence of the cup that cheers, accused him of murdering Lavers. I rather suspect that during a drunken bout he was apt to occasionally say, 'Yes I killed Lavers and I'll kill you too!' In their drunken bouts such a conversation was very likely and probably happened many times. Those who heard it probably regarded it as rubbish – until they learned that there was a reward for information as to Lavers' killer. The two witnesses who claimed McDermott had boasted of killing Lavers were cross-examined at the Royal Commission. They probably did believe that McDermott was guilty. If the conversation was significant their evidence entitled them to a share of the reward and this fact probably encouraged them to believe it *was* significant. This seems to have been the catalyst in the case against McDermott that caused the investigation to be restarted.

Captain Irwin of the Salvation Army was a great McDermott supporter. The captain, as he is remembered (although he was later promoted), was a great supporter of prisoners, both during trials and in prison. He kept accused murderers company while they awaited the jury's verdict; he was the ever-ready friend of society's outcasts, and everyone in the law admired him as a great embodiment of Christianity at its best. In the McDermott Royal Commission he took upon himself the by no means easy task of getting Florrie Hampton to court sober. He succeeded and she gave her evidence, but it was not particularly useful to anyone.

Relevant to her, a witness called as to a conversation he had with her was Sergeant Tracker Riley, an Aborigine, and one of the last of the Special Tracker unit of the New South Wales Police Force. He seemed a fine man to me, and I understand that he had done some great work. This was probably one of the last appearances of the Tracker unit in a New South Wales court. It died out years ago. (The recent film *One Night the Moon* casts some light on the fine men who were members of that unit.)

As I mentioned at the beginning of the chapter, the evidence of recollections 15 years later in 1951 convinced me that Parker's car was probably not bluey-grey at all. The bluey-grey car parts produced at the trial were almost certainly not Parker's car as claimed by the police. In vain the defence called expert evidence to that effect at the Dubbo trial, but this only seems to have been accepted at last by the Royal Commission several years later.

I did my best to investigate Essie May King's evidence by reference to the police diaries. I discovered that she did receive a substantial portion of the reward, and I also discovered that one of the photographs (14 or 15 there were said to be) allegedly shown to her when she identified McDermott was taken well after the date of her alleged identification. Although Inspector Calman 'was confused in some of his answers', Mr Justice Kinsella, the Royal Commissioner, found that there was 'no foundation for any imputation of misconduct or breach of his obligations against Inspector Calman or any of the other officers connected with this case'.

The McDermott story illustrates the danger of convicting a person many years after their alleged crime. Not so long ago the Commonwealth parliament passed legislation to enable accused war criminals to be tried in Australia. I expressed the opinion to John Spender and Peter Reith at the time (they were in opposition) that there were grave dangers in trying people many years after their alleged offences. Identification after 40 or more years is simply too risky, as experience subsequently proved in Australia, and as the Israeli court found in the case of 'Ivan the Terrible' where the defendant was accused of being a particular genocide operator at a detention camp during the holocaust, but it was later shown that he was not, in fact, that person.

Let me illustrate this by my own experience. Stan Howard, John Howard's brother, was a good friend of mine in the mid-1950s. I saw a great deal of him professionally and socially. He instructed me quite often in court. Yet in recent years, 40 years after I knew him, I simply could not recognise his photo in the newspapers.

Jack Shand KC taught me a great deal. He was probably the best cross-examiner at the Sydney bar in my lifetime. He was the great propounder of the idea of 'shutting the stable doors'; that is, cutting off in advance possible escapes from a cross-examination trap.

For instance, when I gave him the information that Parker's photo had been taken well after the date of Mrs King's identification of McDermott from photos, he proceeded in cross-examination of Inspector Calman to obtain innocently and without fuss the following answers:

1. Mrs King's identification was from photos.
2. Parker's photo was one of those shown to her.
3. Calman took Parker's photo himself and recorded the fact in his diary.
4. The date so recorded in Calman's diary was correct.
5. The date of identification was recorded in his diary.
6. That date was before Parker's photo was taken.

Thus all the 'stable doors' were shut and there was nowhere for the horse to bolt when he was asked to explain how Mrs King could have identified McDermott from photos that included Parker's photo. We, of course, submitted that the identification from photos was simply not true.

While closing the doors Mr Shand KC appeared to be fumbling and not sure of what he was doing. This was appearance only. When all the doors were shut he was clear enough, and there was no fumbling.

One further lesson I learned from this case was the fallibility of trying to tell whether a witness is telling the truth by his or her demeanour. If the lie-detector machine is unreliable, as I believe it is, having seen it demonstrated, how much more is the impression one gets from simply looking at the witness and hearing his or her voice?

McDermott impressed many people who completely believed him, and it was this gift to impress people that saved him. He even impressed prison officers. In gaol he found religion and became a changed person. Yet I myself was unable simply to believe what he said because he said it.

I was impressed by the weakness of the evidence against him; the alleged admissions to camp-fire companions, which were obviously suspect; the alleged admissions to police, not that he murdered Lavers but that he had said he had; the clearly unsafe identification by Mrs King; and the real doubt (apart from the tyre tracks) as to whether Parker's car could be the suspect car. McDermott was not associated with any other car.

I believed then, and I believe now, that a witness's evidence is best tested against the known facts and its inherent probability and consistency. As for demeanour, good demeanour is as likely as not to be the characteristic of a confidence trickster or a bent policeman. Bad demeanour is likely to be caused simply by nervousness or a wandering mind.

After McDermott was released I negotiated on his behalf a deal with Tom Farrell of the *Daily Telegraph* for the sale of McDermott's story. Tom had earned my client's gratitude. His own investigations had been invaluable. In particular he had discovered the sale document to Parker of the car in question, and this showed it to be a 1926 Essex tourer. Our investigations then proved conclusively that Parker's car was not the suspect car.

McDermott's memoirs were not all that interesting as articles in the Telegraph. He had little to say that had not been told in evidence, but for one story. He recounted how when he was in the OBS (observation section) which substituted for the condemned cell at Long Bay, after he had been sentenced to death, the sentence still had to be commuted by the State Labor government. That government was fighting an election. In the back of his mind was the knowledge that some time before Labor had lost an election in Western Australia, and a man convicted before the election was hanged, so it was said, and I seem to remember it. Late one Saturday night the Governor of the CIP (Central Industrial Prison) went to see McDermott. 'It's okay Fred,' he said. 'Labor has won the election.'

Actually though, if the Liberals had won, there was no chance that McDermott would have been executed. Labor came into power in 1941, and the last execution under the old UAP (United Australia Party) had been in 1939.

Lavers' body was never found. There was some evidence at the Royal Commission by people who thought they had seen him alive after 1936. This was not strong evidence and Mr Justice Kinsella rejected it, but the particular evidence of his disappearance was consistent with a staged event. As for hiding a body in the country, a ploughed field or an old mine shaft were among the many possibilities.

One witness did come forward who claimed to have seen a lorry dispose of what might well have been a body in an old mine shaft at West Wyalong at the relevant time. Reg Hawkins, the Public Solicitor, and numerous agents of the media went off to inspect the shaft. The witness unerringly took them to the relevant shaft which was among many shafts back then. On examination, this shaft was found to have collapsed. So no one knows even now if that witness did see a body disposed of.

Many years later, in 1977, barrister and one-time journalist Tom Molomby came to see me about a book he was writing about the McDermott case. At that time a Sunday paper ran the story that Lavers had not died in 1936 but staged his disappearance and had only just died in Melbourne in 1977. McDermott had seen hard times after his release. He had lapsed into his previous alcoholic life and ultimately finished up in a nursing home, during which time the story of Lavers having lived seemed to prove that he, McDermott, was innocent. Soon after that McDermott died, believing that his innocence was established.

Tom Molomby thought the story of Lavers' having survived was untrue. I do not think the police ever looked into it. For myself I am not convinced beyond reasonable doubt that Lavers was murdered.

Of all those involved in the McDermott case, witnesses or lawyers, nearly all are now dead. I was only 25 in 1951 and I have survived everyone at the Royal Commission bar table. It was a big case for a young barrister and made a lasting impression on me. Unfortunately the hard work and long hours affected my health so that I was quite ill the following year. A conscientious barrister in a Royal Commission has an enormous burden in studying documents and transcripts of evidence. I was young and enthusiastic and worked very hard indeed. To me, nothing was more important than to correct a terrible injustice.

# 6

# Appearing Anywhere

As I've already mentioned, I married in May 1953, and had three daughters, all of whom have done well and with whom I have a loving relationship. My marriage was and is still a very happy one. I have always considered myself lucky to have a most successful married life. Whether this made me a better barrister is hard to say. Unless urgent work made it unavoidable I did not work at home. Many a good practice was built on an unhappy marriage where the chambers were a refuge from home. This was not so in my case. I got in to chambers early and contemplated my cases in the car driving to town and then back home to Mona Vale, usually about an hour and a half driving every day. Much of this time was spent planning cross-examinations or addresses.

Before I discuss some of the big cases in which I appeared I should relate my transition from a Police Court battler to a rather unusual generalist. Barristers tend to specialise. They always did, but in recent years the laws have become so complicated that few barristers even attempt to cover all jurisdictions. For many years as a junior counsel I did just that.

It is said that a specialist learns more and more about less and less until eventually he knows everything about nothing. If this is so, a generalist learns less and less about more and more until he knows nothing about everything. I was a generalist. On one particular Friday I appeared in the Common Law List, the Equity List, the Divorce List and the Land and Valuation List. In each jurisdiction in the Supreme Court I had substantial experience. In the District Court on both the civil and criminal side I appeared frequently, and as I became a senior junior I appeared in the Supreme Court in its Civil List in equity and at common law and in murder cases. I also appeared in appeals to the Full Court of New South Wales, later the Court of Appeal, and also at times to the High Court of Australia.

My practice as a junior counsel was unique for its variety and was put together over many years. My progress was gradual; there were few high points, just many years of work.

At first, as I have mentioned before, I was known at the bar as 'young Chester', and this lasted for years, until I was in my thirties. As a young man with the excuse of inexperience I received every courtesy from most magistrates. The judges were not so kind. Of course they varied but it was not unusual for me to be on the wrong end of judicial bad temper. On rare occasions judges were quite rude, once very rude indeed, in one case saying, 'I can't understand what this boy is saying' to a crowded court. My humiliation was extreme.

I found that if one was mild and polite one could be the subject of judicial bullying, but if one stood up to the judge and answered back firmly, but still politely, the judge became quite respectful, often friendly. It was common for judges to try out young counsel, and it was not pleasant to fail the test. Frequently, however, one heard at ceremonials to farewell a judge how kind he was to young counsel. In my experience such kindness was rare indeed. However, as I became more experienced and capable, I found the judges much easier to get along with.

In those days, and perhaps still, a great proportion of the work in the common law jurisdictions of the District and Supreme Courts was for injured plaintiffs seeking damages resulting from road and factory accidents. In my very early days I was unlucky in three traffic accident cases and lost before a civil jury. Usually sympathy for the plaintiff prevailed. This initial lack of success probably prevented me from becoming a specialist for injured plaintiffs – an 'arms and legs' man. I am glad now that this was so, but at the time I was very disappointed to lose these cases. I do not think I was incompetent, just unlucky.

To get a reputation as a lucky counsel was to start on the path to prosperity, but a reputation for being unlucky could be a great handicap. Fortunately my reputation was made in other cases, and then I later became quite successful for injured plaintiffs.

By and large, in those days much common law work was before civil juries of four persons. I found such juries usually made sensible findings, particularly for plaintiffs who had been badly treated in business. It was, however, a fact that the attitude of juries to pedestrians injured by motor cars changed over the years. At first they favoured the pedestrian. Later, as more people became drivers, they found frequently for the defendant driver, perhaps because the driver, being able to afford a car, was perceived as socially superior and everyone claimed to be a good driver.

The use of civil juries was greatly reduced in the late 1960s, and nowadays most issues at common law are decided by judges sitting alone. Juries were also abolished in divorce cases whereas previously it was not uncommon for them to decide the issue of adultery. In equity and other courts there were never juries.

Equity judges were usually learned men, chosen for their legal knowledge, and hence equity cases often tended to be technical. Equity started off as a means of easing the strict rules of common law liability, but modern equity judges deal with a great variety of work including wills and company matters. For the most part I enjoyed equity cases. However I did find a tendency in equity to hold people to their contracts, even when there had been considerable unfairness. In this regard I think the old common law jury was better for the battlers trying to overcome the results of being duped or bullied by big business. I think brilliant judges often failed to see the world through the eyes of honest but foolish people.

Very early in my career I started to appear for workers who sought to own their own businesses with very little capital. These were actually Legal Aid cases. There were numerous people ready to trick them into poverty; for example, by selling them motor lorries that broke down soon after purchase, or shop businesses that turned out to have takings vastly below the vendor's alleged figures.

Someone once said to me in my early days at the bar, 'It is no use trying to protect the public. If you tie their hands they will hand the money over with their toes.' Unfortunately there is some truth in this.

In order to succeed for a plaintiff induced to lose money by fraud or misrepresentation, it is necessary to prove that he or she was in fact misled, and that the fraud or misrepresentation actually induced the contract. The problem was that if the plaintiff had been deceived, he or she was going to be a hopeless witness. If the plaintiff turned out to be shrewd and capable, how could one believe that he or she was deceived by the vendor? I have seen a lot of business victims fail in court because they were bad witnesses.

Many a working person tries to be the independent owner of a small business but fails, not merely because of inexperience, but because of deception by one of the many clever tricksters who seeks his or her money. The loss of entire savings can be a small tragedy for the plaintiff. I handled a lot of such cases; they were difficult to conduct and I lost quite a few. On the other hand, I often obtained settlements that eased the pain such losses caused.

As I became more experienced I handled many company cases in the Equity Court. I also helped in the selling off, for tax purposes, of the losses incurred by insolvent companies. The law was later amended to make such sales almost impossible.

One case in which I appeared early in my career was as junior to Jack Shand QC for Sid Barnes, a famous test cricketer. Sid had been unofficially banned by the Australian Cricket Board from playing for Australia, despite his undoubted skill as a batsman and fieldsman. No reasons were given.

The defendant to the case in the District Court had rather conveniently written to a newspaper and his published letter said that he backed the Australian Cricket Board which must have had good reasons for its actions. Sid sued him for libel and he, to defend himself, subpoenaed as witnesses the members of the board who had to disclose as witnesses their reasons for banning a leading player.

They were rather trivial reasons such as jumping over a cricket-ground fence when the gate was locked. The defendant conceded that the reasons were trivial and the case was settled. Sid was publicly vindicated.

Nowadays such high-handed actions by the Australian Cricket Board as banning a cricketer from playing without hearing his defence or even giving any reasons would not be permitted by the courts. The law has moved a long way in the right direction since the 1950s. Now a person cannot be denied his or her profession or job without a fair hearing, if he or she is alleged to have been guilty of some misconduct.

I appeared in many divorce cases, and in subdivision appeals and in all sorts of litigation, as well as equity and common law cases, but I suppose I liked doing criminal cases before 12-person juries more than most other cases. I also had quite a large practice appearing for the prosecution in Supreme Court appeals from magistrates. These appeals on questions of law were usually very interesting and often important test cases.

For example, a man could be prosecuted for having goods in his custody reasonably suspected of being stolen or otherwise unlawfully obtained. The goods were usually forfeited. In a leading case entitled *Purdon v Dittmar* I established that this law applied to drug-sales money that could be thus forfeited and the owner punished. My opponent before the Court of Appeal was Mary Gaudron who, in the days when there were few women barristers, had earned a reputation as a brilliant lawyer and a persuasive advocate. She became the first woman judge in the High Court of Australia where she became a senior judge, noted for her learning, her humanity and her common sense.

In the case of *Tubman v Lucas and Magill* I defended two senior police officers, Inspectors Lucas and Magill, charged with contempt of court for preventing the public entering Central Police

Court during an anti-Vietnam War demonstration in 1970. They were acquitted. In another Vietnam War case I succeeded in upholding on appeal convictions of demonstrators who misbehaved in Waverley Court. I appeared in numerous appeals concerning cases of PCA (prescribed content of alcohol). Breathtesting was initially the subject of many technicality appeals. In one such case it was established that once through the front gate of his or her home a driver could not be breath-tested: the defence of 'home and dry'.

I ultimately lost a leading case on stripteasing at Kings Cross. Was the parading of a naked woman at a strip club that was open to the public necessarily indecent? After one successful appeal from the magistrate's decision acquitting the young lady, I lost the last appeal. During this case I went with my instructing solicitor, Ken Wild, to inspect the strip clubs at the Cross. It is surprising how, after seeing many such shows, one acquires a complete indifference to whether a woman is clothed or not.

I appeared for the Crown in the first model prosecution under the amended Indecent Publications Act. I also appeared for the Crown when hundreds of 'soft-porn' films were seized by the police. The seizure was illegal because of non-compliance with technicalities, but we then tried to convince Mr Justice Mahoney that the films were illegal because they were indecent. This involved watching samples of the films in His Honour's chambers. I lost. My opponent was the well-known Jim Staples, later a judge of the Arbitration Court. One of his submissions was that public opinion in such matters changes and that the films should be allowed to 'mature like good wine' until public opinion accepted them.

His Honour reserved judgment for a long time and, while awaiting this, I happened to meet Jim in the street. 'Chester,' he said, 'You are doing a terrible thing to my client. By the time we get those soft-porn films back they will be worthless. The real stuff is coming out from Denmark!' He was right.

Protecting the public morals was a big issue in the 1960s and 1970s, and of course for many years before. There was the 'Love me Sailor' case about an allegedly obscene novel soon after the war in which a vice squad detective's literary knowledge was tested by asking him if he knew William Shakespeare – he replied that he thought he was a New South Wales detective. Much later there was the *Portnoy's Complaint* case and, in England, there was the *Lady Chatterley's Lover* case which seemed to establish the right to use the 'f' word in films and books, ad nauseam by now.

Throughout the English-speaking world back then the pubic-hairs test was generally applied by police. A picture of a naked woman was indecent if her pubic hair showed. If it did not, it passed. There was no legal case or statute that justified the concept so far as I was able to ascertain, but police applied it in England, America and Australia.

Ultimately the law was amended to permit adults to buy and read anything they wanted to and sex shops proliferated through the city. However, the law had to be amended again to ban, under heavy penalties, child pornography. Apart from the so-called 'kiddie porn' there do not appear to have been any notable indecency or obscenity cases in the courts for many years. Adultery and fornication are no longer civil offences or matters contrary to the public interest. Participants in these activities are now protected by anti-discrimination legislation. One enthusiastic Christian who sought to prevent people 'living in sin' from renting his house was compelled to pay them substantial damages. When the divorce laws were amended it was said that the law would no longer be concerned with people's bedrooms. It was a pious hope.

Today the law sniffs with ever greater enthusiasm into people's sex lives, looking for workplace harassment, discrimination, indecent assault cases and other breaches of the law.

During the amendments of the marriage laws the old action for breach of promise of marriage was abolished. There does not appear to have been any move to restore this law. Mr Pickwick of Dickens' *Pickwick Papers* would be safe from Mrs Bardell today.

I acted in several breach of promise cases, which were all eventually settled. In those days it was notoriously difficult to defend a man sued in such an action. Although the lady's evidence of a promise to marry had to be corroborated, this usually caused little difficulty for the plaintiff. Excuses for changing one's mind were very limited by the law.

I acted in one case where the man had a good factual defence, namely that the lady was entitled to an income dependent upon her remaining single. This fact made the alleged mutual promises unlikely and eliminated any financial loss to the lady from any broken promise. She abandoned her claim.

Men sometimes sued for breach of promise to recover expensive engagement rings and other presents. Such a recovery could also be made under the law of conditional gifts. One of my Greek clients sued for breach of promise to restore his good name. After hard negotiation a settlement was reached restoring gifts and there was a statement in open court by the lady's counsel to the effect that my client bore a good character and the broken engagement was not caused by his misconduct or bad character. So my client was happy until the afternoon paper reported the case under the headline 'Jilted!'. The best laid plans of mice and men 'gang aft awry'.

I have mentioned Mary Gaudron, who was a brilliant advocate and judge, the first female Solicitor General in New South Wales and the first and, unhappily, only female High Court judge.

Besides Mary Gaudron, many other women have distinguished themselves in the law. The first female judge in New South Wales was Jane Matthews whom I also knew at the bar. She became a Crown prosecutor, District Court judge, Supreme Court judge and a Federal Court judge. She had the instinct for the fair thing, the just thing, which is much more important than legal brilliance in a judge. She helped to blaze the way for many female judges.

I remember one attempted-murder case before her when there was a difficult question as to whether and/or how some evidence should be admitted. She discussed what was fair with me for the defence and Mark Tedeschi QC for the Crown and ultimately we agreed under her guidance as to what was fair.

I might add that, in my opinion, jury verdicts improved once juries included women. I particularly noted this in criminal sex cases.

I suppose that as the father of three clever daughters, each pursuing a successful career, and with a schoolteacher wife who pursued her career very successfully while married to me, I have great sympathy for female ambitions. However, to me, the simple fact is that males and females share the same human ability and it was ridiculous in the past not to utilise one half of the available human talents. Great strides have been made in the law, but there is still a long way to go.

Women in the law were at first wary of being barristers, and tended rather to become solicitors. That has changed and gradually the number of women taking leading roles in the courts will increase. It has been speculated that in the past perhaps some women were appointed to the bench partly because of their gender, in order to have women on the bench. If that was so, the appointees have nevertheless distinguished themselves by their ability and sense of fairness. The law is richer for their promotions.

# 7

# The *Voyager* Royal Commission

The first Royal Commission into the loss of the *Voyager* when it was cut in two by the aircraft carrier *Melbourne* blamed the *Melbourne's* captain, Captain Robertson, as partly responsible for the disaster in which over 80 men were lost. This finding was erroneous, I believe, and resulted in destroying Robertson's career. He resigned, naturally bitter at having suffered a grave injustice. There was much agitation to right this wrong. The fact that Captain Stevens in charge of the *Voyager* was held mainly to blame did not save Robertson's career.

The accident occurred near Jervis Bay on 10 February 1964. My client, Peter Cabban, one-time executive officer of the *Voyager*, had sailed with her on a trip commencing 31 January 1963 to Singapore, Hong Kong, Subic Bay (The Philippines), Malaya and Darwin, the cruise extending to 12 August 1963 at Williamstown where some time later Cabban, then a Lieutenant Commander, left the ship and the navy. During this trip, events occurred that convinced him that his commander, Captain Stevens, was an alcoholic. When the disaster occurred he felt responsible for not reporting that his captain was, in effect, unfit to command.

He offered his information to the first Royal Commission into the disaster, firstly to counsel assisting and secondly to counsel for Captain Stevens' interests. Stevens had been lost with his ship. Counsel assisting regarded Cabban's evidence as the ravings of an unbalanced mind, did not call him as a witness, and did not pursue the matter further. No one else offered evidence that Captain Stevens drank too much although there was unchallenged evidence that he had consumed a triple brandy at sea not long before the accident. A blood test from the dead body after it had been recovered confirmed the intake of an amount of alcohol not exceeding the triple brandy.

During the agitation to remedy the injustice done to Captain Robertson, he and his friend Vice-Admiral Hickling heard of Cabban's allegations. Cabban was requested by them to dictate on tape what had happened, and he did so late in January 1965 for the confidential use of Vice-Admiral Hickling RN, as background material for a book he was writing about the collision.

The transcribed tape became known as the Cabban statement and was later used in the House of Representatives as the basis of a brilliant maiden speech by Ted St John QC. As a result there was a second Royal Commission consisting of three judges to ascertain whether Captain Stevens was unfit to command and, if so, but only if so, to reconsider the findings made against Captain Robertson.

These days Cabban would be called a whistle-blower but the term was not used then. I called him an allegator, one who makes allegations. Many of his allegations contained in the Cabban statement were hearsay. The statement was a simple dictation to a tape, not a careful proof of evidence.

It should have been obvious to anyone that if the Cabban statement were to be publicised, the powers that be would brand Cabban a malicious liar. That, of course, was the initial response of the navy and the government. The appointment of the Royal Commission meant that Peter Cabban, not simply the late Captain Stevens, was on trial. If, like so many allegators before him, he was found to be a liar by the Royal Commission, Cabban's character and reputation would have been destroyed. His hope for future happiness in life was at stake for the sake of Captain Robertson.

Of course, as Ted St John saw, there was much more at stake than Captain Robertson's cause. It was of overwhelming importance that modern weaponry should only be in the hands of sober men. There could be no tolerance of insobriety when senior officers were on duty in any service.

I spent hours with Peter Cabban and later with Jack Hiatt QC, my leader, and Tony McDonald, our solicitor. Preparing a complete proof of evidence for such a long voyage, often concerning events suggestive of insobriety, was a time-consuming and difficult task. We had to prod our client's memory and help him to remember, in 1967, events over four years earlier.

What are the symptoms of insobriety or drunkenness? In real life we form superficial judgments that are rarely important. In a court of law or a Royal Commission, a senior officer's hitherto splendid reputation was not to be destroyed on inexact proofs or superficial impressions. What was the significance of a man being flushed, or feeling ill, or staggering or tripping on the ship's gangway? Few serving naval personnel were likely to support Cabban when the navy's attitude towards his allegations was crystal clear. They were false, said the navy.

As it turned out, Captain Stevens was suffering from a duodenal ulcer, and it became at times a matter of some difficulty to sort out what was the cause of the symptoms displayed.

For day after day Peter Cabban went into the firing line as the first witness, cross-examined by counsel for the navy and counsel for the Stevens family. There is something unfair about a witness being cross-examined for days. It becomes a feat of strength or fortitude rather than a useful search for the truth. These days a witness cannot discuss his evidence with his counsel so long as the cross-examination continues. This leaves him or her isolated. This rule did not apply in 1967 when Cabban went through his ordeal. Nevertheless, although he was a courageous man, the strain was intense. In 1967 he was being cross-examined about what happened in 1963, and counsel cross-examining had access to all the contemporary documents, most of which Cabban had not seen, either recently or at all.

There was one important incident. Cabban claimed that he was in command of *Voyager* for five days out of Tokyo, while the captain recovered in his cabin from a drinking episode in Tokyo. Now when a naval vessel leaves port there are inevitable punishment parades on board to deal with offences (for example, being drunk on board or late from leave) committed while in port. The punishment records for a day or so out of Tokyo were produced showing Stevens as the captain administering the punishments. Cabban was literally flummoxed and asked from the witness box, 'Can I speak to my counsel?' This request was refused. Eventually he said that he had forgotten that Stevens, after the five days absent from duty, had the punishment records retyped to show him in command. Under severe threats from Stevens, Cabban gave in and permitted this to be done. He was a naturally strong man and his capitulation led to hysteric amnesia – his mind revolted against the memory and dismissed it. This was why he felt to blame for the disaster but was not really sure why.

I believed him, and other evidence did support him. The person who signed the records was lost in the disaster. Of those attending the punishment parades as delinquents, those still in the navy said the punishing officer was Stevens. Those who had left the navy said the officer was Cabban. In my opinion, it was fairly obvious who was right.

Ultimately, the second Royal Commission neither upheld nor rejected Cabban on this aspect of his story.

Counsel assisting the Commission was 'Red' Burt QC from Western Australia, later Chief Justice, then Governor, of that State. He was an excellent investigator and a shrewd advocate. His cross-examination was at times superb.

As the evidence unfolded, the Stevens party had to justify a lot of questionable behaviour and naturally enough blamed the duodenal ulcer for everything. Thus occurred the most amazing confrontation of a judge that I have ever heard.

Mr Justice Asprey seemed at times hostile to Cabban and when a Dr Birrell from Victoria gave evidence that on the facts alleged so far Stevens appeared to be a chronic alcoholic, he fumed as my leader, Jack Hiatt, continued to question the witness.

Finally His Honour exploded and said, 'Really, Mr Hiatt, do you need to keep on stressing the obvious. If I pass by a hotel and see a man lying outside prostrate, reeking of alcohol with empty bottles beside him, do I need to be told that he is a chronic alcoholic?'

Hiatt replied with a straight but impertinent face, 'Really, Your Honour, in this Commission I should have thought he was suffering from a duodenal ulcer.'

Peter Cabban survived. He was a tough but sensitive man and he suffered under efficient cross-examination. The navy, at first, regarded him as an outcast. Thus all naval witnesses, even ex-naval witnesses, were under pressure to deny that Captain Stevens had an alcohol problem, and to attack Cabban. But there really was not much to attack Cabban about. He obviously believed what he said, and had no motive to denigrate his former captain.

The naval hostility finally became an advantage. A witness who said Captain Stevens was at all times sober and healthy tended to be obviously trying to please the navy. A witness who saw something significant said so very reluctantly and was believed. Red Burt's investigations were thorough and brilliant and much of the hidden truth eventually emerged.

Cabban taught me a lot about giving evidence. It pays to have a good memory and, as one is questioned, the witness should relive the event in his or her mind. In reply to questions the witness should say what he or she sees in his or her mind.

We received no assistance from Captain Robertson, no leads, no witnesses. He had relied reluctantly on the Cabban allegations to reopen the inquiry. Now he distanced himself from them in case Cabban failed. In simple terms, Cabban was on his own. Was it fair to lure a man into this position of peril and then stand aside, ready to disown him?

Captain Robertson's attitude of relying on Peter Cabban to make the accusations against Captain Stevens, but himself standing aloof, was well illustrated by an incident that occurred during the evidence of Commodore Dollard. Dollard had been in Tokyo when *Voyager* was there between 5 and 10 June 1963 and had met Stevens who was affected then by alcohol. The extent of the effects of alcohol was of course crucial evidence. On the grapevine we had heard that Dollard had previously given an account of this meeting with Stevens to Robertson, an account, we understood, that supported Cabban's story.

We felt that if Robertson sat in court while Dollard gave his evidence, that witness would not be so tempted by naval pressure to cut back on the story that we believed he had told Robertson. So we asked Robertson to sit in court during the evidence of this witness for the obvious reasons which were made clear to him. He did not attend but instead sent his wife whose presence was unobtrusive and useless to us. As it was, Dollard gave evidence that gave some restrained support to Cabban's case.

Robertson never denied to us that he had spoken to Dollard about Stevens in Tokyo, but he never told us precisely what had been said to him. Thus we had no evidence of the conversation to put to Dollard in cross-examination.

I am not suggesting that Dollard was not an honest witness. He was, not unnaturally, a reluctant witness and we had no real means of testing his evidence on a very important part of Cabban's case. The Royal Commission accepted his evidence.

So far as Robertson was concerned, Cabban was on his own. If Cabban was held to be a liar Robertson could disown him; if his story was in large part accepted then the way was open to Robertson to exoneration and compensation. Cabban was expendable. At the appropriate time, Robertson, through his counsel, submitted that Stevens was unfit to command, but he never assisted Cabban in any way to prove this.

I felt very strongly about all this at the time. Captain Robertson was a charming, attractive man and he was embittered by a real injustice which had been done to him in the first *Voyager* Royal Commission. He very much disliked attacking Captain Stevens and I suppose he used (*used* being the appropriate word) Cabban as a last resort. Cabban did not volunteer to be an allegator. When his tape-recording, given confidentially to Robertson, was publicised he had no choice. At least he could have been helped.

When the Cabban allegations were in large part upheld, and the way was opened to reassess the navigational questions, when

Captain Robertson was cleared, he was invited to comment on Cabban's struggle and declined. He received a large compensation for an injustice. Cabban went back to his life, thanked by some politicians, but not by Captain Robertson.

Captain Robertson died long ago, but I still feel that his use of Cabban, who was much junior to him in rank, a lieutenant-commander as against a senior captain, was not Robertson's finest hour, to say the least.

Cabban was, to a considerable extent, corroborated by the evidence of Lieutenant David Martin. Martin's reluctant accounts of Captain Stevens imbibing too much fell short of the Cabban statement, but at the same time gave it support of a very substantial nature. Peter thought David had let him down because, he said, David's statements had fallen far short of what he actually saw and heard. Later, David, by then an Admiral and Governor of New South Wales, died. It was said that before he died he said that his evidence had fallen short of the full truth. I think this was almost certainly so.

David Martin appeared at the Commission, as his subsequent career showed, a fine, most impressive young man. In its report the Commission relied heavily upon his evidence. However, had he deposed to the full extent of most of the Cabban statement, had he depicted an alcoholic captain, it may well have done Cabban's cause more harm than good. Martin was known to be a friend of Cabban and had his support been full and complete he might well have been dismissed as a friend putting his best foot forward. His reluctant partial support of the Cabban statement was, on the other hand, accepted without question.

Just what he said before he died I do not know, but he may well have thought that he should have told the full story rather than a watered-down version. On the other hand, the 'full story' was substantially one of impression. Peter Cabban was horrified by what he saw and his impressions reflected that horror. David Martin was a more relaxed character and his evidence may have reflected that character difference. He was not so shocked at his captain's occasional lapses from the high standards expected from a senior officer.

One of the mysteries of the *Voyager* tragedy is that on the night of the collision the captain, while at sea, had a brandy, said to be a triple brandy. It would hardly have affected his judgment, and the Commission so held, at the same time doubting whether it was, in fact, a triple brandy. The post-mortem blood examination seemed to confirm the consumption of alcohol but not to the extent alleged. But Captain Stevens, no matter what criticism may be made of his onshore drinking, never drank at sea. This was the usual rule followed by deck officers. It was strange that he broke his rule on that night. Cabban said himself that Stevens never drank at sea, and the triple brandy was quite a mystery that very much concerned Peter Cabban.

The word 'alcoholic' is often used with quite different meanings. One simple meaning is any person who drinks to their detriment. A chronic alcoholic must have lots of alcohol, much too much and every day. In recent years the 'spree alcoholic' drinks heavily only once a week and then consumes enormous quantities. Probably the best meaning of the word is one who frequently drinks too much for their own good.

The Royal Commission firmly rejected any proposition that Captain Stevens was a chronic alcoholic as I have defined the term and as it is popularly understood. The judges held that his unwise and undisciplined drinking of alcohol during the visit to Tokyo contributed to his condition of health. It was the duodenal ulcer that made Captain Stevens unfit to command, and his usually moderate but occasionally unwise consumption of alcohol on a few occasions was a contributing factor to the illness that made him unfit to command.

What a lot of money was spent on those two inquiries! Still, the lives of over 80 men were lost and the truth needed to be known. Strangely, the second inquiry was publicly regarded as for the purpose of righting a possible wrong done to Captain Robertson. In this it was successful by clearing up an error in the first Royal Commission's finding which cast blame on the captain of the *Melbourne*.

Perhaps Ted St John MHR QC was really on to the main point when he made his maiden speech in the House of Representatives. There can be no tolerance for misuse of alcohol in the context of modern war machinery. I think the second Royal Commission had the effect of reducing the tolerance displayed for alcoholics in the upper echelons of the armed services – and perhaps even in other walks of life.

Finally, it does a great deal of good for a closed service such as the navy, or the police service, to be subjected to a searching inquiry. It is not pleasant medicine, but it is likely to remove inefficiencies, even scandals.

Peter Cabban and his wife, Sue, and their children became quite close friends of myself, Jean, and my children. On the advice of Jack Hiatt QC and myself he made no public statement for many years. But he was an allegator who survived, and not many did, any more than modern whistle-blowers do. His character was preserved and he went on with a successful life. He was very lucky. Those who expose such matters are usually destroyed by those defending the good name of the organisation concerned. It is usually considered better to shoot the messenger rather than expose the scandal. As the whistle-blower's body is wheeled away his epitaph is almost invariably 'He went about it the wrong way'. But there is no right way; there never was, and I doubt whether modern legislation has improved the position at all.

This is not an easy problem. For every useful whistle-blower there are probably many unbalanced idiots, or malicious trouble-makers. One has to beware of the position which exists in the police service today, that numerous spiteful complaints make the lives of good police miserable and hide the genuine complaints.

A would-be informer against his or her superiors would be well advised to obtain good legal advice first. Whistle-blowers should be cross-examined privately as to just what they really know before they put their careers, perhaps their whole life's happiness, at stake.

Better still, proper supervision and proper reporting systems should obviate the need for much whistle-blowing.

Nearly all the members of the bar table at the second *Voyager* Royal Commission went on the bench fairly soon thereafter. Of course, that did not apply to Jack Hiatt QC and myself. I never received any legal instructions from the Commonwealth until Labor got into power in 1972, nearly five years later.

Since writing this chapter David Salter has produced his ABC TV documentary, 'Unfit to Command', about the *Voyager* disaster. The evidence he obtained was to a substantial extent additional to that in the Royal Commission, and it shows that the Peter Cabban statement was very close to the exact truth. The report of the Royal Commission was shown to be not nearly as close to the true picture as the Cabban statement.

# 8

# A Generalist on the Road to Silk

A Queen's counsel was said to take silk because he now wore a special silk robe (and a special bar jacket) that differed from the non-silk, stuff gown of a junior counsel. When I took silk in 1974 not only were silks expected to charge much higher fees than a junior, they had to have a junior with them in court. Now he or she frequently does have a junior but it is not compulsory.

Silks were promoted because of their ability, the extent of their practice and their reputation not merely for success but for ethics and integrity. It was a great honour, conferred by the Attorney-General usually with advice from the president of the Bar Association who made inquiries of judges and senior counsel. Quite recently the government decided that the Attorney-General should not appoint any more Queen's counsels. There were various reasons, some of which may have been related to the move of Australia to become a republic. Now senior counsel (SCs) are appointed by the president of the Bar Association for the same qualities and after similar inquiries to those made for QCs. Probably the references to judges are more frequent these days. SCs are also known as silks.

At one stage it was suggested to the QCs that they should all agree to be SCs. They would not have a bar of it. Eventually we shall all die out as the Sergeants at Law, the predecessors to the modern silks, did a century ago.

Senior counsel or silk is an old tradition and all ambitious barristers hope to take silk. However, taking silk is not necessary for promotion to the bench, or even to the High Court where Mr Justice Starke and Mr Justice Walsh were junior counsel before their respective appointments.

In New South Wales the silk carried nothing to court; the junior carried both their own and their leader's brief. This is still the case, but often everything is wheeled into court on a trolley.

The leader always preceded his or her junior through a door. As a male of the old school I used to wait to follow a female junior, but I was asked not to do this by my female junior, so I changed my habits of a lifetime, if only in this respect.

I suppose I was a bit scared of applying for silk, lest I be refused and lest I received little or no work when my fees had to be increased. For years I had appeared often enough for the Crown as a senior junior against Queen's counsel in appeals from magistrates to the Supreme Court. I suppose the Crown was glad to have my cheaper services rather than pay a senior counsel.

Before I could be a silk I had to have established my reputation and my practice. After the second *Voyager* Royal Commission I suppose it was only a matter of time until I became a Queen's Counsel. I was afraid to apply, believing — wrongly — that one needed a specialist practice to take silk. I was still doing a lot of State government work, company work, divorce work, land-subdivision work, common law — just about everything.

In 1969 I appeared for John Maddison, the Minister for Justice, to oppose an application to evict 72 tenants in a test case. This was a successful opposition and the first, as I recall, of a number of cases I had against Peter Clyne. By this time Peter Clyne had been struck off the roll of barristers, but was acting in the Petty Sessions Courts as a rent consultant, appearing as an advocate. Peter was a brilliant advocate but often spoiled his cases by playing too much for publicity. It was one of the tragedies of the law that his undoubted ability was not put to better use.

I did a number of cases for the State Attorney-General as junior to Harold Snelling QC, the New South Wales Solicitor-General. These were all contempt of court cases. Some were cases of insulting judges, others of publishing material likely to prejudice juries. Broadly speaking, modern decisions allow very wide latitude to journalists and others who criticise judges. The main prohibition is against attributing bad faith to the judge. These days one can say a judge's reasoning is absurd, or even incompetent, but not dishonest.

One must not prejudice the jury in a pending case. Sometimes journalists are foolish enough to disclose a person's criminal record before their trial, or publish their photo when identification is an issue. Any statement that the person is guilty or innocent may well be contempt of court if a jury is to try the case. Nowadays it is considered that a judge will not be influenced by such comments and hence they may not be punishable contempt.

For years, people who wished to avoid public discussion of their conduct filed 'stop writs'. These claimed defamation and made the truth about the plaintiff's conduct a jury issue, hence no further public discussion could be had lest it be contempt of court. Wiser courts and new defamation procedures have put the stop writs into the back pages of legal history.

Briefed by the State government, I had to defend a clerk of Petty Sessions in June 1970, a Mr Wigley, who refused to issue a warrant for the arrest of Mary McNish, secretary of the Australia Party. She and many others had made a statement in defiance of the National Security Act (the Vietnam War conscription). Geoffrey Mullen prosecuted her, he being a sympathiser opposing the Act. She was fined $50 in default of 25 days' hard labour, and apparently wished to be a martyr. I successfully opposed the application and she stayed out of gaol.

Soon after I appeared against six men who had been convicted of contempt of court for raising clenched fists at Waverley Court. They appealed to the Court of Appeal but the convictions stood. This was another Vietnam War case and an example of contempt in the face of the court – being rude, but more importantly disrupting or tending to disrupt proceedings. Tempers ran high in those days. In Victoria I understand that there were actual threatening rushes at the magistrate in one instance.

Company-law cases at the time were less interesting. In 1971 I appeared for Vam Ltd which was eventually saved from liquidation by my old school friend Bruce Smith, then a leading chartered accountant.

That year I also appeared in my first murder case, on my own. It was a sad domestic situation in which the husband was killed by his wife by one shot from a .22 rifle. In this I suppose he was unlucky. It was a wild shot but it hit a vital organ. The Crown eventually after I appeared at the committal proceedings, accepted a plea of guilty to manslaughter.

Leon Tanner, the Crown prosecutor, was concerned lest the dead husband be the subject of heavy attacks for his prior conduct. I assured him that this would not occur and in fact I think I made a much better plea on the wife's behalf by making no attacks on her husband. Domestic misery is by no means necessarily the fault of one party alone, or even either of them. People can be unlucky. She received quite a light sentence.

Murder cases can be neatly placed into two categories. In the first the accused denies killing the victim and in such cases usually does not accuse someone else. The accused simply says that he or she did not do it. Fred McDermott was an example of this defence, as many years later was Andrew Kalajzich. These are usually very interesting cases.

The second category comprises those cases where the accused admits killing the victim but seeks to excuse the killing by accident, self defence, or provocation. In the case of provocation murder is reduced to manslaughter. The other matters result in an acquittal.

These are often cases in which the unlucky face the law – when tempers snap and a weapon is handy. Many a family dispute has the potential to result in a murder case. I have appeared for the husband of a wife who said to her furious husband who was grasping her throat, 'You haven't got the guts.' She was wrong, as was the husband of another client who said to his knife-wielding wife, 'You're not game.' The line between a trivial incident and a tragedy is a thin one. The line between love and hatred is very thin indeed.

Before women were included in juries, the sentimentality of male jurors was sometimes exploited where women killed men, usually husbands or lovers. There were some amazing acquittals – the husband who 'ran onto' his wife's kitchen knife, the girl who shot her fiancé when 'everything went blank'. Once women became part of the jury, crazy verdicts for women male jurors found attractive ceased.

Counsel who appeared in those cases of 'everything went blank' had remarkable courage. They conducted them on the basis of murder or acquittal. They did not raise the obvious question of provocation reducing the offence to manslaughter. When the High Court held that it was the judge's duty to raise provocation with the jury, whether or not the defence did so, juries went for the obvious compromise verdict of manslaughter.

One of my cases in 1971 was a sequel to the famous case involving Mr Brown who threatened Qantas and obtained $500,000 in notes. This, after all, was public money back then, and easily lost. When Reg Ansett's airline was subsequently threatened, he eventually agreed to pay the extortionist $60,000 (beaten down from $200,000).

A Victorian policewoman pretending to be an Ansett employee came to Sydney with what appeared to be $60,000 in notes. Actually there were a few genuine notes at each end and the rest of the wad was blank paper. The policewoman handed the money to my client, Michael Schneider, a young South African nurse, at Mascot Airport. He was then arrested.

He bore the name of an anti-apartheid terrorist and the South African police flew a couple of men over to see him. He was not their man. My Michael Schneider claimed to have advertised for part-time work (this was true) and as a consequence had innocently accepted a job as a courier at Mascot with instructions to fly to Brisbane where he was to be met on arrival. The police should have followed him on the plane up to Brisbane but lost their nerve. All they had to show for their efforts was a young courier, guilty or innocent of knowledge of what was going on. Michael said he maintained his innocence with the police, but at the committal proceedings it emerged that he was supposed to have given an unsigned record of interview admitting guilt.

At these same committal proceedings I found out that when Michael met the Victorian policewoman with the money and both gave each other false names, he told her it was a false name and that he was a nurse working at St Vincent's Hospital, as he in fact was. There was no mention of this in her statement or her evidence in chief, but I found it recorded in her notebook. Why would a guilty courier identify himself?

Eventually the jury disagreed. Michael was not tried again and went back to South Africa. The Crown nearly always spread a story when a jury disagreed that one person was holding out for not guilty. Only one person. This was not the case here. You could see on its return that the jury was split in half, neither half liking the other, to say the least.

The jury room was within hearing of a nearby passage and someone told me they heard a shout, 'The judge thinks he is guilty!' (true enough) and another shout 'That bloody judge wasn't fair!' (no comment: he is dead now and I knew him quite well and liked him despite this case).

Usually one does not know if one's client is guilty or not, unless of course the client wants to plead guilty. Sometimes the story of an accused person is, to say the least, unlikely. However, people are entitled to the court's judgment, not one's own. It is for counsel to put the story of the accused as well as possible; it is for the jury, or the magistrate, to judge the outcome. I might note that a person charged is a defendant before a magistrate, but an accused before a higher court. New legislation will make 'defendants' of everyone.

If a client tells you he or she is guilty, but wants to plead not guilty, it is best that someone else defends him or her, but it may be too late for that. A person charged is entitled to make the Crown prove its case, but you are not able to put up anything positive. You cannot deceive the court with evidence or even a submission that you know to be false. All this rarely happens because a client with a false story usually knows not to tell the lawyer that he or she is telling lies.

Let me illustrate with, as far as I can remember, the only time this ever happened to me in a criminal case. The client, a tanker driver, was charged with stealing petrol and his case was to begin the day after when he confessed to me, much to my surprise. I told him that in my opinion the Crown evidence was insufficient to convict him. He naturally wanted to plead not guilty. He did, and was acquitted without giving or calling any evidence and without any submissions other than that the evidence was insufficient. However, in a related case a garage proprietor who admitted having received the petrol was charged with receiving stolen petrol, knowing it to be stolen.

Since this defendant before the magistrate admitted to receiving the petrol from my now acquitted client, the only issue was whether he knew it had been stolen. For this the police relied upon the very low price paid to my client. However they needed evidence of the normal wholesale price to retailers of petrol. The oil-company officials recoiled in horror. One said he could only give such evidence with instructions from Europe. (It needs more than a little stealing case to disclose the wholesale price of petrol. I wonder whether anyone really knows what it is, still less why it oscillates like a yoyo.) No one gave the necessary evidence and the second defendant was acquitted.

Of course people can *think* they are guilty when they are not. A client of mine was a vendor of cigarettes who bought obviously hot cigarettes from a man in a truck at the door. He was charged with receiving stolen cigarettes, knowing that they were stolen. However there was no proof that the 'hot' cigarettes were in fact the ones that the police could prove were stolen. On my advice my client pleaded not guilty and was acquitted.

Sometimes a guilty conscience can make a person, innocent of the offence charged, want to plead guilty. He wants to punish himself. This is not common but can happen. I acted for a fine young man, a student, who early one morning in what was then a 35 miles per hour area, drove his car into the blinding sun. He killed one little girl on a pushbike and badly injured another.

He wanted to plead guilty but I insisted that he should first hear the evidence. He had said to the police and me that he was driving at 50 miles per hour into blinding sun. On that story he was clearly guilty of manslaughter.

However, when the evidence came out, the point of impact could be clearly marked on the road. The car was not moved after the accident. It was only 20 feet past the point of impact. His speed was certainly not 50 miles per hour, more like 10 miles per hour. He had punished himself with a cruel false memory. He was, of course, acquitted of manslaughter and fined for negligent driving. He should have stopped when the sun blinded him, although he was probably in the process of doing so but was too late.

It is best not to have a firm belief in a client's innocence. Normally one can think if the client is convicted that the court was probably right. If you are convinced that your client is innocent, then the strain of defending him can be dreadful. I was sure that Michael Schneider was innocent.

Fortunately, over the years I have never been sure of the innocence of a client who has been convicted. Where I have had that sure belief, and the occasions were not frequent, he has been acquitted.

Forgive me in this discussion for referring to my clients in the masculine. I have of course appeared often enough for women but they were not the accused in the cases just discussed. Females accused in criminal cases are still fairly unusual, although there are more since sex equality became more real. I do not know why this is so. Perhaps it is because in the past women stayed at home, did not go to work as much as men and did not drive as much as men. Now all these things have changed. There are plenty of women in a position to steal, or kill people while driving. Some do, but not nearly as many as men.

In the old days the Women's Prison had a few prostitutes and petty thieves, and a number of women convicted of murder, often widows. Now there are drug traffickers, swindlers and generally a wider variety of women offenders. But women are still far less likely to go to gaol than men.

Drug addiction is an area where crimes are often committed by women, but still not so frequently as men. This reminds me of another murder case I did that went to trial. My client was a heroin addict who bailed out a criminal to do an armed hold-up, so as to raise the much larger sum of money needed to bail out her boyfriend, also a heroin addict. It was a crazy, stupid scheme dreamt up by a girl under 18 years of age. The bandit selected was out of his league and had no experience of armed hold-ups. They tried to 'hit' a hotel and the attendant laughed at them, the gun went off – only a single .22 shot, but it was fatal. The gunman was convicted of murder. My client, who started it all, was only convicted of manslaughter on the basis that firing the gun was no part of the joint enterprise. She was lucky.

The difference between stupidity and tragedy is often bad luck. The bandit in this case claimed that the gun went off by accident. That the shot killed the victim was unusual in such cases. He was sentenced to life imprisonment, which of course was fair enough. He had taken the life of an innocent man.

Before I took silk I also did many cases for the Medical Board, prosecuting doctors for various offences before the Medical Disciplinary Tribunal. In those days the tribunal consisted of the board itself, presided over by a District Court judge. It was bound by the rules of evidence and there was an appeal to the Court of Appeal. By and large it was a fair and efficient tribunal and most of its decisions were clearly correct.

There were a few sex cases, but they were rare. A patient's complaint against a doctor alleging sexual misconduct would not be upheld under the law back then, unless it was corroborated by independent evidence from that of the complainant, and few such complaints ever even reached the Medical Tribunal. This had its upside and its downside. Doctors are peculiarly vulnerable to false allegations of sexual misconduct, so innocent doctors were protected. On the other hand guilty doctors got away with it, even in cases of multiple complaints.

Now the need for corroboration has gone. This has resulted in the removal from the medical register of a number of guilty doctors who deserved deregistration. I fear, however, that some innocent doctors have been professionally ruined by false complaints that have been upheld. Long after I took silk the legislation governing doctors was drastically altered, mainly at the request of the doctors themselves, who wanted to judge their own and get rid of legal technicalities. Unlike other professions, their tribunal is not bound by the rules of evidence and there is no appeal on questions of fact. Few questions of law can arise since the rules of evidence do not apply. There is an appeal as to penalty, and this has resulted in increased penalties for sex offences.

In a criminal case the charge has to be proved beyond reasonable doubt. A professional charge only has to be proved to the comfortable satisfaction of the tribunal, having regard to the serious nature of the charge, but on the balance of probabilities, not beyond reasonable doubt. Neurotic or spiteful patients can be very convincing, and will adhere to a story despite cross-examination. Some doctors make bad witnesses, and some ethnic doctors speak with an accent that is difficult to understand. The possibility of the ruin of innocent doctors is only too real.

I encountered the Drug Squad in the police force back then in their work of checking on doctors, nurses, hospitals and drug registers. Every now and then a doctor or nurse became addicted to morphine or pethidine, and this was usually revealed by inspection of the drug registers. I would be briefed to appear for the Medical Board against a doctor who was an addict and had abused his drug authority. Only very rarely a doctor had committed some crime requiring his deregistration.

In those early days the Drug Squad in the police force was only a small body, commanded by Sergeant Cec Abbott (later a Commissioner of Police). In the 1970s and '80s heroin became a real problem, as did cannabis. The Drug Squad became very large indeed and had an enormous number of cases. We now know that in these later years corruption penetrated the police force, or police service as it became. All police forces throughout the world are vulnerable to corruption and it has always been common in areas of 'soft crime' – sly grogging, liquor licensing hours, gambling and prostitution. But heroin made sums of cash available of such size as to corrupt police dealing with 'hard crime' such as armed robbery or drug dealing. This problem is still with us.

In my last year as a junior counsel I conducted a prosecution of Sunbeam Corporation for an accidental spill of cyanide into the Cooks River. I believe this was the first big pollution prosecution in New South Wales. It was heard by Mr Justice McClemens in May 1974. This case was so important that it would normally have been prosecuted by a silk. It was defended by a silk. It demonstrated to me and to others that I should take silk myself.

In 1974 it was thought that the Cooks River was so polluted that little life inhabited the murky stream. So with some surprise people found enormous quantities of dead fish and eels floating on the river in the Christmas break of 1973. The state of the river before the leakage of cyanide was obviously much better than had been thought.

Then there were gloomy prognostications from the 'experts' that there would be a sterile river for many years to come. In fact a fall of rain after the spill did much to clear the river, and months later fish were back.

Sunbeam Corporation was most unlucky in one way but lucky in another. The spill was the result of a mechanical failure and only reached a creek that led to the river because of a trench made by building workers for construction going on at the time. However the creek into which the then lethally concentrated cyanide flowed had been, at times, a place where children played. Had any been there playing in the water soon after the spill they would probably have died.

The spill cost the company a lot, in fines and payment for the remedial measures, and not least for the cost of the lost cyanide.

I was appearing in all sorts of civil cases before I took silk.

There were company brawls in which vast sums of money were spent in paying legal fees in the fight to control a company, or to get money from another company. Years later, when I did a civil case after so many criminal cases, I said: 'At least only money is at stake. No one is going to gaol.' It was a relief.

Civil cases involved many facets of human nature. This was

especially so in cases about shop takings. A business would be sold and the purchaser would find that its takings were far less than those warranted or represented by the vendor. I had a bad record of losses in this area. In one case it turned out that the vendor had paid people to go in and buy during the trial week provided in the contract, and thus boosted takings. For a solemn, taciturn but honest purchaser the explanation for the fall in takings after the sale was that his unattractive demeanour in a small corner shop contrasted with the friendly, chatty nature of the vendor.

All shops kept a takings book but if someone produced in court a snow-white pristine exercise book with neat figures all made with the same pen the suspicion did arise that the book had been put together a few days before the case. One client of mine did this but used the wrong year's calendar. Fortunately, bitter experience had made me check the book carefully so it was not produced in court.

It is said that the smart, small shopkeeper kept three sets of books. The first was correct and showed the true position of the business. The second was for the Commissioner for Taxation and showed a somewhat reduced profit. The third showed a vastly improved profit and was for the prospective purchaser.

Some smart Greek purchasers I knew of took little or no notice of the vendor's books. They would watch the shop for days or weeks, counting the customers and observing the business. In those days there were many Greek milk-bar restaurants run by hard-working immigrants, whose children became lawyers and doctors. These businesses were good money-spinners but the work was hard and the hours were long. They provided a good service to their customers. That these businesses are quite rare now is a loss to the community.

Another type of litigation involved the agents' commission of business agents and real estate agents. One often hears people say, 'Get lots of agents to sell your property.' This advice can lead to trouble. After the sale, two agents each claim commission and often the vendor is in the purchaser's hands as to who was the effective cause of the sale. Some owners have finished up paying two commissions. I found these cases difficult.

I remember one regarding the sale of a business. The parties were Greek and our star witness spoke English fluently and effectively, with gestures and emphasis. I was most impressed by him in chambers. The case went on. I was for the defendant and he was my last witness, and I called him with a quiet smile of triumph as my trump card. The case had gone on for some days and there had been much talking between witnesses and others outside the court in Greek while they were waiting to give evidence.

My star witness confidently entered the witness box and took the oath. Again he told his story in good English, fluently and effectively with gestures and emphasis, but this time to the completely opposite effect of what he had said to me in chambers. He was now a star witness for the plaintiff, and I had called him and could not cross-examine him. He had not given a written statement. We lost.

I remember John Cleese as the barrister in *A Fish Called Wanda* when his star witness ratted on him. His woebegone expression was similar to mine.

I did not appear in all that many defamation cases, but I had quite a bit of experience in them. With Jack Hiatt QC I appeared for the ABC in a big libel action brought by ex-Prime Minister John Gorton, concerning a program that was supposed to infer that he had betrayed Malcolm Fraser (then Minister for Defence) by not correcting a proposed story by journalist Alan Ramsay about Fraser. It was quite an interesting case involving the events that eventually led to Gorton ceasing to be Prime Minister. Gorton was quite a charming man. I remember him seeking a light from me outside the court despite the fact that I was the opposing barrister. In those days I was a smoker. (In the early 1970s counsels' chambers were usually full of smoke, as were barristers' dining rooms. One came out of court to a hall with a 'No Smoking' notice barely visible through the clouds of tobacco smoke. At every barristers' dinner we smokers awaited the Royal Toast and then, hopefully soon after the first course, we could light up. How times have changed! Now only a few die-hards and the youngsters smoke. Smoking is forbidden in barristers' chambers, in court buildings, in all restaurants and dining rooms and in most private homes. I gave up in May 1983, just in time to avoid being a social pariah forced to sneak outside for a smoke.)

John Gorton substantially lost his case to the defence of fair comment. He won only one portion where the court held the defence did not apply. After seeing him cross-examined, where he had to match Jack Smyth QC (who appeared for a co-defendant Max Walsh), one of the greatest cross-examiners, I was still attracted by Gorton's charm. I think he was an able man and the circumstances that forced him out of office were, to a great extent, a media-created situation that got out of control. To what extent, if any, it was John Gorton's fault that the media defamed Fraser is for history to judge, perhaps assisted by the transcript of the case of *Gorton v the ABC and Max Walsh*.

Another defamation case in which Jack Hiatt QC led me was where we appeared for the ABC in a case brought by the Honourable Ken McCaw, then Attorney-General of New South Wales. McCaw claimed, with some reason, that an episode of the 'This Day Tonight' program had implied that he was corrupt with regard to enforcing the law against illegal casinos. This case highlighted the difference between a newspaper and a television program. The words in a newspaper article can be read carefully, re-read, and perhaps read yet again, so that defamatory inferences will be discovered and will register with the reader. Television has a big audience but we argued that the pictures and words pass by in a flash. How much is remembered, or even understood? On this argument Ken McCaw recovered quite modest damages for what was a very serious libel.

Many times I advised clients not to bring defamation cases. They are expensive, and the results are often unpredictable. Slander is for spoken words, libel for written words. In slander cases there can be a real dispute as to whether the words were spoken at all.

Very early in my career I appeared as a junior to Jack Shand KC in a slander case for the plaintiff. We were doing very well but on the last day Jack Shand KC had to go to another case and I was on my own. I expected a triumph but fate was against me. The defendant had a pretty daughter who was called as a witness and, in my opinion, charmed 'Jock' McClemens, the presiding judge. He summed up against the plaintiff. I then submitted that his summing up was unfair and he should withdraw it and sum up again. This surprised both His Honour and the jury.

Jock outwitted me by congratulating me in front of the jury for my courage in making the submission that his summary was unfair. The jury, left thinking the judge was a nice man (which was true), followed his lead and found for the defendant. Still, Jock was sincere in what he said and I believe he told a lot of people about my challenge to his summing up, and I always got on well with him in future cases. He became Chief Judge at Common Law. I think his was the first appointment to this position. He was a very humane man.

In the late 1960s and '70s defamation became a highly technical and difficult area. Despite many reforms, it still is.

I do not think that politicians should be able to look on defamation as a happy hunting ground for tax-free money, as was once the case. Nor should it be possible to overwhelm a plaintiff with technicalities, as has been the position for many years when he or she has a real case. These technicalities were built up by the media over the years to defend themselves against fortune-hunters.

Finding the right balance between freedom of expression and reasonable protection of reputations is very difficult, and has not yet been achieved in Australia. In fact, we still have differing laws in the States and territories. Many cases are brought in the ACT Supreme Court to avoid juries.

Contract cases provide much of civil litigation and I was involved in many of these cases. Here the law is mainly the common law; that is, the judge-made law built up from case to case since Saxon–Norman times. It is said to have existed from time immemorial.

When should a promise be binding? What formalities are required? What are the consequences of breach? When is a promisor to be excused from his or her promise, and so on? Contracts was the first subject studied in the law course I started in 1943. Contract law well illustrates the fairness and the efficiency of the common law.

As a 20-year-old in 1946 with my two dogs, Flap and Snuffles. For as long as I can remember I have loved animals.

### CHESTER ALEXANDER PORTER

Chester proposes to go to the bar. He is at present articled to Messrs. Dawson, Waldron, Edwards and Nicholls. With the former aim and the latter experience, he has made debating his chief activity. He is on the Union Debates Committee and is invariably to be found at Union Night expounding the Young Tory point of view. The usually even tenor of his voice will rise a few octaves on the subject of Reds, of whom he is one of the chief baiters. His otherwise gay and placid nature is to be seen at its best in lectures, where he is wont to be ensconced among the fairest of the fair.

A description of 'young Chester' in the University of Sydney law students' magazine *Blackacre*, 1945–46 edition.

My university days were one of the happy periods of my life. I graduated from the University of Sydney with first-class honours in law in May 1947.

I was admitted to the bar on 12 March 1948, a few days before my 22nd birthday. My wig was a present from my mother.

I married Jean on 2 May 1953 at Lindfield Methodist Church.

Artist's impression of aircraft carrier HMAS *Melbourne* and HMAS *Voyager* colliding off Jervis Bay on 10 February 1964. Eighty men were lost in the disaster and there were two Royal Commissions into the loss of the *Voyager*. I was involved in the second.

Captain Duncan Stevens of HMAS *Voyager* was held mainly to blame for the disaster. My client, Peter Cabban, felt that the captain had an alcohol problem. The Royal Commission rejected that he was a chronic alcoholic.

Captain John Robertson (left) on the bridge of HMAS *Melbourne* as the carrier berthed in Sydney on 12 February 1964. In the first Royal Commission into the disaster, Robertson was held to be partly responsible. The second Royal Commission found this not to be the case.

A warden surveying the damage from the Bathurst prison riots of 1974. In 1975, as a result of prison riots and other problems in New South Wales's prisons, the Liberal state government set up a Royal Commission to inquire into the prison system. I was retained to represent the Department of Corrective Services.

Sketch of me (first from right), representing Det. Sgt. Roger Rogerson (second from left). Rogerson pleaded not guilty to attempting to bribe Senior Constable Michael Drury at Darlinghurst Police Station in September 1983.

News Ltd

Roger Rogerson had been a police hero. I do know that he was a very able man capable of great things. His ultimate disgrace was a tragedy.

Peter Rae/Sydney Morning Herald

Mick Drury had suffered dreadfully in hospital after being shot in the stomach during the undercover penetration of a heroin ring. I think he was a strong man but the Rogerson trial was obviously a great strain on him.

Fiona-Lee Quimby/Sydney Morning Herald

Mick Drury in 2002 on a campaign to show the controversial mini-series *Blue Murder* to groups of men on parole.

LEFT: *Blue Murder* was possibly the most controversial drama series ever made in Australia. It delved into the corruption of the New South Wales police force and the criminal underworld of 1980s Sydney, especially focusing on Neddy Smith and Roger Rogerson. I was played by actor John Hargreaves (pictured).

courtesy of Southern Star

BELOW: A sketch of me at the Banco Court in 1985 when I was counsel for Judge John Foord who was facing two charges of attempting to pervert the course of justice.

Tony Rafty

LEFT: Leaving Banco Court after a day in court during the trial of Judge Foord. What an experience the trial was for me! In one week I cross-examined the Chief Stipendiary Magistrate Clarrie Briese, three District Court judges, and Premier Neville Wran. I also managed to make one of my best addresses to a jury.

BELOW: Lionel Murphy and wife, Ingrid, outside the Supreme Court of New South Wales, 28 April 1986. Justice Murphy had just been acquitted at his second trial on a charge of attempting to pervert the course of justice. During the Foord trial he had expressed his surprise to me that his political enemies were so anxious to ruin him.

In many contract cases I found out how quite bona fide recollections differed as to conversations, and how honest people could get into difficult disputes, each genuinely believing that right was on their side. The written word, moreover, could be quite ambiguous in unexpected circumstances.

I do remember a person who was apparently liable under a guarantee for $200,000 back in the early 1970s during a credit squeeze. He came into my chambers a very miserable man, but there was a defect in the wording of the guarantee. I was able to tell him that he was not liable, and he left my chambers with a happy smile.

In other days, many a printed contract contained very fine print embodying nasty clauses for purchasers and consumers. In fact, it was common for goods to be sold with carefully concealed disclaimers in the printed order form. Modern legislation, including the Trade Practices Act, the Fair Trading Act and the Contracts Review Act, has changed all this. When I started at the bar, defending people from the vicious printed word was usually very difficult. Reforms to this area have been effective and very useful.

The Court of Equity was originally meant to supplement the common law and in particular reduce the inequity of the strict common law, and later statute law. I found the Equity Court in some ways disappointing. It handled difficult will cases, company problems and trust problems very well, but its remedies of undue influence, part performance, and he who seeks equity must do equity, always seemed to me to be law-school topics without much relevance to the real world. The court which was supposed to relieve against technicalities was the most technical of all, until the Federal Court arrived. The poor battler who sought relief against an unfair contract found himself in an expensive court where people were expected to know what they were doing and expensive counsel prevailed over the feeble efforts of young counsel. It was rare indeed for a will to be set aside for undue influence, even for lack of testamentary capacity.

Equity did very well in battles between commercial giants, but the poor victim of tough commercial practices or even downright fraud would do far better before a common-law jury. To illustrate, I had such a case, a small businessman oppressed by an unfair contract induced by dubious practices, probably misrepresentation. Now equity should give relief for innocent misrepresentation, not just deliberate fraud which common law requires before it will act. My client was in the Equity Court in the days when if the remedy was to be found in common law it had to go there and be decided by a jury. In the Equity Court before a clever but not so sympathetic judge the other side was adamant against making any concessions. By various processes I forced the case to common law. We no longer had the remedy of innocent misrepresentation, which by itself should have won the case for us, but we now had a jury. Immediately after the transfer of the case to the common law, the other side gave in and there was a good settlement. In simple terms, the equity judge had no sympathy for the foolish victim of sharp practice, even fraud. The other side knew that a jury would take a very different view.

Why was this so? The very clever people who become Supreme Court judges dealing with equity cases are frequently unsympathetic to the stupidity of the ordinary person, even the ordinary small businessman or woman. The cases, after a great expenditure of costs, often boil down to a simple question of fact: who to believe – the efficient, clever but ruthless businessman or woman, or the fool who ought to have known better. In such a case I would prefer a jury, but reforms of the legal system have almost eliminated juries from civil cases, unlike in America. In the ACT this is almost 100 per cent true. In New South Wales, juries have a brief role in defamation cases.

How would the Swiss loans cases against the banks have gone before juries? In these cases the borrowers, usually farmers, were induced by banks to borrow Swiss francs at a low interest rate. Allegedly, the banks did not explain that if the Swiss franc rose in value as compared to the Australian dollar the repayment might be much more than the original loan. This is what happened; the Australian dollar sank in value and those who had to repay in Swiss francs were ruined. Some victims sued the banks but few succeeded.

These days, commercial litigation has become more and more expensive. Photocopiers reproduce numerous irrelevant documents and thus produce briefs consisting of many, many folders. There are preliminary proceedings, complicated pleadings (a written outline of the party's case), written submissions, interlocutory (pending the ultimate decision) orders, etc. This is no place for a small businessman with a small purse.

Thus every now and then we hear of a small businessman or woman told to stop using a business name with some remote resemblance to that of a giant corporation. If he or she came to me I used to say, 'Change your name; forget the rights and wrongs, you are out of your league.' Many ultimately do change their business's name, but only after ruinous litigation.

The Federal Court of Australia has some very good remedies under the Trade Practices Act, and otherwise. But they can be expensive, and there can be many technical obstacles. These days, commercial cases are generally likely to turn into nightmares. I had to advise the loser in one Federal Court case (I did not appear for him) when he wanted to appeal. He had already incurred $14 million in costs (for both parties) and the judgment in question ran into hundreds of pages after months of hearing.

In the District Court, justice is usually much cheaper, although perhaps of varying quality, depending upon the individual judge. Of course, that applies to all courts. Many, if not most, cases depend almost entirely on a question of fact in the District Court. Deciding who is telling the truth is not easy, particularly if it is remembered that a commercial villain is usually an excellent witness with good presentation, whereas his unintelligent victim cuts a poor figure in the witness box.

In business, in investment, we are all idiots at times, and if an otherwise intelligent person has acted stupidly it is hard to give a reasonable explanation for being foolish. In such circumstances the judge may well believe the smart villain rather than the 'idiot' victim.

Fact-finding is difficult. Sometimes documents, undisputed circumstances, even some physical object, can give a foundation of certainty for assessing the sworn evidence of witnesses. Some things are more likely than others. There are those who claim that they can tell the truth by the demeanour of the witnesses, a proposition that receives strong support from Courts of Appeal. I believe that this supposed ability of judges has been greatly exaggerated.

One final word about all of this: if you are ever approached by a person telling such a strange, wild story that you think it must be true, because no one could imagine such a story, think again. My experience, gained the hard way, is that the storyteller in these cases is always lying. I have found no exceptions.

I particularly remember very early in my career, over 50 years ago, a most convincing teller of strange stories. He had just married a young woman who believed completely in his integrity and in all that he said. I was in court when the truth emerged that the husband was a confidence trickster now facing numerous criminal charges for obtaining money by fraud. I can still remember vividly the look on that poor woman's face when her world fell apart.

There were many and varied cases in which I acted as a junior counsel, such as in the Board of Subdivision Appeals (which was very efficient), a Local Land Board, the Council of the Chartered Institute of Accountants (dealing with professional discipline), and many others. I suppose even then I was inclined towards criminal law and my favourite arena was before a criminal jury.

Eventually, still believing that only specialists would succeed as Queen's Counsel I took silk and fortunately found that I was wrong. There was an opening for someone who had been every-where, particularly if he could cross-examine witnesses, and I was certainly quite proficient in this.

# 9

# Taking Silk

In November 1974, at the age of 48, after 26 years in practice as a junior counsel I took silk and became a Queen's Counsel. It was hardly a great success story, but I was nevertheless very proud to be a senior counsel. Upon becoming a QC, I received a Royal Commission, in fact two commissions, one from New South Wales and one from the Australian Capital Territory.

Soon after, in 1975 I appeared for the Commissioner for Corporate Affairs to prosecute one of the first cases of insider trading. The defendant was convicted but the conviction was set aside on appeal. Company prosecutions are difficult indeed: the law is complex, the technicalities are many, and witnesses are often reluctant to give evidence. The Crown should have appealed. I and another silk advised an appeal but there was none and the precedent made future prosecutions much more difficult.

I appeared for the ABC again in a defamation case brought by Stanley Eskell, an MLC, over a 'This Day Tonight' telecast. This case was won by the plaintiff represented by Alec Shand QC. It involved an interesting point as to whether a hint was an allegation, and if so whether a vague hint could be construed by the jury at its worst inference against the plaintiff. I did not appear on the appeal but the law seems to be that if an article hints at wrong-doing, the jury is entitled to act on the basis that the reader or the viewer would infer the worst even though it was not stated. It was quite an important point in defamation law.

Under the new Trade Practices Act of 1975 I appeared to prosecute Sharp Corporation for a pecuniary penalty based on resale price maintenance. A penalty was imposed. I did quite a few of these cases for the Trade Practices Commission which enthusiastically enforced the Act's provisions against resale price maintenance. Before the Act it had been common and lawful for manufacturers to insist that their products should not be sold below a particular price. I wonder sometimes whether the destruction of the local manufacturing industry, mainly due to cheap imports, was accelerated by the law against orderly marketing; for example, resale price maintenance. I also wonder whether crazy discounters can drive their competitors out of business before going bankrupt. Certainly the Trade Practices Act has lowered prices and helped consumers. Whether it has had unnecessarily adverse effects on small traders is something for economists to ponder.

These cases were heard by the then new Federal Court of Australia, a very well-conducted, courteous court, but strict on technicalities. Thus the prosecutions before it were often very difficult to conduct and sometimes failed because of the application of strict rules of evidence rather than because of the innocence of the defendant. However, it was only right to be strict in these cases because the penalties, whether pecuniary civil penalties or fines, were very severe.

Although I appeared in numerous civil cases, my practice leaned quite heavily towards criminal matters soon after I took silk. This was probably because I chanced to have a couple of wins in well-publicised cases. Just a year after I took silk I appeared in Bathurst Supreme Court for Billy Reid, a young Aborigine charged with murder. I had appeared in the committal proceedings at the Bourke Court of Petty Sessions. My junior was Brian Donovan, later a QC himself, and we were instructed by the Aboriginal Legal Service.

On 31 May 1975 there had been a fight between Billy and two brothers in the Aboriginal village outside Brewarrina known as 'Dodge City'. The Boney brothers, unarmed, challenged Billy Reid to come out and fight, but it would have been two to one. Not unnaturally, Billy looked for an equaliser, but perhaps he overdid it. He came out with a machete in one hand and a bayonet in the other. Harry Boney died after being stabbed in the chest by the bayonet, but Billy claimed the defence of self-defence.

Harry Boney was unlucky to die. A stabbing instrument may hit a person's chest and as likely as not will stop at a rib. If, however, it goes between the ribs, there is nothing to stop it damaging the heart or lungs.

As the senior barrister at the bar table in this case I found myself obliged to make a little speech about our impressive surroundings at the opening of the circuit of the Bathurst Supreme Court. Bathurst has a very beautiful Supreme Court building, rumoured to have been based on a plan meant for India and built by mistake at Bathurst. The story has been emphatically denied but the court is suspiciously impressive.

The Crown offered to accept a plea of guilty to manslaughter. This would produce a sentence of some years, but would be very much better than a verdict of murder which would mean nominal life imprisonment and probably then about 12 years in gaol. We decided to go for an acquittal. In those days excessive force in self-defence resulting in death was normally manslaughter. Later it became a question of whether the defence of provocation reduced the offence to manslaughter. So the jury had a choice between murder, manslaughter and acquittal. The obvious compromise was manslaughter and that was the result in Billy Reid's case. He received a very merciful sentence.

In this case, when we were at Bourke, Brian Donovan and I, together with our solicitor, drank at the Carriers Arms, the Aboriginal pub, and we were treated with great courtesy. I danced with a rather clever Aboriginal girl, a very nice person, and met many of the local community. While we were there no one was drunk and everyone was polite. Unemployment seemed to be the big problem, but also there was little doubt that the police dealt out two types of law: one for the whites and one for the blacks, and the latter was at times tough and unfair. Still, the police in Billy Reid's case had been fair and correct in their investigation.

The prison officers at Bathurst Gaol were kind to Billy. They let him outside on a working party, and provided him with art materials in his cell. He drew from memory a magnificent picture of a tree. I should like to have bought it from him, but doubted whether I could do so with propriety, so I did not try to acquire it. He was a talented young man. I hope life was subsequently kinder to him.

Sentencing Aborigines for crimes that are often serious, but are caused by drink and unemployment, is a very hard task for a judge. In my experience most judges tried very hard to be lenient and avoid gaol terms, but the facts of cases often left them with no alternative. The courts have so few other options than gaol in the case of serious offences.

In December 1975 I appeared for the Crown in an attempt by Laurie Brereton MLA to set aside an ex-officio indictment filed by Reg Marr QC, the Solicitor-General when the Attorney-General, John Maddison, was abroad. Mr Brereton had been discharged in the committal proceedings before Mr Farquhar CSM on a charge of common-law corruption. His ruling was that the old common-law offence, in effect of bribery of a public official, had been repealed by the special legislation in the Local Government Act. Mr Justice Taylor refused to rule on the points of law involved. The following year there was a change of government and the indictment was withdrawn. I was then involved in the Prisons Royal Commission and my advice was never sought on the matter by the new government.

I was only concerned with legal points and did not study the facts at all. The case involved a political brawl, and perhaps it was pushing the criminal law further than it was meant to go. Certainly in the end Mr Brereton was in effect found not guilty.

I was concerned in another political case, being the inquiry by Mr Michael Finnane, later Judge Finnane, into the Walsh–Sinclair funeral companies, involving Mr Ian Sinclair MHR. I was simply retained to advise Mr Finnane and I did not meet Mr Sinclair or any other witness. I was not involved in the prosecution of Mr Sinclair – where it was alleged that he forged his father's signature on a company return – when he was acquitted of any criminal conduct. I did notice that at the trial the handwriting evidence, which as I recall, had not been disputed at the inquiry, was successfully challenged by another expert. This trial was noted for the brilliant defence by Mr Murray Gleeson QC, later Chief Justice of the Supreme Court of New South Wales and then Chief Justice of the High Court of Australia. However, to me, the main lesson is the danger of expert evidence, and I may add that I have considerable reservations about the reliability of handwriting evidence.

The two cases, that of Laurie Brereton and that of Ian Sinclair, from opposite sides of politics, show the difficulties involved when politics and the criminal law are brought together. This was later well illustrated by the case of Lionel Murphy. I am not saying that politicians should be above the law, but I do say that it is very hard to provide a fair trial for a politician, whether from his or her point of view or from the Crown's. Where the facts require it, political trials are necessary, but they are very dangerous because of the prejudices both for and against a political figure. I think today that people in conflict, such as those politically opposed to one another, are far too ruthless. People seem to delight in sending their enemies into bankruptcy or gaol. Perhaps this was always so, but I fancy we are more ruthless now than we were when I started in the law.

In the 1950s and '60s few would have prosecuted a person in their seventies. Nowadays it is not all that unusual to prosecute a person in their eighties, perhaps for an alleged sexual assault that was supposed to have occurred over 20 years before. Recently an alleged war criminal was wheeled into court in his eighties not long before he died of his then well-known illnesses.

Of course today people live longer, and fit, healthy people in their eighties are commonplace. Perhaps this is why we are no longer so kind to the aged.

# 10

# The Prisons Royal Commission

In 1951 when I went with Reg Hawkins, the Public Solicitor, and Jack Shand KC to see Fred McDermott in Long Bay Gaol I remember Reg appeared very mournful and I asked him why. He said that he found it very sad to see his fellow men in cages. I do not recall his exact words but I remember his sentiments well. Reg was a kindly man and as part of his duties he instructed the Public Defender and saw many of society's misfits and unfortunates caged by the law.

Who knows whether prisoners deserve what they get? Some are in fact innocent. DNA evidence has exposed a shocking number of innocent men convicted and on death row in the United States. I do not think New South Wales law makes quite the same number of mistakes in murder cases. Our standards of defence of the poor and unfortunate are much better. Standards of the magistrates in the Local Courts, the old Police Courts, have improved greatly and, despite the workload of the courts, I think few innocents go to gaol via the magistrates. In sex cases before juries I think that a substantial number of innocent men have been gaoled and had their lives ruined.

But of the guilty, who deserves gaol? For that matter who among us all would like to receive what we deserve? Gaol is full of the children of broken homes, of poverty-stricken homes, of drunken parents, of people who were the victims of misfortune, and of course today gaol is full of drug addicts, mainly heroin addicts.

In recent years there has been a great agitation in the media for longer and tougher sentences. Victims of newsworthy crimes are asked whether the sentence imposed was enough and of course, according to them, it never is. People who drive home after quite a few drinks demand higher sentences for drunken drivers, until they are caught themselves. People who live dissolute and selfish sexual lives can nevertheless demand enormous sentences for sex offenders who infringe the criminal law. Of course, adultery and desertion of wife and children are not criminal offences, even though such conduct often causes much more harm in the long-term than many criminal offences.

There is so much hypocrisy about sentencing criminals. How many drivers have not committed the offence of driving above the limit for alcohol and causing deaths, only because they were lucky. How many people have 'borrowed' money from various funds contrary to the criminal law, but have got it back in time, or have otherwise never been discovered? How many people have lost their tempers, but through good luck no serious injury resulted?

Instead of remembering Christ's admonition 'Let he who is without sin cast the first stone', the voters of today are apparently prepared to cheer on the politicians who advocate tougher sentences, even mandatory sentences, to be imposed regardless of the circumstances. Some politicians even begrudge the prisoners having television in their cells, and describe barbaric prisons as 'hotels'.

Thus we build more and more brutal prisons which are highly successful as universities of crime, which ruin the lives of persons who are not dedicated criminals and which fail dismally as places of rehabilitation, and fail even more as the means of deterring or preventing crime.

Sex offenders are not infrequently the victims of extreme sentences, at times more than they would receive for murder. Such sentences obviously encourage such offenders to kill their victims to avoid detection.

I have often said that I stood between people and what they deserved. No one wants to receive their just deserts, but, of society's scoundrels, only those who happen to contravene the criminal law *and* get caught, get their just deserts at the hands of the law. In my opinion, they often receive punishments far beyond what they deserve. And the rest advocate more severe penalties.

What hypocrites we are, led by the nose by cynical politicians!

In 1975, as a result of prison riots and other problems in the prisons of New South Wales, the Liberal government set up a Royal Commission with wide powers and resources to inquire into the prisons. It could hardly be said to have been an extravagant Royal Commission. The prison system cost millions of dollars yet prisoners were said, with reason, to be coming out much worse than they entered.

I was retained by Peter Coleman, an enlightened Liberal, then Minister for Corrective Services, to represent the Department of Corrective Services. (I had represented the department in both a public inquiry and the disciplinary hearing into prisoner bashing in the observation section at Long Bay Gaol in 1973. I had also represented the department in a prison bashing inquiry at Goulburn, before that. I had advised the department and I had seen something of the prisons.) My junior was the very capable and enthusiastic Derek Cassidy, now a QC. We were instructed by an experienced solicitor from the State Crown, Leigh Sheridan, and were assisted by Bill Morrow, the senior custodial officer of the Department of Corrective Services, whose help was invaluable. Mr Justice Nagle was to preside over the inquiry assisted by two prominent lay persons, Professor Alexander Mitchell and Sydney Derwent. Sir Leon Radzinowicz, one-time director of the British Institute of Criminology, was appointed a consultant to the Royal Commission. David Hunt QC was appointed counsel to assist the Royal Commission. Special accommodation was found for the Commission – a hearing room, conference rooms, chambers, etc.

The 1975 New South Wales Prisons Royal Commission was a great opportunity, such as comes only once in a generation. Unfortunately it was conceived in the hatred of the Bathurst prison riots which in 1974 almost totally destroyed the old part of the gaol.

I spent many hours with my main client, Walter McGeechan, the then Commissioner of Corrective Services. He was an idealist, an outdoors man with military experience. He was also a reformer, one of the very few in the system, and he thought to get around union opposition and public-service obstruction by being cunning, if not devious. At that time such tactics offered the only prospect of overcoming opposition to any reform. He liked to keep his options open when expressing his opinions and that made him a bad witness in his own interests. But in many ways he was a warm, attractive person and he had many admirers. He had numerous ideas for reform, mainly good ones. There had been many political attacks and counterattacks in which McGeechan had been attacked by the opposition and defended by the government. To a degree he had been politically demonised.

I had hoped to guide the Royal Commission towards the area of future reform and away from digging over past events. It may have been a false hope but Jock McClemens had succeeded in an inquiry along those lines into mental hospitals, and the results were lasting reforms. Still, in the case of prisons, the bitterness was very deep, not merely between prisoners and officers and the department, but between the political parties. A process that could have led to great reforms became payback time. Most of the Royal Commissioner's time was devoted to past sins or alleged sins. Mr Justice Nagle was able to suggest quite a few good reforms, and most were implemented, but fundamentally not much changed for the better. The opportunity for a lot more was lost.

Soon after Labor, led by Neville Wran, gained power in 1976, the arrangements for special premises for the Royal Commission were cancelled as were the appointments of Professor Mitchell, Sydney Derwent and Sir Leon Radzinowicz. The Commission commenced its hearings, firstly with Messrs Mitchell and Derwent, and then without them. My team had compiled much documentation setting out the Corrective Services Department's activities. McGeechan gave his evidence in chief and was being cross-examined by David Hunt QC.

At 9.40 a.m. on 15 July 1976 Mr Justice Nagle received a letter from the Attorney-General's Department removing myself and Mr Tom Falkingham QC as counsel for the department and the prison officers respectively. No prior notice was given to me, but I had been aware of rumours to this effect. So Derek Cassidy had to represent the Corrective Services Department on his own against QCs assisting the Royal Commissioner and representing the prisoners, and also opposing all the other junior counsel representing parties anti the department. This task also involved finding necessary documents and making arrangements for inspections of establishments and doing other things to assist the inquiry.

The prison officers, by threatening to strike, got their QC back. But Derek's task was quite impossible. He had more to do than any other legal team, and he only had a solicitor to assist him.

Eventually Derek Cassidy became, through no fault of his own, entangled in a position of conflict of interests between the superintendent of Bathurst Gaol and the Corrective Services Department. Such conflicts frequently arise in representation before a Royal Commission. While I was acting for the department the decision was made to represent superintendents. Later there was a need to revise this decision but the confidence of the superintendent had been given in conference. Derek retired from the Royal Commission and Neville Wran replaced him with Bill Fisher QC and a junior. Bill Fisher fought hard to save a man who was perhaps the first genuine reformer in prison history in my time. It was too late. McGeechan was trenchantly criticised in the Royal Commission's report and was dismissed. At least in his representation before the Commission McGeechan had a raw deal. He had great faith in our justice system and he was overwhelmed by the findings against himself.

It was easy to blame McGeechan for his, at times, strange ways. In particular he tried to adopt numerous conflicting courses of action without committing himself. However, it was not fair to overlook his achievements. Much of his work was undone –

Katingal, the Parramatta Linen Service, Operation Survival and so on. I do not agree with the strong condemnation of McGeechan's work that appeared in the Nagle Report. But it is fair to say that it is amazing that the emasculated Royal Commission achieved as much as it did. Professor Tony Vinson succeeded McGeechan and implemented much of the Nagle Report. Yet an opportunity was missed that will probably never come again in my lifetime.

As for myself, I had spent months working on the Royal Commission. The State, by its actions in dismissing me, lost the benefit of most of what I could have done. At the same time perhaps I should be grateful to Neville Wran. Working on prisons is very depressing — at least it began to be so to me. Night after night I dreamed that I was a prisoner myself. That dream occasionally returns, even now.

I had had some experience of the inside of prisons but a lawyer sees little when going to interview a client at a gaol. One simply goes to the professional interview room. Then for some three months or thereabouts before the Royal Commission commenced I thought of nothing but prisons and visited prisons every day. I travelled all over New South Wales inspecting country prisons. I had long conferences; I read vast quantities of literature.

The statistics were at times interesting; for example, women convicted of murder were often widows, self-made widows. Prisoners tended to state that they were Roman-Catholic, Anglican or Salvation Army, because these religions had the most frequently attending chaplains not, as it might have appeared, because the Salvation Army's adherents were more sinful. A prisoner who knew the ropes on admission would say his religion was one of the three stated so that he had the services of a chaplain.

There were numerous programs to assist prisoners, some quite successful, others not. I noticed how a prison library could be filled with useless books dumped there from somewhere else, how many young prisoners sat for public exams but few got worthwhile results. I noticed an atmosphere of hatred, particularly when prison workers were on strike and the prisoners were locked up.

I met many famous prisoners, including 'Chow' Hayes, an amiable rogue and a model prisoner; Darcy Dugan; and the pathetic Lenny Lawson, a cultured man, fond of music, yet a hopeless security risk, or so it was said.

I saw Katingal Gaol, and I was not horrified. Katingal was a way of eliminating that centre of horrors – Grafton Gaol – by taking and keeping secure the very worst prisoners and thereby hopefully relaxing conditions for the other prisoners. The places that later replaced Katingal; for example, the cell for the notorious prisoner Peter Schneidas at Goulburn Gaol, were hardly better.

As I attended prisons day after day I became somewhat depressed at times. The atmosphere of fear and hatred in prisons is at times overwhelming. I learned that in some ways the prison officers are also prisoners, shut up in a dangerous workplace. Normally only an officer on the wall is armed. Officers must not carry arms that can be seized by prisoners as officers are usually outnumbered. A riot or escape attempt may well result in serious injury, even death, to an officer. It does not often happen but the threat is always there.

As part of my inquiries, my team went with me to Morisset, the secure hospital ward for the criminally mentally ill. It was strange to be among double and triple murderers, many sedated. There the officers are nurses and the risk of being killed or seriously injured is never far away.

There is no doubt that there had been prisoner bashing by prison officers, particularly at Bathurst Gaol, but also at Long Bay Gaol and probably at many other prisons. Grafton Gaol had been a terrible example of unmitigated cruelty that turned bad men into hopeless cases. Everyone concerned with the criminal law knew Grafton Gaol was bad, but I doubt whether anyone outside the department knew how bad, apart from the people who were there.

The cruelty at Grafton Gaol was mainly towards the intractables who were segregated, but it was a hard gaol, even for local prisoners serving minor sentences. It was intended to be a terrible deterrent, a fearful place to which anyone who caused real trouble, especially by assaulting a warder, went. Naturally it produced hard graduates; for example, Neddy Smith. (One of my earliest cases as a silk was to have Neddy Smith freed on the basis that he was entitled to lengthy remissions that had been withheld. I fought his case through the Supreme Court, the Court of Appeal and the High Court. This was after my appearances in the Royal Commission into Prisons. He went to gaol as a young man, and did time at Grafton. Society paid a price for what gaol did to him and many others.)

The main price paid was the degradation of society itself. Dreadful things happened in the so-called 'Grafton biff', and no one really inquired or cared because the prisoners were bad criminals. Many residents of Grafton were proud of their 'model prison' but they had no real idea what was going on inside.

There is one account I've heard of an ordinary prisoner who after his release met an officer he had seen bashing Darcy Dugan. The ex-prisoner bashed the officer and apparently there was no report to the police. The officer obviously did not want to draw the public's attention to what went on in Grafton Gaol.

On one occasion a senior non-custodial prison officer saw an old prisoner – not an intractable – brutally bashed for looking at him. He was horrified but felt he could do nothing. He was still horrified years later when he told me the story. Grafton was allowed to go on in this way for many years until McGeechan cleared the worst of the intractables into Katingal. After Grafton, Katingal was a Sunday-school picnic.

The main reason for the Royal Commission was the bashing of prisoners by prison officers in the Bathurst riots of 1974. Those bashings, as well as those at Grafton took everyone's minds off a much greater danger to prisoners, their fellow prisoners.

Grafton apart, the chance of a prisoner being bashed by an officer was very much less than the chance of him being brutally assaulted by a fellow prisoner. Informers ('dogs'), child molesters ('rock spiders') and ex-policemen had to be kept in protection. Sometimes protection failed and the prisoner concerned suffered. Many prisoners on protection sought to avoid the closer confinement involved and came back into general discipline. Numerous assaults took place outside protection.

Rape of young prisoners was far too common. I sought to do something about the first night in custody for new prisoners by trying to ensure that they were alone – 'one out' – in the cell or if 'two out' they should not be with hardened criminals.

In a maximum-security prison the brutality between prisoners was, and I believe still is, frightful. If bashed, the prisoner always said his injuries were incurred by slipping on soap, or falling over a chair or some other hardly convincing reason. Had he reported a bashing he would require protection as a 'dog', an informer – a pariah in the prison system.

Years later I remember a client of mine, a white-collar prisoner convicted of company offences, was attacked by two tough men who broke his hand. He imagined he was quite tough himself and in his words, 'I hit the first one with my fist as hard as I could, fair on the jaw. He didn't even jerk his head. I knew then that I was in real trouble.'

Prison labour is not very efficient. Watching an old lag lean on a rake at Milson Island, I wondered how Governor Phillip ever got the colony established. A forestry prisoner's labour is not half that of a paid worker, so I was informed. Workshops have always been a problem. Cheap prison work was naturally resented by trade unions who saw it as seriously detrimental to their members. The Parramatta Linen Service was closed after the Royal Commission. Since 1975 many prison kitchens have been abolished and meals are brought in. Prison bakeries have also been closed. (I think the food was probably better in those days than now, or at least more palatable.)

One great reform of McGeechan's was the sewering of nearly all the maximum-security prisons, except for one wing at Parramatta Gaol. In addition, McGeechan and his Minister, John Maddison, were the pioneers of weekend detention and work-release schemes. The former was intended for minor offenders (for example, unlicensed drivers, participants in pub assaults) and has been a great success even for quite serious white-collar criminals. They do not go to gaol but each weekend go to a detention centre and work for two days doing useful public work. Work release was a way of putting long-term prisoners back into society at the end of their sentences. They went to work from gaol and returned to gaol at the end of the day.

McGeechan had a number of experimental programs of which the most interesting was taking young long-term offenders on bush safaris. 'Operation Survival' was quite successful but did not last after the Royal Commission.

McGeechan also maintained a very easygoing prison at Milson Island on the Hawkesbury River, where previously there had been a mental hospital. The whole island was occupied by the prison, and was intended as a final receptacle for geriatric prisoners, as though to look after the department's oldest customers. At night the officer in charge locked himself up and the prisoners roamed at will over the island. Hopefully no boats were available to them!

Before the Prisons Royal Commission started, one day we got a message that Mr Justice Nagle, who with David Hunt QC and the other Commissioners was inspecting prisons, was coming back from Cessnock Correctional Centre and wanted to drop in at Milson Island. He would have arrived when the officer was locked in his house and the prisoners were roaming the island. Fortunately the boat operator had retired for the day. I did not suggest that he should be recalled.

Prisons are usually dominated by particularly strong prisoners, and this is especially so in maximum-security prisons. While he was my client, Neddy Smith dominated the Metropolitan Remand Centre. This domination by the big men was not necessarily a bad thing. It imposed a discipline on the numerous bullies and thieves who would otherwise be insufferable. Many 'heavy' prisoners prefer the gaol to run smoothly and peacefully. Thus 'Chow' Hayes would guard senior officers serving meals during a prison strike by the other officers.

The 'heavies' spent most of their time keeping fit. They could be seen in groups marching up and down the square. They pumped iron in the gym. Many were very tough indeed (though I could not understand why so many prisoners and criminals wore tattoos, whether acquired outside or in prison since these tattoos often served as excellent identification points in police and prison records).

One part of the prison system that favourably impressed me was the forestry section. There was little farming in prison except that done by the young prisoners at Emu Plains. Prison gardens were rarely extensive. Farming was sometimes attached to a forestry camp. The forestry camps were at one time the only real alleviation for a long-term prisoner. They provided quite healthy outdoor living and it could be said that men emerged from them better, or no worse, than they were before. In fact, in the case of quite a few white-collar company or solicitor prisoners (trust accounts misapplied) desperate, depressed men recovered their health in the forestry camps.

Of course the disadvantage of country prisons is that a prisoner is often deprived of visitors. But the forestry camps permitted contact visits in quite congenial surroundings. Prisons such as Bathurst, in the maximum-security section, forbade physical contact between visitors and prisoners, even husband and wife.

Prison was not so bad for the old recidivists and the perpetual criminals. Most adapted to it. It was a frightful punishment for the young first offenders, and the once-onlys. Many prisoners are not real criminals: they have made one terrible mistake in a car and killed or injured someone; or have lost their tempers with serious or even fatal consequences; or they have given way to temptation in extenuating circumstances, but then things have snowballed. Some cases of misappropriation have small beginnings, an illicit borrowing, then the snowball effect as one offence leads to another. Very frequently such offenders do not offend again after discovery.

I am not making the point that deprived people, especially from broken homes, may become criminals. That is so, but I'm saying that anyone can be both foolish and unlucky in a car, or in a physical argument. People drive home not merely over the limit, but drunk, and reach home safely or have a minor accident. The unlucky ones finish up in gaol. Many a domestic argument leads to a knife or a weapon being wielded, as much for show as with intent. There may be tragedy but in most cases everything blows over without the law being involved.

Sentences are becoming more frequent and longer. Yet in many cases the deterrent effect of two years in gaol is no less effective than three years. The extra year can well make the difference between the offender's marriage holding out or being destroyed.

Based on some experience, I would say that the marriage of a man imprisoned for the first time will rarely survive more than two years in gaol. Yet this is not considered when the sentence is imposed.

Two years in gaol is terrible for a first-timer. It may not be much for an old lag, but even then I wonder whether it has much deterrent effect, either on the prisoner in the case of the old lag, or on other would-be offenders.

Of course prison is intended as punishment, retribution by society and, as I have said in recent years, this is played up a lot in the media. The relative of a victim is asked to proclaim to the world his or her desire for vengeance, and thus no punishment imposed by the judges is sufficient. Judeo-Christian morality requires forgiveness not revenge, but I remember a Buddhist for whom I appeared who claimed to have been framed. I asked did he resent the man who framed him. 'You Christians,' he replied, 'you always want revenge. We Buddhists are not like that; we know his karma will get him.' I did not believe him, but I liked the thought.

Soon after I left the Prisons Royal Commission I was lucky to be able to involve myself in useful work but I am still concerned about the unfortunates in gaol and the public agitations to lengthen their sentences.

Perhaps we should all remember the tax collector's prayer, 'God, have mercy on me, a sinner.' (Luke: chapter 18, verse 13).

It is a mob vengeance instinct that urges heavy prison terms. I doubt whether the vengeance achieved is particularly satisfying in the end.

What we need are alternatives to prison to protect society by segregating offenders, hopefully to reform them, and at the same time to deter others and satisfy the victims. The problem is easily stated but not so easily solved. Special disciplined camps for traffic offenders were trialled in Japan, and the idea is important. Traffic offenders are not usually deliberate criminals and should not be treated as such. Periodic detention and probation are useful alternatives to prison.

Separation of different categories of prisoners has much to

recommend it; for example, youth from age, violent from non-violent, sexual offenders from others.

I do not pretend to know the answers to the questions relating to punishment of offenders. Pure punishment is hypocritical and contrary to many religious ideals of forgiveness. Vengeance – called retribution by judges – is hardly to be encouraged. Deterrence is not achieved by sending offenders to universities of crime so that they emerge much worse than before. Unfortunately we tend to follow the United States, and lock up the deprived, the ill and the unlucky, in conditions that will ensure that if not dedicated offenders now, they soon will be.

Since 1975 the gaols have become flooded with heroin addicts, and heroin itself. Many who seek protection in prison do so because they are in fear of the consequences of not paying for their heroin. Despite strong precautions and 'ramps' (cell searches), heroin gets into and around the prisons.

The maximum-security prison, as it now is, is both expensive and involves often inhumane treatment of criminals. Surely we can do better.

There was and still is so much to learn about prisons, and about how to enforce the criminal law. There is so much need for inquiry and thought. The 1975 Prisons Royal Commission never had a chance to deal in any depth with these problems. They are still with us.

A great opportunity was thrown away.

## II

# Protecting the Weak

In light of the previous chapter it is interesting to reflect that the villainy I am about to describe was substantially unpunished by the criminal law.

For many years, in fact long before I was born in 1926, door-to-door moneylenders operated. They preyed on the poor, the ignorant and the foolish. They particularly exploited lonely housewives.

Their techniques were varied, but the fundamental principles were similar. A housewife was persuaded to buy goods on credit, later converted to a simple loan, or she was given a loan in the first place. She was persuaded to accept terms of a certain amount per week, which she hoped she could afford. She was never told the rate of interest, which, even on the first loan, would be about 48 per cent or more once we were in the 1970s. The 'friendly' collector did his rounds weekly collecting her payments. Usually her husband did not know and the loan was then marked HDNK (Husband Does Not Know). The threat to tell her husband was used to keep the woman in line. In some cases the threat was carried out on a persistent non-payer, and the investigators came across cases of assaulted wives.

Women were encouraged to get further into debt by further purchases and further loans and by 'rolling over' their debts. The debts were put into a new loan so that now interest was being charged on past interest, resulting in compound interest. When we did the sums we found women paying over 150 per cent interest on loans, which they would never be able to repay. The collector was now the 'kind' person who, week by week, staved off disaster.

Of course, the women who got involved were foolish. When cases were investigated many women had no idea of what they had borrowed or how much they owed. In one case the borrower was a gambler and borrowed to bet. She won a big bet and tried to pay off all she owed. The collector would not tell her the amount. He had been making up a lot of it as he went along and had no chance of giving her a proper settlement account. In at least one case the collector borrowed for himself and the housewife paid his account as well as her own without knowing it.

The person who stamped all of this out once and for all was the Honourable Sid Einfeld, the dedicated Minister for Consumer Affairs in 1977–8. His Commissioner, Phil Gallagher, and a team of departmental investigators put the cases before myself and my junior Mike Finnane (now Judge Finnane). We interviewed numerous victims and prepared cases for the cancellation of the moneylenders' licences of the offending lenders. Soon they all either lost their licences, or in one case held the licence but gave up all door-to-door activities. Most gave in either at the door of the court or before, and surrendered their licences.

The police were called in on one case of apparent fraud but were unable to find the evidence that seemed fairly apparent to us. Police time and enthusiasm was, and still is, very limited in the case of white-collar crime.

There were many moneylending companies involved, some in the control of people who should have known better, and who claimed not to have known what was going on. There were many, many victims and the profits must have been enormous. The misery and distress caused to the women involved was quite dreadful. Some of the victims were even pensioners paying their debts to the moneylenders out of their tiny pensions.

Now people use credit cards and pay interest of less than 20 per cent. They are not deliberately lured into hopeless and often fraudulent debt. Such loan sharks as may still operate do so outside the law and often their customers are gamblers. There are not so many lonely wives at home now. Many are in the workforce and are much more familiar with business affairs.

To conclude this story, the victims were all advised that their debts were unenforceable because of breaches of the Moneylenders Act. Those not contacted probably would have read the story in the media. I hope that most did not try to pay off what they allegedly owed, but many did. The honesty of housewives is quite amazing, but not often realised in business.

Sid Einfeld had to administer the Landlord and Tenant Act which protected, as late as the 1970s, elderly tenants on pensions who lived in premises 'prescribed' during the war. The famous Peter Clyne, after he was removed from the roll of barristers, ran an eviction service whereby, for profit, he evicted such tenants. Usually they were paid an amount of money, but by no means always.

On behalf of the Minister intervening I challenged the legality of Clyne's service with some success. On another occasion I appeared for two elderly tenants and saved them from eviction by Peter Clyne. The case that gave me most satisfaction was when Peter advertised his service in an apparently illegal way. Sid Enfield was tempted to prosecute him, but first wanted my advice.

I knew Peter was very cunning and so I went to great pains to research the relevant law. It then became obvious that he had found a loophole in the Landlord and Tenant Act and was deliberately trailing his coat to be prosecuted and triumphantly acquitted. But he had overlooked another offence. I advised Sid Enfield to prosecute him for that and he was convicted. He was only fined, but it was a matter of prestige for the Minister and his department.

Late on the afternoon of the successful prosecution Sid Einfeld rang me. 'Chester,' he said, 'I've had a terrible day but it is all okay now. I've fitted Peter Clyne.' And so he had, and it was a feather in his cap.

I knew Peter Clyne very well. I had known him in university days when he was one of the best team debaters in Australia. Later I acted for him at times; in particular, just before he died I managed to terminate his examination in bankruptcy, and I also won another case for him. At one time, years before, Ted St John QC had led me in an attempt to restore Peter to the roll of barristers. It was a great pity that his talents were never fully employed.

At the time I opposed his tenant-eviction service Peter Clyne regarded it as an adventure in legal points and manoeuvres. He did not appreciate that his activities caused enormous strain and distress to elderly tenants. I became quite irate about his activities in this regard. Possibly because of my attitude and the cases I won against him, he gave up his tenancy activities and, as I recall it, advised Sid Einfeld accordingly. So our litigation had been worthwhile. He then transferred his activities to a crusade against the 'fiscal fiend', the Commissioner for Taxation, and in this cause he had some public sympathy. He no longer concerned Sid Einfeld.

Peter was an entertaining writer, both of legal textbooks and on either autobiographical or legal subjects. Any Peter Clyne book was well worth reading. As an advocate he was interesting and impressive, never boring. His voice could be attractive and persuasive. I once heard him as a barrister addressing a jury with supreme skill.

He was struck off for making submissions not justified by the evidence and in extreme terms. His problem at the time was a stubborn refusal to realise what he was doing, and how others perceived it. In my opinion he did not deliberately break the rules of advocates' ethics, but his foolish conduct made the disaster of his removal from the roll of barristers quite inevitable.

In my dealings with him, as his opponent or when he was my client, he was honest and trustworthy.

Sid Einfeld was the great pioneer of consumer protection and in his time he eliminated many nasty practices. He had a wide range of activities including such things as ensuring that toys were not dangerous to children. Since so many cheap toys have been imported from Asia this has been a most important part of the Department of Consumer Affairs, now called Fair Trading.

Sid Einfeld also administered the Prices Act. The Prices Commissioner, Mr Bob Evans, a magistrate, had the very difficult task of fixing prices under a technical, and at that time unpopular, Act. The main subject of price fixing was bread.

The Bread Manufacturers' Association attacked Bob Evans's prices in the Supreme Court, claiming that they had been improperly and invalidly fixed. The litigation was quite bitter and they achieved a stunning victory at first instance, despite my best endeavours.

With my junior, Mike Finnane, I advised an appeal to the Court of Appeal. That was mainly successful, but the case went on to the High Court and we were completely successful.

Sid Einfeld had, at first, been criticised severely by the Supreme Court, but this criticism was overruled in the High Court and he was completely vindicated. However, during the months that he smarted under unjust criticism there was never a word of reproach to me. He never blamed me at all, and generously congratulated me when we ultimately achieved complete success.

I suppose if I had to pick my favourite client it would be Sid Einfeld. He was loyal to his counsel and as a result he got the best service I could provide.

He and his Commissioner, Phil Gallagher, approached the task of consumer protection with enormous enthusiasm, and they obtained some excellent results. A great deal was achieved by negotiation, and only occasionally was it necessary to go to court.

Even second-hand car dealers were compelled by Sid Enfield to reduce the scams that were common when I first started in the law. In particular, it became dangerous for dealers to wind back the odometer of a car for sale so as to substantially reduce the distance apparently travelled. On one occasion I successfully defended a dealer charged with doing that. The car, a Rolls Royce, had been sold and bought many times over a few years and it was possible by reference to past records to show that the odometer had been wound back more than once. It was not possible, however, to show in the particular case that my client had done any winding back himself. In those days the practice was widespread. I think it is far less common today.

The Trade Practices Act passed by the Commonwealth Parliament produced great advances in consumer protection, and later New South Wales passed its own Fair Trading Act to apply many parts of the Commonwealth Act that covered corporations to other traders as well.

These Acts do provide some means for redressing unfair practices operating to the disadvantage of people in small business. In some cases these remedies have been quite successful; for example, a few of the cases against the banks concerning foreign loans. However, the problem is that such litigation in this area, which is often in the Federal Court, is technical and expensive; in fact, it is quite ruinous if it fails. In the early days of consumer protection the Department of Consumer Affairs took up the little causes of the consumers and usually produced a good result without the consumer risking his or her all against a big company. I suppose the Department of Fair Trading still does this, but I believe not as often or as enthusiastically as in the days of Sid Einfeld.

# 12

# Appeal Courts

Every legal system needs appeal courts to correct errors made by courts of first instance. Australia has excellent courts, but unfortunately, except in the case of appeals from magistrates, the appeal courts can do little to correct errors of fact-finding.

I had always appeared fairly often in the appeal courts when I was a senior junior, and I appeared more frequently in appellate work after I took silk.

In the appeal courts, the New South Wales Court of Appeal (replacing the old Full Court) and the High Court of Australia, the arguments were mainly about questions of law. Questions of fact usually involved argument about the record of the evidence in the court appealed from, but on rare occasions the Court of Appeal heard fresh evidence. The same applied to the Court of Criminal Appeal, which heard appeals from criminal convictions before juries in the District Court and the Supreme Court.

In the '50s and '60s I had been junior to Gordon Wallace QC, who went on to become a Supreme Court judge and then first president of the new Court of Appeal. He was a very capable man, courteous – as were most of the old-time silks – and kind to me when I was a junior. He tended to be overshadowed by the great Sir Garfield Barwick, but it might be said that he was the undoubted choice of those who failed to retain Sir Garfield. Sir Gordon made an excellent president of the Court of Appeal, and under him it was a pleasant experience to appear before that court.

Sir Garfield Barwick as a barrister was very kind to young juniors such as myself and he was a great raconteur of legal stories. He was quite a genius as an adviser on difficult legal questions and I found conferences with him inspiring. As an advocate in court he was never dull – sometimes he was very witty – but his great gift was to make the complicated simple and compelling in favour of his client.

When Barwick became a politician it seemed to me that he lost much of his humour and at times his speeches were quite dull, although he made an excellent speech in parliament when he introduced his Matrimonial Causes Act, which was then quite a massive reform.

When he became Chief Justice of the High Court some thought he was tough on counsel. I certainly did not and he tossed my arguments around many a time. However, the point was that his attacks were not personal, and there was no need for hard feelings. I certainly had none.

We were fortunate throughout my time at the bar to have a very fine High Court. There was always quite a blend of ideas, sometimes conflicting ideas, but the ultimate results were to be admired. I remember arguing a technical point in favour of injustice before Sir Harry Gibbs after he succeeded Sir Garfield. There seemed no answer to my submission, but the court found one and produced a satisfactory fair result. It was a family-law case, but the decision had wide consequences, and useful ones, in all cases where for one reason or another an order was made in the absence of a party.

I found the High Court, when it moved to Canberra, a most impressive court and by and large I have admired its rulings over the years.

Appearing in appeal courts was a hard task. One had to study all aspects of the case carefully and be ready to answer difficult questions from judges who knew the law very well indeed.

When the Federal Court of Australia was formed in 1977, its Full Court was made up of very able men. Its Chief Judge, Sir Nigel Bowen, ran a very efficient court, before which it was a pleasure to appear.

As the first Chief Judge of the new Family Court, Elizabeth Evatt had a Full Court over which she presided with great tact and ability. It had the task of hearing appeals on very difficult questions from judges who had a very wide discretion. I remember her letting me down lightly in argument when I overlooked a section in the Family Law Act. This was easy enough to do when the Act was a very new one, a fact which she, with kind tact, acknowledged.

I have said enough to show that on questions of law the decisions of the appellate courts, particularly of the ultimate High Court of Australia, were likely to be correct. Within the constraints imposed by laws that were not always fair (for example, the Income Tax Act) the appellate courts produced, by and large, fair and sensible decisions, at least in civil cases. In criminal cases there was often more controversy. The High Court and the New South Wales Court of Criminal Appeal laid down numerous 'safeguard' directions, and summing up to a jury in a criminal case is now a complicated and difficult task. Some judges resent this, but I have no doubt that the appellate courts are right in laying down careful directions on numerous matters which must be given to juries.

It is quite surprising how many junior judges are quite convinced that for the most part everyone appearing on indictment is guilty, and that defence counsel are there simply to secure an injustice. Usually such judges have had little or no experience in criminal cases before they came to be judges. It is not surprising that they require correction by Courts of Criminal Appeal, and resent it.

For good reason our judges are appointed permanently, and do not come up for re-election as in the courts of many American States. The idea is that the judge should be fearless and impartial, as well as efficient and learned – quite a lot to expect from any person. Sometimes an acting judge is appointed, but in my experience the performance of acting judges casts little light on how they will perform as permanent appointees. So obviously there are good judges, fairly good judges, and not-so-good judges. There are a few very bad judges.

A judge is the dictator of his or her court to whom all bow and who must be addressed courteously and with respect. Thus counsel cannot say, 'Only an idiot would think that was the law.' Instead they might say, 'With respect (or in extreme cases 'very great respect') the balance of authority would indicate that what Your Honour says is not the correct legal position.' Often judges make mistakes in the law, hence the need for appellate courts, not just to correct the individual mistakes but to keep the currents of the law pure.

Many years ago, I was addressing a judge (long-dead now) known to all as 'Mad Freddie'. I was acting for the defendant in a civil case. The judge told me, 'It is perfectly clear what happened in this case; the facts are quite clear' and proceeded to state them.

I then said, 'On that finding of fact, Your Honour is bound in law to find for the defendant.' To which came the reply, 'I'm not going to be trapped by smart young junior counsel; I change that finding of fact.'

I won on appeal. I remember my opponent was Bob Hope, later Mr R.M. Hope QC and later still Mr Justice Hope of the Court of Appeal. He was then, as always, an excellent lawyer and kept rising to try to get Mad Freddie to decide for his client in a way that would stand up on appeal. To his despair he was told, 'Sit down Mr Hope. I'm for you. Do you want me to change my mind?'

In those days judges and magistrates got away with a lot but things are much tighter now. Appellate courts do their job very well in such circumstances. In extreme cases a judge can be forced to resign or may face removal.

Frequently an obviously guilty person has been convicted but mistakes have been made in the trial. In such a case, if no injustice would occur the conviction may stand, but the law is quite strict and a person is entitled to any fair chance of an acquittal that they may have lost through judicial error.

Of course, many criminal appeals are quite hopeless. When the death penalty applied for murder, appeals were automatic. The habit persisted for some years after such sentences were invariably remitted to life imprisonment. I can remember even some argument back in the 1940s as to whether an accused could plead guilty to murder Now such pleas are common.

The fact that many appeals have absolutely no real merit makes it difficult for the Court of Criminal Appeal. Usually one of the three judges is detailed to study each case before the hearing to try to ensure that a good point is not missed among the not-so-good points. It is a heavy burden on the appeal judges. In my opinion, the Court of Criminal Appeal has improved enormously over the years. One great success was the court as run by Murray Gleeson when he was Chief Justice of New South Wales. He introduced senior judges of appeal from the civil Court of Appeal to sit on the court. Usually they had little experience of criminal law and approached matters with fresh minds, untrammelled by the prejudices and bad habits of those who practised frequently in that area. The results were impressive.

It was the High Court, consisting of mainly specialist equity and commercial lawyers, that produced the first reforms against police verbals. Before that, persons in custody were questioned in the absence of any other witness and were often supposed to have made verbal admissions that they denied at their trial. The summing up in these cases would frequently contain the message, 'Why should these policemen lie?' Often the juries knew the answer to the question that puzzled the presiding judge because they weren't so biased towards police. First the High Court (particularly Sir Harry Gibbs) prevented supposed records of interview that were unsigned going before the jury. Then special warnings as to verbal admissions were prescribed to be made by the presiding judge in his summing up. Then Parliament, no doubt at least in part inspired by the High Court, made it essential for verbal interviews to be videotaped and sound-recorded.

The 1976 Devlin Report in England showed how dangerous is evidence of identification of an accused made by a stranger. Bona fide mistakes can easily be made. Some witnesses are suggestible, others want to be notorious, most do their best, but that best can easily be wrong. The case of Adolf Beck (1895–1904) showed clearly enough how unreliable such evidence is. The Beck case involved an innocent man wrongly identified again and again as a swindler. The real swindler when finally caught bore little or no resemblance to Beck. In one of the cases prompting the Devlin Report a heroic police officer facing an armed man later wrongly identified the accused as his assailant.

I myself appeared in two different cases involving no-doubts, dogmatic identification by a layman where the prosecution was terminated. In one case, someone else was arrested and confessed, and in the other, police expert handwriting evidence proved my client's innocence.

The High Court has now insisted on careful directions by the presiding judge calculated to make such mistakes much less likely.

During my career I was to come up against misidentification in the Blackburn Royal Commission with which I shall deal later. That involved choosing a face from photos. It is said that line-ups take away much of the danger. But in my experience such line-ups were not filmed and properly recorded. Was the accused the only bald-headed man, the only Aborigine, the only man with a beard in the line-up? Will the police reveal that fact to the jury?

In the late 1940s my friend Jack Lindsay agreed to his client, who had been charged with another offence, being lined up on a new charge. He was invited to inspect the line-up and agreed that there was reasonable similarity. The detective left the room to bring in the witness and Jack noticed a raincoat hung up on a peg just behind his client. Quietly he moved the coat a few pegs down behind another gentleman in the line-up. There is no prize for guessing whom the witness picked. Jack walked away with his client.

No one likes to admit he or she was wrong. Shaking an identity witness in cross-examination is very difficult indeed.

When I had only been at the bar for about 10 years I was lucky enough to appear in the High Court instructed by the New Guinea Public Solicitor on appeals by leave from murder or manslaughter convictions in the New Guinea Supreme Court. In those days the only appeals were to the High Court by leave.

My first such case was Sirinjui – whose companion decided to throw four spears into the victim. Apparently for comity my client then threw a further four spears on the spur of the moment and not pursuant to any common purpose or pre-arrangement. This was the first of several appearances before the great Sir Owen Dixon who was very amused by my submissions that the appellant could not be charged with murder since his spears may well have been thrown at a corpse nor could he be charged with mutilating a corpse because the victim may have still been alive. Sir Owen cited a famous Harvard puzzle:

> A man has two deadly enemies when he is about to make a trip across a desert. One poisoned his water in his water-bag, the other slashed the bag so that it leaked. The man died of thirst. Who, if anyone, was guilty of murder?

Ultimately Sirinjui was acquitted.

I was led by Doctor Frank Louat QC, a great silk and a very pleasant man, in the famous case of Wendo. Since this case involved about 20-odd appellants I suppose I did more murder appeals to the High Court than anyone else. (Frank had not been in the other homicide appeals I did on my own from New Guinea.)

In Wendo's case the appellants had wiped out the village of Maga and justice found them in the person of a police inspector who told his men to bring in all witnesses. Who were witnesses? Anyone who ran away. In due course the witnesses, handcuffed and secured, appeared before the inspector, now a coroner, who held an inquest during which each witness was asked did he kill the victims. The questions went through two translators from Kukukuku to pidgin to English. The answers were boastfully yes. Were these answers voluntary? The High Court said yes and the convictions stood.

The common law was a bit too sophisticated for these tribesmen, but training in the common law had to start somewhere. In those days it was considered that all murder cases had to be proved by proper evidence.

I think this was the last big tribal massacre in New Guinea. The appellants were proud of what they had done. They were trained to put their hands over their mouths when asked to plead. By standing mute they were deemed to plead not guilty.

Nowadays pleas of guilty to murder are common. Of course, back then there was a death penalty, usually not enforced but still there.

The appellate courts have a lot to do besides criminal cases. One area that takes up much of their time is income tax, and at one time Sir Garfield Barwick's court was vigorously attacked for up-holding tax schemes that artificially avoided tax. It was said that the court should have set aside technicalities and have had more regard to the objects of the legislation. However, it must be appreciated that the Income Tax Act is quite draconian in its operation, viciously taxing the simple, honest operator who does not have a tax adviser at his or her elbow. It long ago gave up any attempt to be fair. As a struggling young barrister I found the income in my tax returns far exceeded subpoenaed evidence of tax returns of wealthy businessmen who operated strings of companies. Only employees, professional men and small businessmen paid full taxes. The big boys never did and never will.

How else can a court interpret such an Act other than strictly? That was Barwick's attitude, and that of the majority of the court at the time. Perhaps they went too far.

Instead of the government drafting a reasonably simple statute that could be understood, the Income Tax Act was plugged up with vast new anti-avoidance sections. New legislation obliges the court to pay more regard to the objects of the Act. The ultimate result is that sophisticated tax advice is much more expensive, the ordinary battler tosses on a hopeless tax sea, and the big boys sail smoothly through, as they always did.

I appeared in some tax appeals years ago for the Commissioner of Taxation. In those days there were a lot of hard-working, dedi-cated people in the Taxation Department who did their work very well. That was back in the 1970s. I rather fancy that there is a smarter but not-so-dedicated breed today, so that tax officers learn their trade and then join private enterprise. I hope such persons may still be in a minority.

The law gets more and more complicated. The Corporations Law, replacing the old Companies Acts, is a maze. Generally, local government, planning, and administrative law are new fields of difficulty to add to the old fields of equity, common law, family law, property law, taxation and probate. An appellate judge has to learn enough on any topic to decide a case. In the High Court the community expects a first-class judgment on any legal subject from the court of last resort, and it gets it. We have good reason to be proud of the Australian High Court, which must be one of the best appellate courts in the English-speaking world.

Appellate-court wit is not always gentle, as evidenced by the following interchanges.

'That,' said pompous counsel, 'concludes the first branch of my argument.'

'Branch?' said one judge. 'I should not have thought it was a twig!'

In a criminal appeal Sir Frederick Jordan had been quiet while his two brother judges hammered the famous Jimmy Kinkaid with hostile questions. There was a brief break in the interchange and Sir Frederick looked up.

'By the way Mr Kinkaid, don't get any encouragement from my silence, will you?'

I have spent many difficult but enjoyable days before appellate courts. One of my problems was that I have a bad memory for names. I remembered everything about precedent cases except their names. Often I angled a clue and remembered, for example, that the mysterious name bandied by the bench was the case, for example, of the man whose wife drowned in the surf. Then I was back in the picture.

Sometimes the Court of Appeal, sitting as three judges, had to decide original questions of fact. This was the case when Wendy Bacon – a prominent agitator and later journalist in the '70s and '80s – applied for admission as a barrister after she was refused by the Barristers' Admission Board. I appeared, not for the Bar Association, as has been reported at times, but for the Prothonotary, the chief Supreme Court administration officer at Common Law. This was in September 1981.

I cross-examined Wendy Bacon at some length, mainly over an allegation of providing false bail; that is, bail not independent of the accused, for one Stephen Sellars. Ms Bacon is a very intelligent woman and was unlikely to wilt under questioning. The court was full of her supporters, and I had the impression that their loud support did her no good, because her answers at times were more likely to impress the audience than the three judges.

Looking back at the case now, with the wisdom gained from the Police Royal Commission, Ms Bacon was undoubtedly a brave political agitator who may have been much more useful to the community than was then realised. At the same time she went to extremes in demonstrations and her actions were held to be seriously illegal in the bail matter. Her strictures about various police officers, including my client Roger Rogerson, were, to say the least, courageous, much more so than most of us realised.

Later when I defended Rogerson, Ms Bacon and her entourage were frequently at the court. She was not pleased with the result.

Ms Bacon was not believed by the Court of Appeal, and her application to be admitted as a barrister was refused. Ultimately I think this result was inevitable having regard to the evidence. Fortunately she recovered her prestige as a journalist.

The appeal courts perform the function of supervising the judges, even at times senior judges. Readers of Dickens' *Oliver Twist* will remember the fierce magistrate Mr Fang. His image was rare but not completely unknown in my days at the bar, particularly the early days. When his like emerged, the appellate courts usually acted quickly, and effectively.

Of course magisterial errors were not often in that category. However, in busy courts, often without adequate library references, it was easy for a magistrate to depart from proper practice, called 'natural justice' at the time – now procedural fairness. I was frequently the counsel briefed by the Crown to defend the magistrate's conduct. Sometimes the task was not easy, but usually the mistakes were honourable errors. In fact, the appellate courts were imposing higher standards than had existed before.

It was perhaps natural for a magistrate to try to shorten cases (which were then often two or three times 'not reached' after the parties attended in vain because there was not time to hear them). One magistrate discouraged addresses, and to one advocate who said 'But Your Worship has not heard me address,' he replied 'Neither I have, go ahead address me, address me as long as you like; see if you can change my mind'. This was very soon after the war and there was no appeal. Nowadays such conduct would be misconduct on the part of the magistrate, not merely an error.

Natural justice seems a simple enough proposition but it is fraught with difficulty. What particulars of an allegation is a party entitled to? How long must a court put up with a long, useless cross-examination? How long is a party entitled to address the court for? Common sense and judicial tact usually solve such questions.

More difficult perhaps are the questions of bias and prejudgment.

I remember George Amsberg in the District Court had to hear a case of mine in which a motorist was suing a pedestrian for causing an accident in which the car was damaged. I think the car swerved to avoid him. George was quite incensed. The case was sound in law, but to him an insurance company covering the motorist (as he believed) was going too far in suing the pedestrian.

I got on well with George and we had quite an argument. Finally George said, 'All right, go ahead Mr Porter, but I shall be doing my best to find against you.'

I replied, 'I regret that Your Honour has now disqualified yourself from hearing the case.'

I suppose the word 'regret' was legal hypocrisy. He had to concede, with quite good grace. Another judge heard the case and I lost it.

George had said to me as I left his court, 'The next judge may not be as frank as I was.'

If a judge's wife has a few shares in a very large public company should he hear a case involving that company? If a judge has expressed firm views as to the relevant law in another case, should he hear the same point again?

These problems are not always easy to solve. Very broadly, a judge may approach a case with firm views as to the law, but not as to the facts gained otherwise than from the evidence.

The preliminary directions to a criminal jury these days are especially aimed at keeping it to the evidence and nothing but the evidence. The same should apply to any judge deciding questions of fact.

By and large the appellate courts have ample powers to deal with mistakes of law or errors in procedure. On other matters they have far less power.

If a judge makes a decision in the exercise of a discretion – for example, in deciding how much of a husband's property a wife should receive on their separation; what sentence a convicted offender should receive; how much of an estate a testator should have left to his widow – the appellate court normally can correct it only for an error of law, or a clear error of fact, or perhaps for a hidden error indicated by the actual result. The appellate court cannot simply substitute its views for those of the judge at first instance.

On simple questions of fact – for example, how fast was a car going; did the parties reach a verbal agreement; did the defendant assault the plaintiff? – the appellate courts (apart from appeals from magistrates to District Courts) have few powers. They can only override a finding that does not depend upon the view of the judge of first instance as to the demeanour of the parties, unless in very rare cases the finding can be shown by the other evidence in the case to be clearly wrong.

Except in esoteric equity and commercial cases most disputes depend on a conflict of evidence, a dispute as to what actually happened. This, of course, is essentially so in criminal cases.

One might ask what human judge can hope to be usually correct in a conflict of evidence, where there is a real and genuine dispute as to the facts. Injustices must abound in civil cases where the onus of proof is bare probability. In criminal cases the onus of proof is beyond reasonable doubt, but this formula can easily deteriorate into 'Who do I believe?' Again, the case of appeals from magistrates to judges is quite different because the appeal judge is entitled and bound to form his or her own opinion, usually assisted by hearing the crucial witnesses give their evidence again.

While witnesses give false or inaccurate evidence, justice will always be in danger. Where the wrong decision is given on a question of fact at first instance, it will very rarely be corrected on appeal.

# 13

# Fighting the Drug Trade

I suppose I have a great experience of the law's efforts to suppress the drug trade, mainly as a prosecutor but sometimes as counsel for the defence. I have also acted for parents and am familiar with the devastation heroin causes within families. Heroin and other drug cases are usually sad cases involving people who would not normally be criminals.

Australia copies America, and as we watched American films about the drug trade, heroin reached Australia.

In 1980 a Commonwealth–State Task Force into Drug Trafficking was formed as the result of a recommendation by the New South Wales Woodward Royal Commission. The Task Force consisted of both New South Wales police and Australian Federal Police officers, and it had some success.

By 1980 I had had some experience in prosecuting federal drug cases, and I was chosen to prosecute the first case for the Task Force. My junior was Nicholas Cowdery, who later took silk and then went on to become the New South Wales Director of Public Prosecutions. There were nine accused in this case, of whom the principals were Desmond Bennion and Kenneth Harrison. The scheme involved sending numerous letters containing small quantities of heroin from Malta to a person in Mount Druitt.

Nick Cowdery did most of the work in obtaining the extradition of the heroin sender from Malta – quite a difficult task.

The committal proceedings were lengthy, involving a great deal of evidence as to what happened in Malta and in Mount Druitt when the letters were received. Numerous relatives and acquaintances of Bennion were involved. In the end, every accused person was convicted and sentenced.

This case was followed by others. Few accused were acquitted. The Task Force did its work with skill and care.

Drug enforcement is difficult. Those involved dare not speak, lest they be murdered (as quite a few were). Ingenious ways are found to conceal drugs. In one case I dealt with, a tin of shaving cream was altered to contain a quantity of heroin while still being able to puff out shaving cream.

I prosecuted quite a few cases both for the Task Force and for the Australian Federal Police. At first, the latter had quite a deal to learn from the New South Wales police, but they were soon very capable by themselves. One case I prosecuted involved a barrister engaged in the importation of Buddha sticks (potent cannabis) as part of the famous Moylan conspiracy. This was originally a Narcotics Bureau case before the Australian Federal Police absorbed the bureau.

The Moylan gang used pretty female couriers who used Samsonite suitcases to bring drugs through customs at the airports. Such an enterprise would be foolhardy today because incoming suitcases are now inspected by sniffer dogs under the carousel before the passengers receive them. Cannabis has a strong smell, even to humans, and I should think no dog would miss it.

I remember once defending a Sri Lankan man accused of drug trafficking. A sniffer dog signalled his bag. He was taken into a room where he denied that there was anything in his bag. Eventually, after some discussion, the bag was opened by the customs officers, but no cannabis could be detected. Perhaps my client smiled too soon. The dog was brought into the room and chewed the lining of the bag. It was packed with thin strips of hashish (very potent cannabis) and it was very cleverly packed indeed. Only a knife through the lining revealed it after the customs officer was encouraged by the dog's enthusiasm.

Dogs can also sniff heroin but probably not as reliably. One client of mine packed a bag (Samsonite of course) in Singapore and the dog sniffed out the heroin upon arrival in Sydney, but the bag was actually leaking white powder. Can the dog claim much credit for that one?

In the 1980s probably a lot of drugs came in by passenger planes. I doubt whether much gets through that way now. Shipping containers are more likely to be used. There are thousands of containers and they cannot all be searched. Whereas to my knowledge the maximum suitcase content found was 10 kilograms (the suitcase contained nothing else), a container can hold a very large quantity, literally five or 10 times that amount.

The Wood Police Royal Commission later heard evidence disgracing the Task Force, but this was all as to matters occurring after 1983 when I ceased to act for the Task Force because I was injured in a car accident. I met some good men in the Task Force and some went on to impressive careers.

In 1985 I acted to assist the New South Wales Coroner, Mr Kevin Anderson, in a second inquest into the death of Dale Payne. She was a drug addict, not infrequently arrested by the police. Each time she traded leniency for her supplier's name, and one name given was that of 'Macaroni Anderson', alias 'Liverpool Tony', who was murdered during the inquest.

Dale Payne died of an overdose only possibly by accident. She had been off heroin for a while and had lost much of her tolerance for the drug, but there was plenty of motive for someone to give her an overdose. A girl used to about 10 per cent (the then common street strength) might well die if given 50 per cent pure heroin.

How was she to tell the strength? I sought the assistance of reformed users and medical people in finding this out. Apparently tasting the powder, as so often used to happen in films, only indicates the presence of heroin. It gives no clue as to the strength. Perhaps the only way of finding out is to inject a small amount into the vein (most users become mainliners into the vein if they persist) and then wait for the body's reaction. If not too bad, then inject more. But what junkie hanging out for a fix has the patience to follow that routine?

Before injecting it, heroin is often dissolved in water from a hotel toilet. The user thus achieves privacy at the risk of blood poisoning. Heroin addiction is quite crazy. The 'grey death' involved heroin mixed with cement used by some idiots. Usually heroin is 'cut' with glucose or glucodin. The effort to find a vein has, so I am informed, resulted in some injections behind the eyeball.

One terrible side effect of heroin use is little known. A client of mine had a bad traffic accident causing quite agonising injuries to his face and palate. Pethidine and morphine had little or no effect to ease the pain because he had a high tolerance for heroin. Heroin was originally invented as the most powerful pain reliever.

I get quite angry when people in this country are denied heroin as a legitimate painkiller. Of course, any attempt to legalise heroin, not for addicts but for cancer sufferers, meets enormous opposition from the same people who deny euthanasia to such sufferers. I appreciate that 'expert' evidence can easily be obtained that morphine is as good as heroin. If so, why not ban morphine? In fact, in other countries, including England, heroin still has a merciful use for which it was originally intended.

Quite recently, heroin strength on the street was very high and people were dying of overdoses. The use of Narcan in time is quite miraculous, but its effective use can only be ensured through shooting galleries where heroin addicts can be monitored and advised. If these places are used to save lives and counsel addicts off heroin, then I fail to understand the opposition to them. I do not know the answer to the drug problem. In my many discussions with addicts it seems that addiction is usually the result of fundamental unhappiness with life. While enjoying drug intoxication these people know their happiest moments. But I do not think that this dissatisfaction with life is caused by the miserable state of society. Rather it is because people expect, or at least want, so much more from life than their parents had.

One thing I might usefully add: films such as *The Man with the Golden Arm* and a great deal of material in the media suggest that withdrawal from heroin addiction is a frightful experience, so much so that many addicts fear to attempt it. In fact, withdrawal effects vary a great deal and many people go on and off heroin with little discomfort. Others find it hard, but usually it is not nearly as hard as the media suggest.

When I was appearing in the Dale Payne inquest in 1985, it suddenly occurred to me that Macaroni Anderson and his ilk were only middlemen at worst. I doubt whether the big-time operators have ever been caught. Judging by the dishonesty of corrupt police, as revealed from time to time, I doubt whether this will ever happen.

One can argue that drug enforcement has in fact failed dismally. But one can also argue that due to police corruption, drug enforcement has never seriously been tried. Not all detectives are dishonest, but it only takes one to inform the targets of an investigation. The opportunities for graft are so great that one wonders whether it is possible to have an honest drug squad. Most of what has been done so far has merely targeted users and lower distributors. Perhaps the Customs Department and the Australian Federal Police have been more successful.

I have little doubt that many minor players in the drug scene are deliberately betrayed by the higher-ups. This way the police keep up their arrest rates, the gaols find customers and the public can believe something is being done.

Under the former New South Wales Police Commissioner Peter Ryan there were some big drug hauls and arrests. It is also fair to point out that the corrupt police from the Manly area were exposed by other New South Wales police. This is a hopeful sign but we are a long way from any real enforcement of the drug laws.

At the same time there have been some brave, dedicated people fighting the drug trade. Their efforts have achieved some results, but the trade goes on.

I remember, at the request of the Australian Federal Police, acting for the main witness against Robert Trimbole, alias 'Aussie

Bob'. The witness was carefully guarded by federal police officers and I could only see him after being picked up in the street and driven to a secret destination, which changed every time. There was a reward of $150,000 payable by the underworld simply for this witness's address.

The witness first gave evidence at Paddington Court. The New South Wales police were supposed to check everyone with a metal detector, but on the first day the battery was either flat or the machine was not working efficiently. I complained to the magistrate, Mr Bruce Brown SM, and things were much better the next day. Since then we have become much more sophisticated. An attack on the court with machine guns would not have been pleasant, especially as I was at the bar table which would have been in the line of fire from the court door to the witness box.

The Narcotics Bureau and the Task Force were good ideas, but they failed because of a few people. One person in such an organisation can ruin everything.

I am intrigued by bodies such as the National Crime Authority. I am not a very good figures man, but skilled accountants following the money trail might achieve a lot. The heroin trade involves billions rather than millions of dollars. Those in gaol did not get much money, in my experience.

Where did the money go?

I did a lot of prosecuting of drug offenders. I was left with the impression in the end that I was only convicting the lesser idiots. I never got anywhere near the really big operators. I doubt whether anyone ever has.

# 14

# A Car Accident

It is a kind dispensation that we cannot see into the future. Otherwise I would have suffered in advance the consequences of a car accident, an event that changed my life.

On 30 October 1983 I was with my wife, Jean, and our two cocker spaniel dogs, driving home on Mona Vale Road at Ingleside. One Thomas Gilbert, well under the influence of the cup that cheers, came over onto the wrong side of the road, probably asleep at the wheel. We were each travelling at the permitted 80-kilometres-per-hour speed limit. Thus there was a 160-kilometres-per-hour impact.

Most people involved in such an accident, if they live, remember little or nothing because of concussion. My seat belt saved me from serious head injury so I still have a clear memory of the accident.

When I had suddenly seen the car coming towards me, I remember thinking I must not swerve to the right. In legal cases I had heard such swerves led to much worse accidents, so I swerved hard to the left and the impact came on the driver's side.

I clearly remember an incredible sound of impact, then everything seemed red. It took me months to realise that a gash on my forehead and eyebrow filled my eye with blood and hence the red vision. After the crash, at first there was silence.

I was badly injured. Apart from the head injury and some glass in my eye, I had a shattered left upper arm which caused agonising pain, a broken left ankle and a fractured right hip, plus enormous bruising of my legs. I was trapped in the car by my feet and rescuers were not able to get me out for over two hours. I was comforted by Mrs Hill, the wife of Graham Hill (later Justice Hill), a fellow barrister who was passing by at the time.

Jean was badly shaken and shocked, but not seriously hurt. One dog, Emily, had her back fractured and had to be put down. The other, Bobby, was simply bruised and shocked. He was a good dog and lived for some years, but I think the accident shortened his life.

I must have lost consciousness while trapped in the car. I remember, after being in the car helpless and in pain, being dragged out by rescuers who cut my boots off. The process of being freed from the car was very painful. I remember being in the ambulance and then waking up the next day in Intensive Care in Mona Vale Hospital.

While I was unconscious in casualty my daughter Mary saw I had a label attached saying 'Thomas Gilbert'. She pointed out the error in no uncertain terms to the staff and it was corrected. Blood tests were taken from each of us. I had had no alcohol, while Thomas Gilbert was well over the limit. I like to think that the mistake would have been corrected eventually, even if Mary had not interfered.

I spent a long time in Mona Vale Hospital, about six-and-a-half weeks, and then the hip did not knit. A further operation at St George Hospital healed the hip so that today I do not even limp. I still have a metal splint in my left arm which sets off metal detectors at times. I am indebted to Doctors David Sonnabend and Bill Cumming that I made substantially a complete recovery, but it was a long, painful process.

I don't find hospitals pleasant and I spent time in three hospitals and underwent three operations, the last of which was to remove the metal pieces in my hip just before I appeared in the Chamberlain case in early 1986.

Thomas Gilbert was fined $1000 and disqualified from driving for 12 months. This was quite a light penalty but that certainly did not worry me. I was glad that he did not go to gaol. I should not like anyone to be in gaol on my account. It was a one-off event for him. He had a good record and perhaps he was unlucky, but so was I.

I find it hard to understand the modern emphasis on retribution for crimes. It may be that the offender has to be punished, but punishment of the offender is no real comfort to the victim or at least it was of no comfort to me. In the end, in most aspects of life, revenge is bitter in the mouth, and no comfort at all.

The discipline of suffering is not pleasant. Pain is very hard to bear at times, but it is an experience that helps one to understand one's fellow man better.

I returned to work early in 1984 with my left arm in a sling and my right arm grasping a crutch. I appeared in several cases, quite successfully, but since my hip did not knit I was away again around March and did not return to work again until July, when I was well on the mend but still on crutches, two this time, because my left arm had recovered.

Soon after my return I appeared for two police officers charged with corruption. As the case progressed I realised that I had a new power. I had suffered, and I now knew much better how my fellow men suffered in their lives. As a result, my address to the jury was one of my best ever. The accused were both acquitted, and I was about to become a criminal-law specialist. I was about to acquire a very difficult practice appearing by and large for once-onlys – people who were of previous good character, now accused of serious crime.

Quite a few of these clients were policemen. There was an anti-corruption drive on at the time, but those conducting it were inexperienced and often incompetent. Hence police were being charged on the evidence of criminal drug dealers with no real corroboration. The investigators often tried to compensate for their own incompetence by dubious means, on the basis that the end justified the means.

It is worth remembering that New South Wales Police Commissioners John Avery and Tony Lauer pioneered the work of reforming the New South Wales Police Service and stamping out corruption. Some of their reforms were very worthwhile, but the Wood Royal Commission showed that much more drastic means were necessary, and the task is far from complete today.

# 15

# Roger Rogerson

Very soon after New South Wales Detective Sergeant Roger Rogerson was charged with attempting to pervert the course of justice, I was retained to defend him. Two or three days later I was asked to prosecute him. Thus sometimes one's life is at the crossroads.

In that year, 1985, Murray Farquhar, ex Chief Stipendiary Magistrate, was convicted of attempting to pervert the course of justice. So was Justice Lionel Murphy, although the conviction was subsequently set aside on appeal. Roger Rogerson was considered a certainty to be convicted. The first part of 1985 was the time of lopping the tall poppies, the time when high-profile people were accused of serious crimes.

This type of trial after trial of tall poppies can have its dangers. As more flowers fall, fresh accusers come forth and further poppies are accused. It is not long before the innocent are accused and convicted. It is important to appreciate that the conviction of a guilty man on inadequate evidence is only a short step from convicting an innocent man.

Roger Rogerson had been a police hero. As he is today it is hard to imagine the clever, charming man of yesterday. Had he fought in a war he would have been a candidate for a VC, a man who defied danger and won many times. No one knew the underworld as he did. His informants were everywhere. He solved many crimes. He was kind and courteous to his neighbours and friends. He has now been publicly disgraced and a TV film has depicted him as a criminal.

If there was another side to him, as depicted in the ABC film *Blue Murder*, few saw it. I doubt very much whether he ever went as far with Neddy Smith and others as is shown in the film. I do know that he was a very able man capable of great things, and his ultimate disgrace was a tragedy.

I knew Rogerson once gave evidence for Neddy Smith in a trial where I did not appear, although I was briefed on the appeal, and succeeded. It was, after all, his duty to give relevant evidence, even if it helped a noted criminal. Rogerson was alleged in *Blue Murder* to have a criminal association with Neddy Smith. No one alleged this at the time I appeared for Rogerson.

I knew about Rogerson shooting Warren Lanfranchi (for whom I had twice appeared on appeals) but I had no real knowledge of the circumstances of the killing. Rogerson was alleged to have, in effect, murdered Lanfranchi, but a coroner's inquest found differently. The story now told in *Blue Murder* was never proved in the Coroner's Court or anywhere else.

At the time I first met Rogerson I was impressed by his frankness and his ability. My clerk remarked upon his polite and friendly manner. It was not my task to judge my client, but I did form the opinion that he was probably innocent.

Mick Drury, Roger Rogerson's accuser, had the self-confidence common to undercover policemen. He was a very capable undercover man, and, perhaps like many such police officers, had an exalted opinion of his own ability. Of course, he had reason for pride in his achievements. The problem of the policeman who in the course of his duties pretends to be a criminal is an intriguing and important one. Normal life is impossible, and so his family life may well be shattered while he lives a lie in the course of duty. In later years I acted for another undercover policeman who suffered a nervous breakdown. He was not alone.

I think Mick Drury was a strong man. He certainly appeared so to me, but the Rogerson trial was obviously a great strain on him. Many of his fellow officers were on Rogerson's side, probably a majority.

In his first trial it was Rogerson's word against Drury's. The other witnesses added only a little as the case turned out.

Rogerson had, at that time, a magnificent unstained record of service. Not only was he a very capable and brave police officer, he was a kind man. An elderly neighbour gave evidence that Rogerson painted his house for him, a not insignificant act of kindness and generosity.

I suppose all of us are mixtures in character of good, bad and indifferent. When some bad is proved, it's easy to allege more, which will then be readily believed. I very much doubt whether Rogerson was as bad as he has since been depicted. I note that he was later tried for conspiracy to murder Drury, and acquitted.

The trial in which I appeared was his first, and in substance he was charged with trying to bribe Drury, in order that he should give false evidence so as to acquit one Williams, a heroin dealer from the Painters and Dockers Union, on trial in Victoria. There had undoubtedly been conversations between Rogerson and Drury about this Victorian trial, but the two men had two very different versions of what was said.

The undercover penetration of this particular heroin ring was dangerous in the extreme. Before it was over, several participants, or in one case a person mistakenly believed to be a participant, had been murdered. Drury had been shot and dreadfully wounded in the stomach by an unknown gunman, said to be Christopher Dale Flannery (now dead). No one to my knowledge has suggested that Neddy Smith had anything to do with these matters.

A mistake by police in Victoria had let Williams, the drug dealer, escape before he was caught in possession of heroin. Had things gone according to plan, at the arrest Drury would have faded away, leaving the arresting police with ample evidence of the culprit's possession of a large quantity of heroin which Drury, posing as a buyer, had persuaded him to produce. As it was, Williams got away but was followed and ultimately arrested. The case against him then depended almost entirely on Drury's evidence. He thus had to discard his cover.

Of course the strength of the Crown case against Rogerson was why should a fellow police officer accuse him if he was innocent. The two men hardly knew each other. Drury claimed that Rogerson had approached him to change his evidence. Rogerson said he was giving Drury some useful information he had picked up from an underworld contact. Certainly Rogerson had many such informers, and had he received such information it was his duty to tell Drury. But why would Drury accuse him of corruption if the conversations were innocent? That was my problem as Rogerson's counsel.

It must be appreciated that many false accusations are made without the motives ever being apparent. This is particularly so in the case of alleged sex offences.

In the committal proceedings when I cross-examined Drury I concentrated on the fact that he had been trained to lie. He had been successfully deceiving people as an important part of his profession. Thus he had successfully penetrated the Painters and Dockers Union heroin ring by pretending to be a dealer looking for heroin to sell. He was obviously good at lying.

Drury's pride took over during the cross-examination and he answered me as one who was dominating the scene. This I cheerfully permitted in the hope of getting a useful answer when he thought he was doing well. Very foolishly he looked around the Magistrate's Court and said words to the effect that he could tell lies in the court, and nobody could pick him.

He tried to retreat from this statement at the trial before a jury, but it had been recorded and was very damaging to his credit. He again made a smart answer to me at the trial when I suggested he would have been shocked at Rogerson's alleged suggestion to him of money for perjury. He said something along the lines of 'I would have a few hundred years ago'.

Drury had suffered dreadfully in hospital. To what extent he may have been bullied by superior officers when he first accused

Rogerson I do not know. Rogerson had been a hero, perhaps even an icon at that time. To accuse him of corruption was almost sacrilege. Drury gave a number of accounts to various people of what he said had happened, and there were inconsistencies. This was not surprising in the circumstances, but these inconsistencies were important in the defence case.

I went to great pains to cross-examine Drury gently lest I gave him reason to break down in tears in front of the jury. However when he was re-examined by Mr Hiatt QC for the Crown he burst into tears. I doubt whether this appeared genuine to the jury, but they were in a much better position to judge than I was as an advocate.

Rogerson had always been noted as an excellent witness and he did well in his own trial. We put his character in issue and thus Hiatt could throw any dirt at him in the Crown's possession. Of course he had no convictions and no disciplinary findings against him, but Hiatt cross-examined him about a number of matters, brandishing big files in his hands and on the bar table. In re-examination I was able to show that these matters had never previously been the subject of any inquiry or even a call upon Rogerson to explain. Numerous good witnesses gave Rogerson a splendid character.

The jury was out for over 24 hours, locked up as deliberating juries were in those days. On the second day of their deliberations at the lunch hour I was told by another barrister 'The Crown says only one man is holding out for not guilty'. This did not come to me from the Crown direct, if it came from them at all. How would they know? But it was the sort of rumour that is often heard when a jury is divided.

About half an hour later the jury brought in a verdict of not guilty. There was quite a roar of protest from those who hated Rogerson and cheers from his supporters.

Rogerson went back into the police force but not long after he was the subject of departmental charges and further criminal charges. He never asked me to appear for him again.

On the evidence I believe the jury's verdict was correct. They could not properly find beyond reasonable doubt that Rogerson was guilty.

Years later Drury came up to me in Queen's Square. I told him I thought he would not want to speak to me but he said, 'I have nothing against you. You were doing your job.' We had a friendly chat then, and on another occasion outside Central Criminal Court.

I do not know whether being an undercover agent did Drury any serious mental harm. If it did his being shot subsequently would not have helped matters. He had an agonising wound and he suffered a great deal of pain in hospital. He had good reason to believe that he was going to die. He had risked his life and suffered in the service of the community.

As for Roger Rogerson, I think I only met him once after this trial, a casual meeting at some magistrate's court when he was facing the charges that ultimately put him in prison. He was a tragedy, not just from his own point of view, but from that of the community. He had been a very able man, highly intelligent, well suited from that angle to high rank in the police force. He was a polished, well-mannered man who was in many respects kind and considerate. He was also a strong family man, very fond of his daughters. His other side I never saw, but I have read about it with interest.

Normally I did not stay with my client for the whole time he was awaiting the jury's verdict. In his case I did because I respected him, liked him and was sorry for him, and my company may have eased the strain. The summing up had been strongly against him but the jury's questions during their deliberations were highly intelligent and right on the issue. It was clear from questions the jury asked the court that they understood the issues perfectly. Rogerson, for once, was downcast and depressed when the jury retired, and was sure they would find him guilty. As soon as their questions started I knew there was hope and I turned out to be right.

I had watched one member of the jury with interest and hope. He was taking careful notes and, I could see from when he wrote, relevant notes. I think he was the man who rang me some time later because he wanted to tell me what had happened in the jury room. I had to tell him that I was not allowed to hear what he had to say because what went on in the jury room was secret. This was the rule applying to everyone, but often disobeyed, even then before special legislation made any inquiry from an ex-juryman as to the reasons for the verdict, a criminal offence.

I do not think I had ever met Roger Rogerson before he was charged and I was retained to defend him. I got to know him well over a short period, and I liked and admired him – as I thought he was. It was a great disappointment to me to find that his character left much to be desired, to say the least.

Frankly, I did not expect to win Rogerson's case. Drury was a hero. Why should he lie? There was an atmosphere of conspiracy about the case, in which witnesses seemed to be reluctant to give evidence for the Crown.

I was elated by the jury's verdict. It was a great win because everyone expected me to lose. However, to my mind it is very clear that the jury doing its duty deciding the case on the evidence had to find that at the least there was a reasonable doubt. Roger Rogerson was entitled to a fair trial on the evidence, not on suspicion or rumour.

Today, having lost his character by one conviction he is now, more than ever, the subject of suspicion and rumour. He is fair game for any defamatory allegation. How much of what is alleged against him is true I simply do not know.

# 16

# Judge John Foord

Roger Rogerson's acquittal broke the procession of tall poppies being cut down in 1985. It added much more to my prestige than would have been the position had I been his prosecutor and he had been convicted. Such is fate. The rule of the bar is that counsel takes the first brief offered, whether he or she likes the client or not. Otherwise the unpopular, the oppressed, the unfortunate, might be deprived of counsel of their choice.

Soon after the Rogerson case I was approached by the late Ken Hall (who had been John Foord's clerk when he was a barrister) to defend Judge Foord, then facing trial on two charges of attempting to pervert the course of justice. The first charge related to a conversation with Clarrie Briese, the then Chief Stipendiary Magistrate, and the second to a conversation with his fellow District Court judge Paul Flannery. In these conversations Judge Foord was alleged, in effect, to have urged Briese to lean on the magistrate hearing the committal proceedings of Morgan Ryan and urged Flannery to go easy as trial judge in the trial, in order to improperly secure the acquittal of Morgan Ryan. Lionel

Murphy, then a Justice of the High Court, had been tried on similar charges regarding Briese and Flannery, and had been convicted on the Briese charge. Some time later he was successful in an appeal on legal grounds, and was now expecting a second trial on the Briese charge.

The Morgan Ryan affair was a case of politics and law mixing badly together into an unholy mess.

Morgan Ryan was a prominent solicitor who had political connections with Lionel Murphy. He was charged with conspiring to import Koreans illegally but eventually the charges were not proceeded with. He was also a friend of Murray Farquhar, the Chief Stipendiary Magistrate prior to Clarrie Briese.

Clarrie Briese is entitled to great credit for securing the independence of magistrates and for the renaming of Courts of Petty Sessions to Local Courts. Justice Lionel Murphy was a close friend of Neville Wran, the Premier of New South Wales, and Murphy appears to have supported Clarrie Briese's excellent submissions to the New South Wales government, and assisted in securing these very important reforms.

Much later it emerged that the New South Wales Police had been quite illegally tapping telephones and had picked up conversations of Lionel Murphy which were supposed to be not to Murphy's credit. Clarrie Briese learned the contents of these tapes, some of which had been published in the *Age* newspaper (so they became known as the *Age* Tapes) and took a very serious view of them. I think these may have affected his conception of conversations he had with Murray Farquhar and Lionel Murphy.

Murphy, as a one-time Labor icon, having been a Labor Federal Attorney-General in the Whitlam government, was politically attacked and Briese was counter-attacked by Murphy's supporters. Judge Paul Flannery had had some conversations with Lionel Murphy that he felt supported Clarrie Briese, and the result was a number of Senate inquiries which concerned allegations that Lionel Murphy had improperly tried to influence Clarrie Briese to lean on the magistrate who heard the committal proceedings, and had tried to exert improper influence on Judge Flannery, the trial judge, to secure Morgan Ryan's acquittal.

There emerged, as I have said, an unholy mixture of politics and law. Then it was alleged that Judge John Foord had tried to lean on Clarrie Briese similarly to Lionel Murphy's alleged efforts. Foord was alleged to have said that he was doing this on behalf of Neville Wran, the Premier of New South Wales. Then Judge Paul Flannery accused Judge Foord of improperly trying to influence him.

I should make it clear at this stage that judges are human and no doubt often talk to each other about pending cases. However, it would be an attempt to pervert the course of justice – a criminal offence – if one judge tried to persuade another judge to decide a pending case other than on the evidence and according to law.

John Pritchard QC, whom I knew very well, had appeared for John Foord until then, and in particular had appeared for him at the committal proceedings. He was now asked to step down for me to take over and he did so graciously. Later, when Foord was acquitted, John was the first person to ring and congratulate me. He was a fine gentleman.

My junior was Des Andersen (later a QC), a wily criminal-law barrister with whom I had worked very happily before. With him I spent many hours in conference with our client and our solicitor Steve Masselos. We worked very well as a trio.

Ken Hall had said to me that the cases against Foord were stronger than those against Lionel Murphy, in that the words alleged against Foord were less ambiguous and therefore stronger for the Crown. I replied that Foord would be easier to defend. He was such a nice person that no jury would want to convict him. John was one of those amiable people who would do anything for anyone. It was now claimed that he had done too much for Neville Wran.

The inference in the Crown case was that someone high up, apparently the Premier, had put Foord up to approaching Briese and Flannery in an impermissible manner on behalf of Morgan Ryan. But no such person could be proved to have done this and Foord hardly knew Ryan well enough to act as alleged on his own initiative.

The Judge Foord allegations arose out of the allegations made against Justice Murphy. The Murphy allegations had been the subject of Senate inquiries, committal proceedings and the first

Murphy trial. Murphy's defence had sought to explain the differences between the conversations he had had, as he remembered them, and the alleged conversations on the basis of faulty recollection by the witnesses against him. I read the Murphy trial transcript and the Senate inquiry transcript plus some *Age* Tapes, the Foord committal depositions and numerous other documents. Eventually I decided, with the concurrence of Des and Steve, that in the Murphy case and in Foord's case the difference between the Crown versions of conversations and the defence versions was such that mere faulty recollection was not a sufficient explanation. If Foord was telling the truth, Briese and Flannery were not.

Foord was supposed to have said to Briese, 'Neville [Wran] wants something done for Morgan Ryan.' Foord firmly denied saying this and Neville Wran firmly denied that he had asked Foord to say it. Foord was also supposed to have told Flannery, then a fellow judge and a close friend, 'Lionel Murphy and I have read the evidence of the [Morgan Ryan] committal proceedings and we can't find any evidence of conspiracy.' Foord denied this. These were the fundamental allegations.

To us it seemed clear that there was a battle between Briese and Flannery on the one hand and Murphy and his supporter Neville Wran on the other. Wran denied any involvement in the Morgan Ryan case, and he denied that he had asked Foord to intervene with Briese.

We noted that neither Briese nor Flannery on their own versions protested to Foord at the time of the conversations, and the allegations did not surface for more than a year later in Flannery's case, and two years in Briese's case. It appeared to us that the cases against Foord were incidental to the war against Murphy and the New South Wales government. In simple terms I submitted to the jury that 'Foord was a casualty in someone else's war'.

After many proceedings in which they had given evidence we decided for the first time that Briese and Flannery needed to be approached, in effect, as persons pursuing their causes who were not telling the truth. It was not a pleasant task and we took a long time deciding that it had to be done. Clarrie Briese had left himself open in the many conversations he had had with Murray

Farquhar CSM, the Chief Stipendiary Magistrate whom he succeeded, by appearing to agree with Farquhar that prominent persons should be looked after in court. This was when he hoped that Farquhar would support his application to be the next Chief Stipendiary Magistrate.

Briese had become involved in the politics of the *Age* Tapes. He was making his accusations long after the events occurred, with no contemporary note of the conversations. He had made no protest at the time. He was alleging a rather ridiculous approach by Foord to himself, put, as I submitted to the jury, with all the tact of 'a hippopotamus running through an ornamental garden'.

Paul Flannery had been a school friend, a close adult friend and a fellow judge of John Foord. When the Briese allegations were made, and when Briese was very fiercely attacked by Murphy's friends, he felt obliged to disclose what he considered to be an approach by Murphy to himself concerning Morgan Ryan, when he, Flannery, was to be the judge at Ryan's trial. He had discussed the Ryan case with Foord and he claimed Foord had said that he and Murphy had read the Ryan committal proceedings and concluded that there was no evidence of conspiracy. Foord denied that he had any discussions with Murphy about the Ryan case, that he had ever read the Ryan depositions, or that he had had the alleged conversation with Flannery. There were other alleged conversations, also denied by Foord.

Of course the conversations alleged by Briese and Flannery were very much longer than the portions I have mentioned. The recollections of all parties were no doubt coloured by a highly charged political atmosphere. With the best will in the world, this could hardly be avoided. The case was not made easier by the fact that I liked and respected everyone involved – Foord, Briese and Flannery.

It was strange that Flannery did not ask his then good friend Foord for an explanation of their conversation before he made his allegation to high authority without Foord's knowledge. Further-more, during Foord's committal proceedings before the magistrate, Flannery made a small bet with his judge's associate (similar to a secretary) that Foord would be committed for trial. Paul Flannery was and is regarded as a reasonable, pleasant person. This was a strange and foolish action on his part, of which I knew, from the committal proceedings, and I used it to some effect in cross-examining him.

In many ways this trial was the trial of the century. Andrew Kirkham QC (one-time junior to John Phillips QC for Lindy Chamberlain in Darwin) was the leader for the Crown. His junior was Nick Cowdery. Every day the courtroom in the old Supreme Court Banco Court was packed.

The presiding judge was Justice Maxwell, a very fine, upright and impartial judge, a model as to how to conduct a criminal trial. It was my privilege to have 'Maxie' preside over quite a few trials in which I appeared. He was polite and efficient, with a charming, friendly personality. A hip replacement gave him a lot of pain, often when he was sitting in court, but his iron will prevented it showing to those before him. He always appeared pleasant and cheerful. The Supreme Court lost a lot when he retired some years after the Foord case.

What an experience the trial was for me! In one week I cross-examined the Chief Stipendiary Magistrate, Clarrie Briese; three District Court judges – Judge Flannery, Chief Judge Staunton and Judge Thorley; and the Premier of New South Wales, Neville Wran. My cross-examination was quite successful and I managed to make one of my best addresses to a jury. Kirkham QC was an efficient and fair prosecutor and 'Maxie' gave a typically impartial and impeccable summing up.

The questions that the jury had to decide were, in effect, for each charge:

1. What was said during the conversations?
2. Did what was said have a tendency to pervert the course of justice?
3. Did Foord intend to pervert the course of justice?

The jury, after quite a long deliberation, found John Foord not guilty on each charge, and the courtroom rang with cheers. John was a very popular and kind man, and he was cleared at last. By then it was night-time and Des Andersen and I walked out of the court to media lights everywhere and cheers from numerous spectators. It was quite a night!

John Foord was one of my favourite clients. Unlike Lionel Murphy in his first trial, he left everything to his counsel, and listened very carefully to any advice he was given. Most clients in criminal cases want to forget the trial and the counsel who appeared for them after they have been acquitted. Perhaps they feel that they do better to believe that their innocence was such that they did not really need any counsel for the defence. There are notable exceptions and I still hear from some clients. John was one of these exceptions. He has always welcomed me at any gathering and gone out of his way to show that he has not forgotten his trial.

He was acquitted on 1 October 1985. Since then, the offence of attempting to pervert the course of justice in cases where someone talks to a judicial officer seems to have faded into oblivion, and a good thing too. There are numerous conversations between judges about pending cases, and sometimes between judges and their friends. Only a little twist to such conversations can make them appear sinister and criminal, when they are not.

Lionel Murphy was convicted for allegedly saying to Clarrie Briese, after helping him achieve the great reform of transforming Courts of Petty Sessions to Local Courts with full independence 'and now what about my little mate?' meaning Morgan Ryan. These words were supposed to suggest improper interference in the committal proceedings against Ryan. In my opinion there was no case to go to a jury. The words, after considering all the circumstances, are too ambiguous to prove beyond reasonable doubt that Murphy intended to secure improperly the acquittal of his friend. I know that in expressing this opinion I differ from the five judges in the Court of Criminal Appeal who upheld Murphy's appeal on other grounds. I think there are some good criminal-law experts who would agree with me.

I knew Lionel Murphy as a fellow student at the Sydney University Law School, although he was not in the same year. We exchanged Christmas cards for years, but we had no other social contacts, except sometimes at law functions. We were at opposite extremes politically, although perhaps I was a left-wing Liberal until I gave up politics in the late 1960s. I did not particularly like Lionel, but I did feel he was being persecuted.

During the Foord case hearing Lionel rang me nearly every day at the end of the day to find out how the case was going. I did not mind in the least and was in fact anxious to help him as much as possible. He did express to me his surprise that his political enemies were so anxious to hurt and ruin him. I myself felt that there was a most unpleasant political venom about his case and, of course, that of my client John Foord.

Ian Barker QC appeared for Lionel Murphy in his second trial and he used the transcript of my cross-examination of Clarrie Briese to assist his own cross-examination on the same lines. Murphy was acquitted.

It is worth noting that some time after the Foord trial I shook hands with Clarrie Briese and Paul Flannery (on different occasions). Each said that they bore no grudge for my having done my duty. I appeared quite happily before both of them in their respective courts after the Foord case was long over. They were each fine persons caught up like Foord in a political controversy that should never have been a court case at all.

I have no doubt that the jury's verdict in the Foord case was correct. It had to consider whether it could find the relevant conversations and the relevant intent against John Foord 'beyond reasonable doubt'. At the very least there had to be a reasonable doubt. The verdict does not carry any inference that anyone was lying.

I have a particular memory of reading the Song of Solomon, waiting in chambers for the verdict. I think the jury went out about 4 p.m. and did not return until after 8 p.m. That is quite a long time for a criminal jury, although in recent years jury considerations often extend over 24 hours.

I was fairly confident of the result. Years of experience told me that many of the jury – in fact, it seemed like all of them – were with me. Obviously one or more contemplated a verdict of guilty, but not for very long.

Waiting for a criminal jury is hard indeed on the accused, but it is also hard on counsel, even a Crown prosecutor. One's nerves are on edge until the jury returns. Usually I could pick the verdict by the expressions on a few faces, and it is often the case that looking away from the accused is an indication of a guilty verdict. But one is never sure.

A federal police sergeant told me years ago – in May 1983 to be precise – that the best way to give up smoking is to pick the worst possible time and then do it. So I waited for my worst time – when a jury retired – to stop smoking. When they returned a few hours later I had not smoked and I have never smoked since then.

Some time after the Rogerson and Foord Cases I was requested, more than once, to give a press interview. In those days, back in the mid '80s, barristers were not supposed to publicise themselves, and, in any event, perhaps I was shy. I refused.

This did not stop John Slee doing an article about me for which he consulted my friends and enemies. The article was published one Saturday morning entitled 'Sydney's Deadliest Counsel' on the front page, so that I turned with interest to the article itself, headed 'Phillip Street's Smiling Funnel-Web'. To my complete astonishment it was about me. No one had told me that the article was coming. He stated that I was a deadly cross-examiner and was known as the 'Smiling Funnel-Web', hardly a pleasant nickname. I had never heard of this before nor do I know anyone else who had heard it, but the name stuck. I got used to it. In some ways it was a compliment. (Later, my young solicitors in the Chamberlain case presented me with a great funnel-web embedded in glass as a paperweight. I had it on my desk thereafter and still have it. Many of my juniors liked the nickname, and there was nothing I could do about it.)

What the article said was very mixed. My anonymous enemies had a field day, but everyone seemed to agree that I was a good cross-examiner. That did me no harm.

# 17

# Lindy Chamberlain

After the John Foord trial I said to Jean that I could expect to be regarded as Sydney's leading criminal barrister for a few weeks. Some media genius had created the rhyme 'Chester Porter walks on water' and a clever cartoonist had illustrated the concept. This was an example of the necessity of finding a rhyme to create a fiction. Actually, my fame lasted a little longer than a few weeks, and as a result my practice became even more specialised. I appeared in numerous criminal cases, mostly for serious crime. I had my wins and I had my losses.

However, I still did other types of work, in particular administrative law. I especially remember appearing for the Public Service Board in the Court of Appeal in the case of *Osmond v the PSB* which was presided over by Michael Kirby, the comparatively new president of the Court of Appeal. The point of the case was whether natural justice required the Public Service Board to give reasons for refusing Mr Osmond's appeal against not being appointed chairman of the Local Lands Board. In the past it was not the practice to give reasons in such appeals. I remember submitting to President Kirby that he could not make law, only apply law. The question was: what was the law?

The Court of Appeal by majority found against me with a long, very extensively researched judgment by Michael Kirby, but in the High Court I had this judgment overruled. Some time later I met Michael, who congratulated me on my win in most fulsome terms. Having regard to the work he had put into his judgment, he was very generous in his praise. He was a fine judge and a fine president of the Court of Appeal, and this was typical of him. He has gone on to become a very good High Court judge. I had many an appearance before him, with varying success.

Early in 1986 I obtained bail for Andrew Kalajzich, the proprietor of the Manly Pacific Hotel who had been charged with murdering his wife, Megan. He was lucky to get bail for murder, and in fact he only succeeded because of authorities dug out for me by my industrious junior, Robert Baker. Bob Baker and I were due to appear many times in the future for Andrew Kalajzich.

In April 1986 my junior Bill Caldwell and I were retained to assist the Royal Commission into the conviction of Lindy Chamberlain. This, I felt, was a great compliment and I knew the case would be very interesting. I knew Justice Trevor Morling, the Royal Commissioner, and I was to enjoy working with him. My task was to conduct any necessary investigations and to present all the relevant evidence to the Royal Commission. It was a fascinating, if strenuous, task. Normally counsel is there to advocate some cause or point of view, but counsel assisting an inquiry is there simply to ascertain the truth so far as possible. I had had quite a bit of experience of inquiries and I had assisted the Coroner the previous year in the Dale Payne inquest. I knew what I had to do.

I had the enormous task of sifting through a great amount of evidentiary material to ascertain what was relevant and then present it to the Commission. I had to keep in mind material that seemed irrelevant, lest it be important later. I had to clarify and organise the evidence. I had to make my own investigations, particularly of Aboriginal trackers, and I also had to interview the witnesses from the trial before they gave evidence again.

I had to conduct quite a scientific study to understand the

forensic evidence. In this I had Jean's assistance, she being a scientist.

I had to pursue every crazy rumour and, by and large, interview every improbable witness, lest valuable evidence should emerge. I had to try and be familiar with every bit of evidence given before or during the Commission.

All this involved long hours and hard work, but it was interesting and never boring.

Probably everyone around in 1986 in Australia knew a lot about the Chamberlain case. Azaria Chamberlain, aged nine-and-a-half weeks, disappeared from the Chamberlain's tent at Ayers Rock shortly before 8 p.m. on 17 August 1980. Mrs Chamberlain said that she went to the tent and saw a dingo leave it, and that a dingo had taken her baby. The search for the baby or her body was unsuccessful. A week later a tourist, Mr Goodwin, found the jumpsuit and other clothing belonging to the baby not far from a dingo den and some kilometres from the tent. The clothing was damaged but not so much as might have been expected had a dingo consumed the baby. There was a lot of blood on the jumpsuit. The Chamberlains had left Ayers Rock on 19 August, five days before 24 August when the clothes were found.

On 20 February 1981 the Coroner, Mr Barritt, after a widely publicised inquest, found that a dingo had in fact taken the baby, but that there had been some human intervention in the placing of the clothing where it was found. He criticised the Northern Territory Police – I thought unfairly – and perhaps this helped to activate more inquiries resulting in a further inquest which on 2 February 1982 decided that Mrs Chamberlain should be tried for murder and her husband Michael should be charged with assisting her conceal that murder.

The second inquest was open to very serious criticism. The finding of the first inquest had been set aside by a closed – that is, a secret – session of the Supreme Court after a great deal of further evidence had been discovered by the police and their forensic experts. Thus the new evidence was not available to the Chamberlains. An effort was made to get Sally Lowe, the last witness to see the baby, to change her evidence. She had said, and always maintained, that she heard the baby cry after Mrs Chamberlain returned from the tent after checking on Azaria, when on the Crown case the baby had been murdered.

The Chamberlains were called to give evidence in ignorance of the new Crown evidence against them. Under the glare of publicity they could hardly claim privilege against self-incrimination and refuse to give evidence, which was their right. Common fairness demanded that they should not give evidence until the Crown revealed all its case against them. Thus they were cross-examined in a most irregular and unfair procedure as this common fairness was not afforded to them.

Furthermore, Mrs Chamberlain was asked whether she was prepared to submit to a test of her hand supposedly against blood fingerprints on the jumpsuit which Professor Cameron, an English pathologist, claimed he could see. At the later Royal Commission I asked again and again for particulars of the proposed test. It turned out that there was no such test, and in fact the alleged fingerprints were in the main not blood but desert sand. Professor Cameron's evidence that the jumpsuit found showed that the baby had been murdered was a big reason for reopening the case.

Mrs Chamberlain, on good legal advice, refused to take the mystery test, and this was widely interpreted as evidence of her guilt. It was not a good thing to happen before her trial.

After a trial in Darwin of 35 days both Michael and Lindy Chamberlain were convicted by a jury, but only Lindy was imprisoned – for life.

No motive was alleged for the murder. Medical evidence stated that Mrs Chamberlain was not suffering from postnatal depression. There was some evidence of marks in the sand to support the story of the dingo, but there was forensic evidence of blood in many parts of the Chamberlain's car, but particularly a spray under the dashboard consistent with the baby's throat having been cut while she was held near that position. There was Professor Cameron's evidence that the jumpsuit bloodstains were very strongly suggestive of the baby's throat having been cut. In fact, Professor Cameron, as previously stated, purported to see a woman's finger imprints in blood on the jumpsuit. Hairs found in the tent were said to be cat hairs, not dog or dingo hairs. Some of the damage to the jumpsuit was, on expert evidence of the highest calibre, said to be cuts made by a knife or scissors, not by a dingo's teeth. A test for dingo saliva on the jumpsuit proved negative, and Mrs Chamberlain was not believed when she said that the baby was wearing a matinee jacket over the jumpsuit which would have absorbed the dingo's saliva. No matinee jacket had been found. The considerable amount of blood detected in the car was said by the experts to be foetal blood; that is, a young baby's blood.

There was a strong defence case, in particular the evidence of the witness Sally Lowe who heard the baby cry just after Mrs Chamberlain returned from the tent, when, on the Crown case, the baby was dead. Mrs Chamberlain then went to the tent because of the cry and said she saw the dingo.

Lindy Chamberlain's defence team, John Phillips QC (later Chief Justice of Victoria) and Andrew Kirkham, did an impressive job demolishing the expert evidence as to blood. Subsequent appeal courts held that they had established that the experts' finding that the blood in the car was foetal blood was unreliable. They not only proved a lack of motive but established that the witnesses who saw Mrs Chamberlain at Ayers Rock were convinced that she was a loving mother of the baby. They stressed that the marks on the sand were suggestive of a dingo resting the burden of a baby after taking it from the tent and they stressed the evidence of nearby campers who heard a dingo.

The trial was conducted on the basis of murder or dingo, which seemed to cast an onus of proving the latter proposition on the defence. Although it was emphasised to the jury in the trial that the onus was the other way I have some doubts whether the emphatic warnings from the trial judge had their full effect.

The Chamberlains were regarded by many as unusual. At the time of Azaria's disappearance Michael Chamberlain was a pastor of the Seventh Day Adventist Church. He was probably anxious to prove his faith in life hereafter for his lost daughter, and this gave an impression of being callous. His mania for photography had him taking photos of the tent and sending them the next day to an Adelaide newspaper.

Lindy, I am sure, believed she would meet Azaria again in another life. This, combined with a desire to warn others about the dangers of dingoes, made her appear much too unmoved and detached when she gave numerous media interviews. When someone tells a story many times in an emotional context, inconsistencies are inevitable. Such was the case with Lindy and so there was the material available on which to found allegations that she was lying. At the times she spoke she probably had no idea that she was in danger.

I do not intend to give anything like a complete account of the evidence, but I have set out some of the salient features. What happened to reopen the case was firstly a widespread agitation on Lindy's behalf, backed up by a lot of forensic-opinion evidence and secondly, when at the same time doubts were arising in the minds of those who mattered, by sheer chance the missing matinee jacket was discovered. An English tourist had fallen off Ayers Rock and his body was later found missing a limb or two, taken probably by dingoes. This was not far from where Azaria's clothes had been found years before, and a search for the missing limbs revealed the matinee jacket. This discovery apparently prompted the decision to hold a Royal Commission and to free Lindy Chamberlain immediately, not to be returned to custody in any event.

It is worth noting that before the baby's clothes (minus the matinee jacket) were found on 24 August 1980, Mrs Chamberlain had described in detail how the baby was dressed and her detailed, in fact almost minute, description of the matinee jacket corresponded exactly with the article found. Botanical examination showed that it had been there since about 1980.

I was due to go to hospital early in 1986 to have the metal splint removed from my recovered hip. Before going in and while there I was reading the transcript of the fairly lengthy trial in Darwin. I was struck by the fact that no blood was seen on Lindy's clothing, nor was any blood smelt in the car when she was driven to a motel that night by a nurse. According to the evidence at the trial there was a lot of blood, fresh blood, in the car at that time. Can one smell blood? I came out of the anaesthetic asking that question. The answer seems to be that some people can and some people cannot. The nurse later claimed that she could smell blood, but on this particular occasion there was no such smell.

We had a lot of work to do. John Davis, my instructing solicitor, was assisted by Mark Buchanan and Fiona Cosgrove, two younger solicitors. Between them they set up a very efficient organisation of documents so that we were able to find what we wanted quickly as the paper mounted up into formidable volumes. Many people wrote to us with lots of information, much of it useful. For example, we had a large file of reports on dog, dingo and wolf attacks on humans. Wild dogs and domestic dogs have many times wounded and killed humans. So, I found, have the yellow-footed wolves of India, the species that formed the Seeonee Pack and reared Mowgli in Kipling's *The Jungle Books*. They killed many more humans than tigers according to the Bengal Natural History Society's papers (supplied by one 'Birdie' Swift, a dedicated Chamberlain supporter who had spent some years in India). But attacks by dingoes on humans were very rare. There were some terrifying accounts, well over 100 years ago, but in the twentieth century very few indeed.

The strongly held belief that dingoes do not attack humans made many people believe in the murder theory for Azaria's disappearance. During the inquiry it did emerge that unwise feeding of dingoes by tourists had made those at Ayers Rock lose their fear of humans. Something of this had emerged at the trial but much more came out at the inquiry, including the story of 'Ding' who had attacked a child and been shot by park rangers not long before the Azaria disappearance.

Since the Chamberlain Royal Commission dingoes have attacked humans at Fraser Island and killed a child, because, having been fed by tourists they had lost their fear of humans. The same thing has happened to grizzly bears in North America and polar bears in Alaska.

Early in the inquiry the Victorian Forensic Science Laboratory was appointed to assist us and we received the invaluable assistance of Tony Raymond, a biologist skilled particularly in blood tests. There was quite a dispute between the parties as to access to the numerous blood fragments thought still to be left in the car.

Obviously Tony Raymond had to have first access, and he was to preserve any residue for access by the Crown and the defence. As it turned out, he was closely observed in his examination of the car by scientific experts representing both the Crown and the defence. He went over the car with Ortho-tolidine (O-tol) which is a presumptive test for blood reacting to minute particles. To everyone's surprise he found no blood.

At the trial a car had been produced by the defence with an under-dash spray similar to the supposed arterial blood spray in the Chamberlain's car. It did not go much further than that. Since then, Les Smith, a capable, practical scientist working for the Sanitarium factory at Cooranbong, had done work suggesting that the spray was not blood at all but sound deadener. Les Smith and others had also done some work on the alleged cuts on the jumpsuit, proving that a domestic dog's carnassial teeth could cut cloth in a manner similar to a knife or scissors.

I asked Tony Raymond to investigate the spray under the dash first, and soon I made my first trip to Melbourne with Jean (at my expense) accompanying me. As she is a science teacher she was familiar with most of the blood tests which she was able to explain to me. In fact, I had a lot of science lessons from her during the inquiry.

When we got to Melbourne we were invited to look through a microscope at the under-dash spray in the Chamberlain's car and we could clearly see specks of duco on it. The paint must have been applied to the spray during manufacture. The spray could hardly be blood.

As we studied the blood aspect we found that O-tol reacts to copper oxide in a way very similar to its standard reaction to blood. The Chamberlains came from Mount Isa, a copper-mining town. Was the 'blood' found before the trial, in truth, traces of copper oxide? Bill Caldwell, a brilliant man, was detailed by me to deal especially with the blood side of the case. His contribution towards the inquiry, particularly on this aspect but also on others, was invaluable. Certainly the impression given at the trial of a car almost awash with blood had been quite wrong. A great deal, if not all, of what was thought to be blood was something else. The spray under the dash was in fact only sound deadener. Professor Cameron's 'bloody fingerprints' were, at least in large part, red desert sand.

There has been much argument as to how these mistakes were made. Certainly one of the lessons of the case is that forensic laboratories should cover a wide area of skills and have good equipment. Before the inquiry the sound deadener had apparently never been studied under a microscope or been chemically analysed. The Northern Territory's facilities were in some respects quite primitive, as were those in New South Wales where much of the forensic work had been done. A lot of the forensic evidence involved previously unexplored areas.

It is so easy for an expert to be wrong. The hairs in the tent turned out to be dog hairs, not cat hairs, and the Chamberlains did not have a dog. They were thus quite significant pointers to a dingo having been in the tent. It is not possible to distinguish domestic dog hairs from dingo hairs.

Some of this new forensic evidence was discovered before the inquiry, and had contributed towards the decision to reopen the case. A lot more was discovered in the Victorian Forensic Science Laboratory. Tony Raymond and David Gidley were sources of impartial and accurate advice to me and my team in a turmoil of controversy.

There was another source of expert evidence of a different kind which was probably first exposed by Detective Inspector Graeme Charlwood who was the police officer in charge of the case at the trial. He subsequently investigated wild and unfounded claims that the dingo 'Ding' had not been destroyed, was a pet of the people at the Rock, had killed Azaria, and there had then been a con-spiratorial cover-up involving numerous respectable people. His report on the 'Ding' story showed that the male Aboriginal tracker, who was half blind and therefore had been discarded by everyone, was in fact only the spokesman for the women who did the tracking, the main tracker being his wife, Barbara Tjikadu. As a result I arranged with the Aboriginal Legal Service to interview the female witnesses at Ayers Rock.

It was most important that in my interview I should not make any suggestions or 'lead' in any way. I had the interview tape-recorded and interviewed Barbara Tjikadu through an interpreter fluent in her native language. I also interviewed another lady.

Ms Tjikadu was a highly intelligent woman who later gave impressive evidence in Darwin and showed ability as a witness under cross-examination. I doubt whether my precautions against 'leading' her were necessary. She knew her own mind. (Later she became a member of the Aboriginal council administering Ayers Rock, by then renamed Uluru. When I visited Uluru years later I heeded her request and did not attempt to climb it.)

Ms Tjikadu had tracked the day after Azaria's disappearace and her evidence confirmed that a dingo had taken the baby. On the night of Azaria's disappearance a fine Aboriginal tracker, Nui Minyintiri, had reached the same conclusion by torchlight. Derek Roff, the Chief Ranger of Ayers Rock, who I ascertained had learned tracking in Kenya as well as in Australia, saw the tracks himself the next day and supported the findings. His evidence at the trial became much more effective at the inquiry, supported as it was by the evidence of the Aboriginal trackers.

The desert sand they were inspecting would have been excellent for track imprints. To my mind it was difficult to cast aside their evidence.

I have heard the suggestion made that the Aborigines had a motive to lie, namely to protect a guilty camp dog of theirs which may have taken the baby. Mrs Chamberlain emphatically rejected any suggestion that she saw a camp dog, not a dingo. Of course, if a camp dog did take the baby, and all the evidence is against that idea, then the Chamberlains were just as innocent as if a dingo took her. However, there was no evidence implicating any camp dog.

Once it appeared that the car was not awash with blood and there was no under-dash blood spray, there was much less reason to question the tracking evidence.

Much time was spent during the Royal Commission on the question of whether the jumpsuit when found had been cut by human hands. It was an intriguing question, involving a lot of conflicting evidence. It was perhaps suggestive of guilt of Lindy

Chamberlain if the suit had been cut because this might well have occurred at the time of the alleged throat cutting or stabbing by her. On the other hand the cuts, if cuts they were, could have been made long after the Chamberlains left Ayers Rock and either before, or even after, the clothes were found.

As it was, the conflicting evidence of cuts or dingo damage made it hard to reach any conclusion.

The Crown case was that baby Azaria's throat had been cut by Lindy Chamberlain, at a time when Aidan, her son, was either with her or nearby. There were time difficulties about the Crown theory, apart altogether from the evidence of Sally Lowe. However, I was impressed by the lack of blood on Lindy Chamberlain's clothing on the night of the baby's disappearance.

I think most criminal-law practitioners would agree with me that murder by knife without blood on the murderer's clothes is almost, if not completely, impossible. Surgeons at the inquiry expressed the same opinion on the particular facts of the case. Had Lindy Chamberlain cut her baby's throat, substantial blood on her clothing (she might have washed her hands) was just about inevitable. No witness saw such blood.

Of course she could have changed, and at one stage did change her clothes, but at the time of the alarm she was seen by many people and had not changed her clothes since her visit to the tent.

There were many stories about the Chamberlains, few of which were permitted to intrude on the trial, but they did influence public opinion.

Azaria does not mean sacrifice in the desert, as was reported. It is the Hebrew name for Abednego (the Chaldeean name) of Shadrach, Meshach and Abednego who survived Nebuchadnezzar's fiery furnace (Daniel: Chapter 3, and there is of course the popular spiritual song). Azaria means: He whom God has loved. The confusion of the name Azaria with Azaziel, the devil to whom was committed the scapegoat in the desert, led to this dreadful story about Lindy Chamberlain's baby.

It is also true that the Chamberlains had a miniature coffin, which was used by Michael as a prop in anti-smoking lectures. It is also true that Azaria had a black dress, but when it was produced with its pink ribbons it was pretty, not sinister. There were many stories of Lindy Chamberlain assaulting the other two children and putting them in hospital. These stories were patiently investigated and I found them to have no basis in fact. In one case the story arose out of a completely unrelated person named Chamberlain, an adult, attending a hospital, and no more than that.

One strange feature was the correspondence I received to the effect that the last photo of Azaria taken that day at Ayers Rock was not of a baby of nine-and-a-half weeks, but of a much older child. Admittedly, to myself and others, Azaria, held in a standing position, did seem older and we referred the matter to a leading paediatrician who assured us that the photo was consistent with the stated age.

Many parents have expressed the opinion that it was strange to take a nine-and-a-half-week-old baby to Ayers Rock. I myself am the father of three daughters. I should never have thought of taking our first baby on a long trip. I was terrified that the little mite was so small and weak. But I suppose I was much more confident as to our ability to look after a small baby by the time we'd had three children and we were experienced parents.

Lindy Chamberlain was a strong character, otherwise she would not have survived her ordeal as well as she did. I think at times she may have been indifferent to public opinion, but this was not surprising. Public opinion must have seemed cruel to her, although numerous members of the public rallied to support her and to demand the inquiry that cleared her. I found her an amazing woman who could come through such an ordeal supported by an enviable inner strength.

Was she innocent? In my opinion, of all the possible explanations to explain Azaria's disappearance, the dingo is by far the most convincing, supported as it is by strong tracker evidence apart from the mother's evidence. The least convincing explanation is murder by the mother, which on the facts revealed by the full inquiry now seems ridiculous.

The mystery is the clothing. Animal conduct continues to surprise naturalists and I am an amateur naturalist. Yet I consider that there is quite a strong argument that a dingo did not tear the clothes (or cut them) as they were found, and that had the clothes been left there by the dingo the damage to them would have been more extensive. The clothes were not far from a dingo den where there was a milking dingo bitch, which supports the argument that a dingo left them there. The Chamberlains could hardly have done so. They had few unobserved moments after the baby disappeared; they did not know the dingo den was there, nor did any white person, including the Chief Ranger of the park and his deputy. They were found nearly a week after the Chamberlains left Ayers Rock for Mount Isa and were dry when found. That morning it had been raining at the Rock, at least at the rain gauge some short distance away.

The clothes when found were quite close together, more consistent with having been placed there by human hands on the morning when they were found than animal scattering. There were numerous predators around to scatter bloodstained clothing within a week. Perhaps the long-lost matinee jacket (bloodstained like the jumpsuit) was removed by a hawk because it was quite a distance away.

If there were human cuts on the clothes, and this is a highly arguable if, then they had five days to occur after the Chamberlains had left Ayers Rock. The clothes were in police and expert hands for over a year before the trial. In fact, they were damaged by moths during that latter period

If the clothes were cut by human hands by no means does it follow that this was done by the Chamberlains, either to simulate dingo damage or in the course of wounding the baby. As to the latter, the jumpsuit shows a great deal of blood which should have stained Mrs Chamberlain's clothing extensively, according to the Crown case.

This was a case in which the experts tended to be advocates. Some were giving dogmatic opinions on matters that were far from certain, so that there were opposing dogmatic opinions from highly qualified experts. The experts came from all over the world.

I may remark that a scientist writing for a scientific journal, submitting his work to the judgment of his peers, exercises very great care. I doubt whether such care was always exercised in the case of Lindy Chamberlain.

She ultimately survived because the Seventh Day Adventist Church gave her enormous support. Her counsel at the trial, competing against State experts when most of the samples (for example, the biological slides) had been destroyed, achieved a great deal. They only missed the tracker evidence because of a rather loud-mouthed alleged tracker whose evidence was useless, but who hid the evidence of the other trackers.

By and large the Royal Commission revealed the dangers of expert evidence, and more importantly suggested reforms, many of which have been adopted. In particular, Justice Morling's report triggered the formation of NIFS, the National Institute of Forensic Science, and it has helped to raise standards throughout Australia. The Splatt case in South Australia, where Splatt was convicted on entirely forensic evidence, prompted drastic reforms there, and NIFS has endeavoured to lay down standards throughout Australia.

The important matter to be remembered is that few accused persons have the able counsel and support that the Chamberlains had. It is quite unusual for forensic evidence even to be challenged, let alone successfully challenged. The Guildford Four, the Birmingham Six and other IRA cases in England have illuminated the dangers of wrong expert opinions. Mrs Chamberlain's case is often cited as the awful example of how wrong expert conclusions can send an innocent person to gaol. Certainly there are many lessons to be learned from the Morling Report.

Yet of all the lessons from the Chamberlain case I think the most important one is the danger of convicting a person of prior good character of a serious crime when no motive is proved or even suggested for the crime.

It is clearly stated in criminal law that the Crown does not have to prove a motive. Sometimes crimes have been committed without a motive ever having been revealed. But convictions in such cases are, in my opinion, always dangerous. Later I shall deal with the case of McLeod–Lindsay where the same point emerges.

Murders by mothers within 12 months of their baby's birth are, in many legal systems, treated as the special crime of infanticide. These cases are very sad. The mother has suffered postnatal depression. I know of no case where the mother really persisted in a denial of guilt and in most cases a merciful judge gives a sick woman, by then overcome with remorse, a bond. Lindy Chamberlain was not suffering from postnatal depression and there was a great deal of evidence that she was a normal, loving mother. I tried to call every person who had seen her on the crucial day and all who gave evidence, and all whose statements were tendered in their absence, said she was a normal, loving mother. She had no history of mental illness. I inquired about that, even of the Superintendent of Berrima Gaol whom John Davis and I interviewed. Lindy Chamberlain revealed no mental abnormality when in gaol or anywhere else.

Being mentally normal, apparently a loving mother, can one just simply say the law does not require proof of a motive? Common sense requires extra care if it is sought to convict someone of murder if there appears to be absolutely no motive.

Justice Brennan in the High Court and others have given weight to inconsistencies in Lindy Chamberlain's evidence. As I have said before, there were quite a few inconsistencies. Mrs Chamberlain did not think herself in danger, and gave many, many recorded interviews to both the police and the media. Anyone who tries to tell the same story many times will finish up with self-contradictions. If the story comes out exactly the same way each time most people will say that it is a lie learned off by heart. Consistency is not always a reliable indication of truth. Still, there are contradictions and there are contradictions, and those of Mrs Chamberlain were said to be significant.

I do not think she was a good witness; that is, a skilled and careful witness, but a good witness is often a liar, and a poor witness is often telling the truth.

As for significant contradictions and variations in a story, I had a very interesting experience years ago. My client had been accused of being the suspect in the still unsolved Wanda Beach girls murder of many years ago. In appearance he was quite a match for the described suspect. He gave a long record of interview which, if he had ever been tried for the offences, might well have sunk him before a judge and jury. It was crammed full of unconvincing and contradictory answers. It was a prosecutor's dream, a clear case of apparently guilty lying. There was only one catch. The true suspect's blood group was known and my client was proved to be innocent.

What I have written so far is what is now in my mind after hearing and reading all the evidence and after still thinking about the case for years afterwards. It was not always so. I have looked up my contemporary notes and I repeat those of 12 May 1986 when I was still inquiring and before the evidence started:

It is very hard to see where the truth lies in this case. Nothing really makes sense.

Everything is illogical. What will ultimately eventuate is certainly not clear now.

Nothing seems to stay firm under careful examination.

Two things clearly emerged later: the Aboriginal trackers' evidence and the fact that there was never a great amount of unexplained blood in the car. This latter point, had it been known before the High Court hearing, in my opinion certainly would have swayed the majority judgment of Chief Justice Gibbs and Justice Mason in favour of the Chamberlains, and I think Justice Brennan would also have reached a different conclusion.

One thing which I and my team achieved was an efficient inquiry. We received great co-operation from the Northern Territory government, and the Royal Commission's secretary, John Flynn, was a very able man. As a result, evidence flowed freely and this inquiry never dragged as many have done in the past. The inquiry stuck to the issues and, in fact, I took it upon myself not to call far-fetched and fringe witnesses.

Early in the hearing I rejected the 'Ding' story. It was a media beat-up and the subject of a book. Ding, the pet dingo of the people at Ayers Rock, had allegedly not been shot after attacking a child not long before Azaria's disappearance (as had been believed) and was supposed to have killed Azaria; the rangers and others supposedly joined in a conspiracy to pervert the course of justice and ensure that the innocent mother would go to gaol.

I had read Inspector Charlwood's report that investigated the claims and I carefully considered all the supposed evidence in support of the theory. I designated the 'Ding' story to be rubbish at the beginning of the hearing. For this I was roundly abused by telephone for some hours by some dedicated Chamberlain supporters.

It was to Lindy Chamberlain's credit that she would have no part of this attack on the Ayers Rock residents. It was to the credit of the rangers, particularly Derek Roff, the Chief Ranger, that they gave evidence supporting the Chamberlains despite having been so defamed by the 'Ding'-story book. Ultimately there was an action for libel and this was settled for a substantial payment. In fact, Ding *was* shot for attacking a child some time before Azaria disappeared.

Keeping up with the flow of witnesses in the inquiry was a big job, particularly the non-forensic witnesses, the people around Ayers Rock at the time, including Constable Morris, the policeman on the scene whose evidence was very useful and, in my opinion, remarkably detached and impartial. From each witness I or Bill Caldwell ascertained what relevant evidence he or she had to give and ensured that the evidence was given in chief. We led every witness in chief except the Chamberlains.

I did not interview the Chamberlains because they had their own legal team, and any conference with me might have been misconstrued. I interviewed nearly all the lay witnesses myself. Bill Caldwell saw a few, and he also did a great job with some forensic witnesses. He was concentrating in the main on the blood evidence but unfortunately when those witnesses were called Bill had to appear in the Spycatcher case. However he read the transcript and became an expert on the blood evidence. His ideas and his summaries were a tribute to his scientific skill.

Of course, scientific method and the legal appraisal of evidence are closely linked intellectual exercises.

The forensic or expert evidence was a very big part of the inquiry. Unfortunately reputations were in danger, so witnesses were reluctant to make concessions, still less alter previously expressed opinions. Experts were not infrequently extreme advocates for either the Crown or the defence. Having said that, some experts were most impressive.

On the other hand, I do remember a controversy as to how wide a dingo's jaws could go in order to lift an object as wide as the baby's skull. Experts with maths and diagrams clearly and conclusively proved quite a small limit. Then a zoo dingo was videotaped lifting a frozen chicken with a gape much wider than the experts' limit. In another instance, an expert laid down a proposition of dingo behaviour and I received a layman's letter giving evidence of his own observations to prove the expert was wrong. A great deal of what the experts said was widely publicised and as a result people wrote to me if they disagreed.

Once the blood in the car more or less disappeared from significance, attention concentrated on the clothes found near Maggie's Springs on 24 August 1980, five days after the Chamberlains left Ayers Rock and a week after Azaria disappeared. Could the dingo have removed the clothes doing so little damage to the jumpsuit? An experiment at Adelaide Zoo before the trial indicated a dingo's ability to remove a jumpsuit from the body of a young goat, doing more damage than to the relevant jumpsuit but less than expected. Derek Roff, whose knowledge of dingoes was extensive and who was a man with a well-balanced mind, thought a dingo could have removed the jumpsuit with as little damage as revealed by the evidence. One tracker thought the dingo prints not far from the jumpsuit (there was a den nearby) matched those of the dingo at the camp site. So it could be that there was no human intervention, that the baby was taken by a dingo, and the clothes were left by it not far from the den.

However, to many people it seemed unlikely that a dingo would have removed the clothes so neatly and left them rather unscattered. To me it seems unlikely that the clothes stayed as they were found for a week after the baby disappeared. There were numerous predators to scatter bloodstained clothing, as the matinee jacket itself was removed. There were numerous tourists around Ayers Rock who might have found the clothes and then put them back lest they had to become witnesses.

I wish the numerous questions arising in the Chamberlain case could all be answered. I did my best. One clear fact emerged to my mind: there was simply no real evidence that Lindy killed her baby. Another fact that emerged was that it was likely that a dingo took the baby.

Even as I write this I seem to be falling into the old trap. Either a dingo took the baby or Lindy murdered her. The proposition completely lacks logic, even though the trial and the public controversy tended to be conducted along these lines. A better approach seems to be that once the forensic evidence fell apart there was simply nothing to incriminate the Chamberlains. One might then say why not believe the trackers, why not believe Lindy herself, why not believe Sally Lowe and numerous other witnesses nearby? Why not indeed!

As for the clothing, it is an exercise for the mind to try and sort out conflicting forensic evidence, but if someone did cut the clothes there is, in my opinion, no reason to suspect the Chamberlains of having done so.

I did hear a rumour years later that the clothes were cut by a policeman in order to compare a real cut with the tears in the jumpsuit. When the later controversy arose, had this in fact happened, it is unlikely that the policeman who did it would proclaim the fact.

Of course, that was a wild rumour but it does serve to illustrate that there could be unknown pieces in the Azaria puzzle. I stress however that there is no reason to believe, or even suspect, that any unknown fact would incriminate the Chamberlains. Indeed they have been put under a very searching microscope, not once, but at least four times, at the two inquests, the trial and the inquiry. And in this regard I did not leave any stone unturned.

Quite recently Mrs Chamberlain held a function at her home to unveil a memorial to Azaria (*New Idea*, 16 March 2002). To this function came most of the witnesses I called back in 1986, the people there on the night of 17 August 1980. They saw Lindy Chamberlain then, and not one would be in any way persuaded that she killed Azaria. In fact, these people, who were in the best position of all to judge, became her loyal supporters and I note that they still are.

All of them were good, sincere people. Some had been put under pressure by police or lawyers to incriminate Mrs Chamberlain, or at least to not support her. But they gave her unswerving support. They were and still are convinced of her innocence, convinced that she suffered a frightful injustice. There are people in Australia who know little of the facts, but despite the findings of the Royal Commission, still condemn Lindy Chamberlain. It is hard to understand them, especially in view of the unanimous attitude of those who saw her the night of Azaria's disappearance.

She has received monetary compensation, as has Michael Chamberlain. She has married again and is apparently happy. She is remarkably free of bitterness.

She survived. She was supported by a church and by an able solicitor, Stuart Tipple, who never lost faith in her. She had very able counsel at her trial and at the inquiry (particularly John Winneke QC, a great cross-examiner, now president of the Victorian Court of Appeal). Eventually she was vindicated.

How many people are there who have been wrongly accused, who have had no support, who have been wrongly convicted, and never ultimately vindicated?

The Northern Territory government, to its credit, enthusiastically supported the reforms suggested regarding forensic evidence. There were no scapegoats in the end, just careful reforms of procedures and standards. We did not know then that the advent of DNA testing was not far away, requiring very careful procedures and the highest standards of care and reporting. In the end a lot of good came out of the Chamberlain case.

I look back on some fine people I met, the witnesses at Ayers Rock who saw Lindy with her baby, the rangers, the trackers, and some good police officers who were first on the scene of what they rightly judged to be a tragedy, not a murder.

Finally I conclude with the miracle. Few cases have divided public opinion and dinner tables more than that of Lindy Chamberlain. Yet Justice Trevor Morling so conducted the inquiry, and was so fair and careful in his findings, that by and large the controversy ended, and Mrs Chamberlain was cleared not merely by the Morling Report, but by public opinion also.

# 18

# Kalajzich

In 1986 Andrew Kalajzich was the owner of the Manly Pacific Hotel, a highly successful enterprise on the northern beaches of Sydney. He was a self-made man, the son of a fish-shop proprietor, and he had built the hotel and become a leading citizen of Manly.

On 27 January 1986 Andrew's wife Megan died in bed beside him, shot in the head. Andrew was not injured, although the murderer had fired two bullets into his pillow, missing his head. He said he was woken by the noise, saw his dead wife, and rang the police. Megan's mother, Mrs Carmichael, and Andrew's adult son were sleeping in the house at the time of the murder. The police were very suspicious as soon as they heard Andrew's story. One George Canellis confirmed these suspicions when he told the detectives that he had been paid by Franciscus Vandenberg to shoot Megan Kalajzich but kept the money and decided not to commit the murder. This led the police to Vandenberg who immediately confessed to being the murderer. He said that he was instructed by Warren Elkins, an employee of Andrew Kalajzich.

It seems that a friend of Vandenberg, Kerry Orrock, furnished

Vandenberg with the murder weapon, a sawn-off Sterling .22 repeater. The said weapon was recovered by the police from the Lane Cove River, where Vandenberg said he had thrown it.

During 1986 the Chamberlain Royal Commission adjourned in July and I appeared for Andrew Kalajzich in the committal proceedings against Andrew Kalajzich, Franciscus Vandenberg, Kerry Orrock and Warren Elkins. We were instructed by John Webb, then a Manly solicitor.

In the old-style committal proceedings that prevailed at that time one learned as one went along. Now, all the pertinent facts are received in advance by way of statements in a full Crown brief of evidence. Back then in 1986 it came in dribs and drabs and the first we knew of Andrew Kalajzich's previous love affair with Lidia Iurman was when she gave evidence. Lidia's story of a long, secret love affair with Andrew was corroborated by a bundle of love letters, and the police prosecutor tried to infer it as supplying Kalajzich with a motive to kill Megan.

However, the Lidia Iurman affair came to an end years before Megan died and Kalajzich had gone back to his wife. Unfortunately at the end of the affair there had been an accident in which Andrew's car went over a cliff with his wife and baby son on board. It was suggested that this had been a murder attempt, but if so it was stupid in the extreme. The cliff was so low that no one was injured. Of course, the story would not make good listening for a jury, but I believed (correctly) it could only be used at the trial if Andrew claimed to be a man of good character and thereby made an issue of his life history. Otherwise it was an old story happening far too long ago to throw light on Megan's murder.

Marlene Watson, Andrew's secretary, had denied that there was any love affair between herself and Andrew. Marlene Watson's denial of an affair between herself and Andrew deprived the police of any motive for Andrew to kill Megan, although the chief detective in the case, Inspector Inkster, did not accept Marlene's denial. Although there was no evidence, there was great suspicion that Andrew Kalajzich had engaged Warren Elkins to murder Megan Kalajzich.

In the end the Crown had clear cases against Vandenberg, Elkins and Orrock but no real case against Andrew Kalajzich. Consequently, Greg Glass, the magistrate, discharged him. I shall always remember that day. It actually snowed in Sydney and as I stood outside the Coroner's Court with Bob Baker and John Webb, the victory helped us endure the biting cold.

I returned to the Chamberlain Royal Commission and soon after this Andrew went on a trip to Croatia, his parents' homeland, returning to Australia at the end of the year. He was re-arrested on his return, although there was then very little additional evidence available to the Crown. Soon after, Elkins made a deal with the Crown. He pleaded guilty to a lesser charge of conspiring to murder and, in return for a very lenient sentence, would give deadly evidence against Kalajzich. Vandenberg after pleading guilty himself would give evidence which would not directly incriminate Andrew, but would corroborate Elkins.

A love letter from Marlene to Andrew (then in prison awaiting trial) was intercepted and provided the motive for the murder, although both claimed that they had only fallen in love after Megan's death.

This love letter was incredibly foolish. It was written in extreme terms and finished up with words to the effect of please destroy this letter because it would be fatal if it were found. It was taken to the gaol by a friend of Andrew's, but as I learned from Phillip Player (Andrew's cell-mate) the officers were expecting the letter and seized it before Andrew saw it. John Webb suggested that Andrew should not be shown it – a shrewd idea. Not having received or read it, it was hard for the Crown in cross-examination to incriminate Andrew with the contents of someone else's letter.

The revelation of this letter shocked Andrew's relatives. It did not altogether amaze me because I live at Mona Vale, not far from Manly, and I'd heard the rumours floating around.

The Crown attempted to have Andrew indicted on charges of conspiring to murder Vandenberg but in those committal proceedings I was successful and Andrew was discharged. Ultimately, Andrew appeared before Mr Justice Maxwell and a jury at Darlinghurst in April 1988 charged with murdering his wife Megan.

Kerry Orrock was his co-accused. Elkins and Vandenberg were the most important Crown witnesses.

If Andrew was in fact guilty, and a jury and a later inquiry have said that he was, it is strange that he should have gone about the murder in such a stupid fashion. Whoever fired the shots – and Vandenberg said he did – fired two shots to kill Megan and two that went into Andrew's pillow. Vandenberg had no experience with firearms, but of course the shots were fired only inches from the targets. Andrew claimed the latter two shots were fired in an unsuccessful attempt to kill him; Vandenberg said they were fired after Andrew rolled off the bed. Obviously suspicion fell on Andrew and never shifted. Yet, if he was guilty, he could have spent the evening working at the hotel, thereby giving himself not only an alibi, but the defence that all the circumstances pointed to a stranger intruding on to the premises.

It was a very difficult trial. If I had made a mistake, such as raising good character on the part of Andrew, evidence of his affair with Lidia and the incident of the car over the cliff would have got before the jury. Witnesses other than Kalajzich himself would have hurt him more than they would have helped him, because they contradicted him on vital issues. Eventually only Kalajzich gave evidence. Both he and Orrock were convicted.

It is worth noting that Mrs Carmichael, Megan's mother, maintained that Andrew was innocent, as did his relatives, particularly his son and his brother Tony. Eventually there was an inquiry into his conviction by Justice Slattery who, after a long hearing, held that there were no reasonable doubts about his guilt. At Kalajzich's insistence my records were made available to Michael Finnane QC, counsel assisting the inquiry, and I was called as a witness in 1994. I did not help Andrew's case. I had warned him about seeing Elkins, and he apparently had many meetings with him after the committal proceedings, unknown to his legal advisers. These meetings were deadly evidence against him, especially as telephone conversations to arrange the meetings were secretly taped by Elkins.

I remember well the tapes being played to the jury. It was bad enough Andrew having secret meetings with Elkins, but his voice over the phone was sinister indeed, the voice of a man fearful of being discovered. Kalajzich had a great deal of evidence against him, but I think that these tapes were the worst. I was able to prove that both Elkins and Vandenberg were liars about many things, but their essential stories of how the murder was planned and carried out provided an obvious link between a great deal of circumstantial evidence.

I had, as the evidence in the Slattery inquiry revealed, warned Andrew that he should not have any contact with Elkins, just as I had warned him to beware of close contact with Marlene Watson. The failure to follow my advice did not help him in the long run, but if innocent he would be curious as to what really happened to his wife, and who was behind it.

As for Marlene Watson, although the police, popular rumour and the Crown have always put Andrew Kalajzich's love for her forward as his motive, I have never been persuaded. If he did kill Megan I doubt whether Marlene was the motive. There was nothing in the evidence to indicate such an urgent passion that murder rather than divorce had to be the way to marrying Marlene. The police certainly looked for such evidence and never found it.

George Canellis was the interesting character involved in this case. He was known as 'Black George' Canellis and after being paid to murder Megan he went as far as shadowing her and then decided not to kill her, but kept the money. He was a reputed standover man and criminal thug available if not to kill then at least to injure for money. It may well be that he was much more talk than a real standover man, but even in the witness box he purported to be a very tough customer, and he certainly handled a sawn-off .22 rifle with practised expertise.

When Canellis heard of the murder he feared that he might be implicated, and so he bought immunity for himself by informing on the others. It was amazing to see him in the witness box posing as a tough criminal, to such an extent that he was almost a romantic character, with the jury highly amused by his antics.

Elkins had received a sentence with a non-parole period of only five years and with the remissions then applicable he was out of prison in a much shorter time.

Vandenberg committed suicide in prison soon after the trial. It was inevitable that there should be rumours that he was murdered but I am sure he killed himself. Vandenberg quite enjoyed being cross-examined. At times it was clear to me that he was playing with me. I think he also played with Alan Saunders QC, the Crown prosecutor. Being a confessed murderer made him more important than he had ever been before. He enjoyed his moments on the stage. When he went back to prison there was nothing left to live for.

Why did Vandenberg shoot Megan? It was not for the money which, by and large, he gave away. He said he was scared of whomever was ordering the murder, but I really doubt that. He was a lonely man with few friends, but no prior criminal record. I think he got himself into a crazy adventure, and may well have suffered remorse afterwards, as he claimed.

Kalajzich always maintained his innocence to both his lawyers and the world and he still claims that he was innocent. His supporters have not put forward any feasible alternative architect of Megan's death, nor have their theories been supported by evidence. Yet it is still astonishing that a man of Andrew's intelligence should murder his wife in such a foolish way – in such a way as to make it absolutely certain that he would be immediately suspected – and have no real answer to that suspicion. I spent a great deal of time with him inside and outside prison. I could not help but pity a man for whom life had been going so well until it turned into this nightmare.

I appeared in many murder trials before and after Kalajzich. In some my client was acquitted; in others the verdict was manslaughter only. In no other case in which I appeared can I remember a jury bringing in a verdict of guilty of murder against my client. As I have said before, murder cases fall into two categories: firstly, where the killing is admitted but explained – for example, as self-defence or provocation; and secondly, where the killing is denied. These latter cases are much less common than the former and are usually harder to defend. Sometimes the defence can point to another killer, but usually the defence can only say, 'I don't know who the killer was, but I was not.' That was the position in which Andrew Kalajzich found himself. It is dangerous indeed to say of a person accused of murder, 'Well if you didn't kill her, who did?' but the circumstances of this case made that question inevitable, and the defence never found an answer.

Justice Maxwell gave Kalajzich a fair trial and we only had one ground of appeal, a legal point as to whether a piece of evidence could corroborate an accomplice when the significance of that evidence as supposed corroboration depends on the evidence of the accomplice. It was quite an important point, but when we lost in the Court of Appeal, the High Court refused special leave to appeal. The law on this aspect of corroboration; that is, what is true corroboration, is still uncertain.

Ultimately, under the new sentencing laws, Kalajzich's life sentence was altered so as to impose a minimum term of 25 years, a very severe sentence even for murder. This case seemed to establish a rule that anyone who procures a contract killing will be placed in one of the worst categories of murderers, even more so than the actual assassin.

When the High Court appeal failed, Andrew Kalajzich not unnaturally lost confidence in his then legal advisers and we were all sacked. In his letter to us he informed us that he was angry with me and solicitor John Webb for advising him that he was putting too much faith and power in his accountant John Thomas. We had strongly advised him to secure his own control of his own money, being the proceeds of the sale of the Manly Pacific Hotel – well over 20 million dollars. He ignored our advice and in fact in his final letter rejected it with scorn.

In Pippa Kay's recent book *Doubt & Conviction* Kalajzich says (at page 241): that John Webb and I warned him about John Thomas.

In December 1991 John Thomas went bankrupt. Kalajzich's money (which Thomas held) had disappeared. We tried hard to save his money but, as he said himself, he could not bring himself to doubt John Thomas until it was too late.

Pippa Kay, on page 338 of her book, sums up her doubts as to Kalajzich's guilt – he was too intelligent to plan such a stupid murder, and there was no evidence that he and his wife Megan had fallen out. The latter is a surprising fact, supported by Megan's mother, Mrs Carmichael, believing in Andrew's innocence.

Justice Slattery's report of 30 May 1995 following the section 475 inquiry (section 475 of the Crimes Act provides a machinery for a public inquiry into doubts about a conviction) into Kalajzich's conviction is very thorough and for myself I see no reason to quarrel with any of His Honour's conclusions. Kalajzich now continues to pay a dreadful price for murdering his wife.

# 19

# The Blackburn Royal Commission

I appeared in many cases after the Kalajzich case, quite a few being in defence of fellow barristers, mainly on charges of professional misconduct. My practice was mainly criminal law and usually for people who had never offended before.

I appeared for a young accountant involved in the 'Bottom of the Harbour' tax-evasion schemes. He was a man of charm and ability, and fundamentally a good person, but had got carried away by the mad atmosphere of the time. I did my best for him but he had gone too far as it turned out, and I could not save him from a finding of guilt and a prison term.

I acted in many cases for a Yoga Swami whose Ashram empire broke up in a welter of accusations. He was accused of sexual misconduct and was convicted on some charges and acquitted on others. Ultimately in the High Court his convictions were overruled on legal grounds. I remember visiting the Ashram in a wonderful bushland setting, with golden whistlers – most beautiful birds – singing a pretty melody around the buildings. It was a pity that human frailty should spoil such a pleasant place.

Since the Wood Royal Commission into New South Wales police corruption, which exposed so much corruption and incompetence in the New South Wales Police Service, people forget that Commissioners John Avery and Tony Lauer tried very hard to break down the power of detectives and eliminate corruption. Many of their reforms were successful. It is not fair now to judge them on the basis that corruption remained. The task of cleansing the service was beyond any one or two men. Even after the Wood Royal Commission report and the subsequent purges, corruption on a large scale has been revealed yet again.

The Blackburn case and the circumstances leading to the Blackburn Royal Commission were strange indeed. There were apparently two serial rapists at large in Sydney but there was a theory that there was only one rapist responsible for both series of rapes, each series occurring many years apart. Many years ago a police officer, Thornthwaite, conceived the idea 'Harry the Hat' Blackburn, then a fellow police officer, was the serial rapist sought for the Georges Hall rapes, being 14 attacks in 1969 and 1970 in the Georges Hall/Sutherland area. The police had made up a description and picture of the suspect based on victims' descriptions. Thornthwaite, then a detective-constable first-class, claimed that Blackburn, then a sergeant first-class in the police force, was very similar to the picture.

I pause here to comment that in many, if not most, cases where a suspect picture has been published by the police it bears little, if any, resemblance to the person subsequently convicted of the crime (although in very recent years these pictures have improved). Rather, suspect descriptions and pictures are usually of great assistance to defence counsel when identification is an issue because they bear no resemblance to the accused.

Thornthwaite's identification of Blackburn became an obsession, but no one seems to have taken much notice of him back in 1970. The obsession only grew over the years. When a serial rapist operated in Sutherland and Botany between 1985 and December 1988, he was sure Blackburn was the culprit. It was by no means certain that all the Georges Hall offences were committed by the one man, and the same doubt applied to the Sutherland offences. There was a very substantial doubt, to say the least, that the one man committed all the Georges Hall and all the Sutherland offences.

In September 1988 Thornthwaite, then in charge of the Tactical Intelligence Section (TIS) of the New South Wales Police began a process of targeting Blackburn, by then a retired Superintendent working for the War Crimes Commission. 'Operation Photo' was set up as a very confidential investigation run partly by the TIS and mainly conducted by Detective-Sergeant Minkley and Constable Paull, two detectives from outside the TIS. It is yet another dreadful example of the dangers of police targeting rather than investigating.

There was an O-type blood grouping recorded for Blackburn in hospital of which the investigating police were aware. This was inconsistent with various blood groupings recorded for the Sutherland rapist, so that Blackburn was not that offender. Nevertheless, on minuscule identification evidence, and ignoring contrary identification evidence, Blackburn was arrested. Not only was Blackburn arrested but he was paraded as a rapist in front of the television and other media, a parade that cost the New South Wales government quite a bit in a settled action for damages after the Royal Commission. This parading of Blackburn was quite crazy. Normally the police do not disclose the name of an arrested person. That is done when the defendant comes before the magistrate. He is normally never paraded before the media at the police station but Blackburn was paraded before television cameras before being taken to Central Police Station. Then a police statement was broadcast and telecast as to his arrest in terms that would certainly have been understood as, 'We've arrested the right man.'

What happens in court is protected from defamation proceedings by absolute privilege. What happens when a suspect is paraded and labelled in the media is wide open to an action for damages, and rightly so.

This was just the most spectacular part of a police fiasco. It was the culmination of a procession of quite inexcusable blunders.

The arrest was on Monday 24 July 1989 and Blackburn was held without bail until 26 July.

There seems to have been no attempt to record any interview with Blackburn or even interrogate him. He saw a chart in the room showing the dates of the various offences. When he claimed alibis for some days it did not influence the police other than to drop some charges relating to those days. Yet the crux of their case was that one man had committed all the offences and that man was Blackburn.

The performance of the arresting police was remarkable, in fact quite absurd. Unfortunately Sergeant Minkley was seriously injured in a car accident on the way home after the arrest and Chief-Inspector Thornthwaite had a nervous breakdown, so neither gave evidence at the Royal Commission. In particular it would have been interesting to ascertain how they proposed to proceed with the committal proceedings against Blackburn with, in effect, only one identifying witness against him being the boyfriend of a victim who said her attacker was not Blackburn.

Minkley's accident meant that another police officer had to take over the inquiry. This was Inspector Clive Small. He very soon appreciated that the arrest was a blunder, particularly after he obtained a blood sample from Blackburn who was advised by his lawyers to supply one. This proved his innocence. Small prepared an excellent brief which exposed only too clearly how ridiculous the case was against Blackburn. For this he was hardly thanked. He was rebuked for advising that the charges should be withdrawn and a story was started that he was a 'black knight' who had 'gutted the brief' to save Blackburn who was really guilty.

One cannot expect senior officers to admit that they have been fooled by nonsense. They were supposed to have closely supervised the investigation. Now they looked incompetent themselves.

It would appear that Minkley and Thornthwaite were given their heads, and the matter had been kept secret from the regular detectives (who might have been corrupt in favour of Blackburn; they might have been 'black knights'). So the very obvious stupidities of the Minkley brief passed unobserved by people who should have known better.

Once the Director of Public Prosecutions, Reg Blanch QC, examined the brief he instructed his officers to withdraw the charges in the Magistrate's Court.

I appeared as counsel assisting the Blackburn Royal Commission. This time my junior was Peter Johnson, now a senior counsel, who gave me enormous help and who applied a record of evidence system of mine to such effect that we were able to find evidence very quickly. It was a system based on what I had done in the *Voyager* Royal Commission back in 1967 and was also based on what was taught to me by Keith Stewart, a master at Shore in 1940. I had used it right throughout law school. My team had also used it in the Chamberlain inquiry. It was a simple system of main-paragraph headings and sub-paragraph headings that made finding any particular topic a quick operation, and ensured a complete coverage of the matters summarised in a small space.

Peter Johnson, with my solicitors Ross Klugston and Jane Elliston, and later a second junior, Robyn Burgess, was able to give relevant transcript references within a few minutes, and in fact faster than the computer.

It was an interesting bar table at this Royal Commission. Kevin Murray QC with Clive Steirn (now an SC), appeared for Blackburn. Kevin was then dying of cancer and came to court from hospital, but his contributions to the case were shrewd and at times inspired. Nicholas Cowdery QC appeared for those responsible for charging Blackburn, including Detective Chief Inspector Thornthwaite. Alec Shand QC appeared for the then Commissioner of Police, John Avery, and his senior officers.

The Royal Commissioner was Justice Lee, noted for his quick mind and a very good knowledge of the law. He had years of experience in the criminal law in particular, both as a leading counsel and as a judge. He could sum up to a jury with a simplicity that ensured that its members understood the relevant law and the issues in the case.

I was retained for this case by phone at the end of 1989 when I was stopping over in Hong Kong on my way home from a trip to Israel and Switzerland. At the time there was a suspicion around that Blackburn, now discharged in the magistrate's court on numerous charges of sexual assault, had been freed because of corrupt friends in the police force who were the 'black knights' and who had 'gutted' a good brief against Blackburn according to police rumours at the time. As it turned out, nothing could have been further from the truth.

I used the Director of Public Prosecution's file as my first reference, so I was able to see why the charges were withdrawn. It became obvious that there never was a case against Blackburn and the more I investigated the more obvious this became. Fairly early in the inquiry Justice Lee held that there was no case – that in effect there was no brief to gut. In his report he commended Inspector Small for his excellent report on the case. Thereafter the inquiry was concerned with the reasons for the fiasco.

The hearing of evidence commenced on 13 November 1989 and concluded on 27 April 1990. Addresses were concluded by 11 May 1990. Having regard to the issues involved, despite the most efficient conduct of the inquiry, there was not time to hear and fully cross-examine all relevant witnesses but the essential witnesses were dealt with thoroughly. An extension of time for completing and making the final report was sought until 31 July but only granted to 30 June. I think the powers that be did not like the way the senior officers of the police force were appearing as incompetent and at times foolish, so they wanted to cut everything short. This was a pity because this inquiry and this report could have, to a receptive government, advanced the progress of reforming the police force.

This Royal Commission was the first exposure of a top-heavy police administration but the government took no notice. Some years before, I had appeared for the police with regard to an asthmatic who had died in the police cells at Darlinghurst. Questions arose as to whether the custody police should have taken away the deceased's Ventolin. There was a great fuss and after numerous reports a solemn Police Commissioner's direction was issued to the effect that prisoners in the cells should retain their Ventolin tubes. In the Blackburn Royal Commission we visited the main police custody centre in Sydney with reference to Blackburn's custody. As a matter of interest I asked the custody sergeant about Ventolin for those with asthma. He had never heard of the Commissioner's direction and as a matter of course Ventolin was always taken from prisoners. I wonder how many other directions were similarly buried under piles of paper and lost forever.

The Commissioner had given a direction about enforcing

search warrants, which failed to instruct officers to give a list to the occupier of property taken from the premises, despite the statutory regulation requiring this. In fact whereas the Australian Federal Police always gave such a list, the New South Wales Police hardly ever did. If an occupier complained of money being stolen by the searching police no court would believe him. Few bothered to complain officially, but plenty did to their lawyers. At the Royal Commission, at my instigation the direction was corrected to require the giving of a list.

Interestingly, the police did give Blackburn a list. However, when a listening device was inserted lawfully but secretly into Blackburn's unit, a photo of Blackburn was secretly removed without any authority to do so in order to assist the investigation. This was done by Sergeant Minkley, not the listening-device police. The secret entry into premises to insert listening devices must be authorised by the statute which requires the order of a Supreme Court judge. The police who do it are skilled in the extreme and no one ever knows that they have been. These police were very annoyed with Minkley for taking the photo. He should not have been there at all.

The more the Minkley brief was examined, the more it fell apart.

The investigation was one of the earliest involving DNA samples. At that time DNA could not be identified in New South Wales so Minkley and Paull went to England with samples. It was a farce. The only sample to yield DNA was unrelated to the case.

The case was important as to photographic identification. One of the greatest areas of injustice in the criminal law is wrongful identification. The police and prosecutors want dogmatic witnesses who will never concede any doubt and will remain firm under cross-examination. These are obviously the witnesses who are most likely to be wrong. Many witnesses like to be key witnesses, important witnesses, and the police may well play up to this human weakness. Quite a few witnesses, having been persuaded to identify a suspect from photographs, then become determined advocates for the prosecution.

In the Blackburn case, when witnesses failed to identify Blackburn as the offender from photographs of various men, police actually pointed to him and tried to persuade them that he was the man. More subtly, as Kevin Murray QC put it, when the witness paused on the wrong photo police might say, 'Keep looking' and when he or she paused on the correct photo they might say, 'Congratulations, you've got the right photo; everyone else has picked him.' Minkley actually hypnotised one witness to get him to make an identification of Blackburn's car.

I had hours of cross-examination of the investigating police, and the senior officers who were meant to supervise them. I suppose I was not very popular at the time in some police circles.

During the Blackburn Royal Commission I had a couple of conferences with John Avery, the then Commissioner of Police. He had an impressive appearance and an attractive personality, even at a time when the inquiry was showing up his senior administrators in a very poor light.

Although he was humiliated by the Blackburn-case revelations he told me that he would not penalise Small, as I have no doubt some of the senior officers would have done, for indirectly exposing them. Avery kept his word. He was that sort of man.

As I mentioned previously, Thornthwaite and Minkley did not give evidence, the former on psychiatric evidence as to his health and the latter because of brain damage suffered in the car accident. It was hard on their subordinates who had to bear the cross-examination that the absent witnesses avoided. Yet if the powers that be had really considered Justice Lee's report they might have initiated reforms to prevent such a farce happening again. The problem was not so much the individual police but a police system that obviously permitted the end to justify the means. The other major problem involved the alleged supervision, which was in this case completely ineffective. The police administration had permitted a farcical investigation to go unsupervised, despite the involvement of many senior officers. There was a top-heavy administration in which everyone had a hand and no one took responsibility and in which paper directions were buried and lost.

It should be emphasised that there was no corruption involved in the Blackburn case of the nature revealed in the Wood Royal

Commission. There was much deception of superior officers and the investigation was often inefficient, stupid and improper. However the superior officers were trying to efficiently investigate serious charges against a one-time superintendent and they were anxious to spare no resources to do this properly. Suspecting that other police might protect the suspect, they tried to keep the operation secret. They were inefficient and unlucky in the detectives they chose to conduct the investigation. The supervision of those detectives was farcical in its inadequacy.

Yet most of the superior police officers were decent honourable men doing their best. Some lacked essential experience in detective work, but fundamentally a top-heavy inefficient administration came to grief and the consequences were quite horrific. I cross-examined them at length, as did other counsel. At the same time I was sorry for many of them. Each was rather let down by others, but no one did his job well.

There is no doubt that Chief Inspector Thornthwaite was an honest man. I conferred with him. His obsession about Blackburn brought about a nervous breakdown, which prevented him giving evidence, so he was never cross-examined except perhaps by me in conference.

Obsessions are not uncommon, even in otherwise reasonable people. In this case Thornthwaite was able to make the men under him in the TIS as enthusiastic as he was.

There was a lot of talk about police corruption at the time and there was a solid basis for such talk. When the case against Blackburn collapsed the idea grew like wildfire that he had been saved by police corruption. This turned out to be complete nonsense.

Blackburn himself was a very capable man. He seemed to me to be a rather reserved, almost aloof man, but he bore his troubles with great dignity. As a result of his arrest he lost his job with the War Crimes Commission. During the Royal Commission quite ridiculous efforts were made by senior police to discredit Blackburn by examining old travel expenses, for which he had been reimbursed, but such efforts led nowhere. Eventually he emerged from the Royal Commission a man who had suffered a terrible injustice, but whose reputation was now completely restored.

I do not think that the police-service hierarchy or the government paid much attention to the detailed, accurate and thoughtful Royal Commission report of Justice Lee. There were many ideas therein that would have improved the police administration and the standards of police investigation. However I think the powers that be were first sold on the story that Blackburn was really guilty and 'black knights' gutted the brief. When they found that this was absurd and the administration had blundered they lost interest. I know of no reform that followed the excellent report the government received from Justice Lee.

I conclude with a simple story. While I was in the course of rather severe cross-examination of various senior officers during the Royal Commission I reached Friday and went up for the weekend to my cottage at Blackheath. I had told numerous people at the inquiry that I was going.

At Blackheath on the Saturday night I went with my wife to dinner at a restaurant and we shared a bottle of wine, Jean having less than half. We got in the car late in the evening and drove off. Immediately lights flashed and sirens sounded and I was pulled up within a few hundred metres of the restaurant by a police car that must have been waiting outside the restaurant.

Police cars are not supposed to wait outside licensed premises for the purpose of stopping drivers. If this were permitted they could put particular establishments out of business or obtain bribes to stay away.

When I stopped, the policeman approached me in the driver's seat and told me to blow into an Alcotest. I was somewhat surprised, even shocked, by the sudden pulling up of my vehicle. The policeman was obviously hostile. I was then accused of not blowing but sucking and was told that he was going to arrest me for refusing the test. I told him, as was the truth, that I had never undergone a test before and I blew into the gadget, this time apparently to his satisfaction. He seized it from me – there is no other word for it – and looked at the measure. I knew then that I had passed because his face fell, very obviously. I was in fact .04, not over .05 as he had apparently hoped.

On quite a few occasions since then I have been stopped for random breath-testing. The police have been polite and friendly. The contrast with the Blackheath occasion was, to say the least, unmistakable.

My particular 'random' breath test involved myself and no one else. No other motorist was tested at the time.

# 20

# The McLeod-Lindsay Inquiry

There are some resemblances between the case of Alexander McLeod-Lindsay and that of Lindy Chamberlain. In each case the Crown could offer no motive to explain the alleged actions of the accused; in each a verdict of guilty was obtained because of overwhelming forensic evidence. The case of McLeod-Lindsay was a pioneer case in what became known as the science of 'bloodstain dynamics', a field of knowledge which over the years has become a useful aid to the investigators of violent crimes involving the spilling of blood.

The type of bloodstains left in an assault or murder can indicate the direction of the blows, the type of weapon used and, in particular, may identify an offender because stains which appear on a person's clothing can be very strongly indicative of the proximity of the person to the crime. Thus, impact spatter on the clothing of a person may indicate that he or she struck the blows, so as to be so close as to be stained by the blood from the victim. Such impact stains are quite different from the smears received by someone later rendering aid to a wounded person.

I gained greater knowledge of bloodstain dynamics when I appeared in the case of a man who had killed his fiancée with a hammer. In that case the wielded hammer cast weapon spatter on the ceilings, and the pattern of bloodstains throughout the premises carried clear indications as to the localities of the assaults. The evidence was given by Dr John Duflu of the Institute of Forensic Medicine. I think it is fair to say that at that stage he was only newly versed in the study of bloodstain dynamics.

In March 1991, the accused, David Low Woy On, was convicted of the manslaughter of Cherry Kou Kai Wen, his fiancée. I argued that because Cherry hit David first with a hammer and thereby temporarily deprived him of his power to reason, he was thereafter a mere automaton, unable to control his actions. The fact that he told a false story to the police probably lost him this defence before the jury. Nevertheless, there was a story of months of extreme provocation leading up to the very severe hammer blow, which was ample to reduce the offence from murder to manslaughter. The effect on his power to reason occasioned by the blow also provided a basis for reducing murder to manslaughter.

Initially the defendant was put on a bond by way of sentence, but on appeal this was increased to, I think, two years minimum.

Appearing for David gave me a lot of experience in bloodstain dynamics. The flat's walls, ceilings and bath were covered in blood from hammer blows. However these really only proved that he had gone berserk in his attack and that he had apparently followed the victim from room to room with frenzied blows to her body. He was a patient, long-suffering man who had suddenly snapped.

McLeod-Lindsay's case was a strange one. The Crown case alleged that shortly before 9.30 p.m. on 14 September 1964 Mr Lindsay (as he is now known) left his employment at the Sylvania Hotel without permission and before he was due to leave at midnight, and brutally assaulted his wife with a steel jackpick used to prop up the garage door. She was shockingly injured to the head and was not expected to live. Their son Bruce, then aged four, was apparently accidentally hit and severely injured by the assailant. Thereafter, Lindsay, on the Crown case, went back to the hotel, finished his work and left just before midnight when he drove home and purported to discover his injured wife. The police observed bloodstains on his trousers and windjacket and experts later said that the stains on the windjacket in particular were impact spatter; that is, they could only have been received if Lindsay struck the blows.

There was no motive ever proved for what was obviously an attempt to murder Mrs McLeod-Lindsay. Furthermore, Lindsay had an alibi through witnesses who saw him at the hotel. He denied ever leaving his work. However, the alibi was incomplete, there was a window of opportunity not adequately covered by witnesses at the hotel and the expert evidence was apparently quite conclusive. The bloodstains on his windjacket could not have come from arterial spurting when he bent over his wife and, as it were, disturbed the wounds to her face. These stains could only have come from him being the assailant, said the experts.

McLeod-Lindsay was convicted on 5 March 1965 of attempted murder and on 8 March 1965 was sentenced to 18 years imprisonment.

In 1969, because of public disquiet over a man of good character with no apparent motive being found guilty of such a serious offence, there was an inquiry into his conviction by Mr Justice Lee under section 475 of the Crimes Act. On 2 October 1969 Mr Justice Lee reported that in his opinion there was no doubt as to Lindsay's guilt. This opinion, expressed in a careful report after quite a lengthy hearing, was based on the simple fact that according to the experts Lindsay could not have received the bloodstains on his clothing unless he was the assailant.

Now McLeod-Lindsay was not an accused seeking to excuse a killing. He fell into the much more difficult category of accused who say, 'I don't know who did it, but it was not I' and the jury knows that its verdict of 'not guilty' will mean no one will be punished for an undoubted murder, or attempt, in the case of McLeod-Lindsay.

The frightful wounds to Mrs McLeod-Lindsay broke her facial bones and her teeth, and in fact were so severe that it is probable that she would have died within the time lapse of 9.30 p.m. to midnight had she lain there without assistance. This idea was first advanced by Dr Duflu who, though a witness for the Crown, was quite impartial in his approach. Dr Kevin Bleasel, a leading neuro-surgeon confirmed this likelihood.

One might wonder why a man who had assaulted his wife with intent to kill, and left her dying, would two-and-a-half hours later seek medical assistance for her, rather than complete the unfinished crime.

Inquiries revealed a normal marriage and no reason for Lindsay to want to kill his wife. He had an alibi for nearly all the relevant time, save for a small window of opportunity around 9.30 p.m., sufficient for him to have committed the crime. Of course a partial alibi is no real defence, but it may make the suspect's guilt less likely.

According to the Crown case Lindsay would have worked for over two hours wearing bloodstained clothing, but the most noticeable item, the windjacket, was not worn then, but put on when he went to the hospital. Why put on a bloodstained windjacket if he was guilty?

It can be simply said that everything pointed away from Lindsay's guilt except the bloodstains on his clothing, but the inference from those on his jacket was apparently unanswerable.

At the trial his wife said that he was not the assailant, but she was so brain-damaged that her evidence was discarded, even though she had made a miraculous recovery from injuries which had made her death the very likely outcome.

Lindsay was in prison from his arrest on 28 September 1964 until he was released on parole on 3 August 1973, nearly nine years later. In 1982 his parole expired, but he had always maintained his innocence, and continued to do so long after his sentence expired.

In the Chamberlain case one might say that there were many mistakes in the forensic evidence that should not have occurred. These were caused by over-enthusiasm for the Crown case and by numerous other reasons such as insufficient skill, inadequate equipment, and lack of overall liaison between experts. In the McLeod-Lindsay case it would be wise not to criticise those who originally gave forensic evidence that seemed to establish guilt beyond any reasonable doubt.

The study of bloodstain dynamics has advanced, and the new

knowledge tended to exonerate McLeod-Lindsay. Justice Loveday ordered there be a second inquiry into the guilt of McLeod-Lindsay. I was appointed counsel to assist the inquiry.

I had known Justice Loveday at the law school as a fellow student and had seen a lot of him as a fellow barrister and as a judge, particularly as a District Court judge. He was then promoted to the Supreme Court. He once led me when I was a junior barrister in a most abstruse land-title case. I appeared before him when he was a judge in criminal cases and in an environmental case involving the smells from a 'tank farm' (where dangerous and difficult chemicals are stored). He was versatile, able and had a great feeling for justice. McLeod-Lindsay had been convicted, there had been an extensive inquiry by Justice Lee which confirmed his guilt, and now there was to be a second inquiry into the guilt of the man who had been convicted of attempting to murder his wife and had long since served his sentence. This inquiry was a Crimes Act inquiry similar to a Royal Commission.

The second inquiry was founded almost entirely on new forensic evidence of bloodstain dynamics, as the study was now called. The experts now gave their opinions based on photos and diagrams of the previous exhibits, namely the clothing which no longer existed. Fundamental to the application was a report by Ms Anita Wonder, an expert from the United States. Her report said, in effect, that far from being impact spatter the relevant bloodstains were consistent with having been put onto the clothing long after the assault, consistent with Lindsay's claim that he was stained when he went to the assistance of his wounded wife. Ms Wonder's report made some compelling points as to the bloodstains being in part from clotted blood, which meant that there was a long time-lapse between the assault and the stains.

Since the Crown case had depended entirely on the bloodstains it is not surprising that the extraordinary step of ordering a second inquiry was taken.

This time I had Bob Greenhill (now a senior counsel) as my junior to assist the inquiry. He had been my junior in the previous case of David Low Woy On.

Peter Hidden QC (now Justice Hidden) the Public Defender

and John Nicholson (now Judge Nicholson) appeared for Lindsay. My junior from Blackburn, Peter Johnson, appeared for the Crown. Anthony Restuccia, an old friend, was my instructing solicitor. It was a credit to our justice system that the successful application to reopen the case was made by the Public Solicitor and the Public Defender. Lindsay did not have the funds to retain private lawyers.

Some might think that these were expensive proceedings concerned only with a very old case where, after all, guilt had been decided against Lindsay twice, and his sentence had long expired. But the law learns a lot from these inquiries and, in any event, injustice is something that is worth spending money to remedy, even years afterwards.

Anita Wonder was totally deaf but she could speak in a rather strange voice at times. Equipment was put in court that translated spoken words into printed words on a screen so she gave her evidence effectively, and was subject to a full and efficient cross-examination. She was an intelligent woman with a good sense of humour. She was obviously well versed in the close study of bloodstains and bloodstain dynamics, and had degrees from the University of California and California State University.

Now the real issue in the forensic evidence was could there be any explanation for the bloodstains on Lindsay's clothes other than impact spatter; that is, was he the assailant, splashed with blood while inflicting the blows? His explanation was that when he moved his wounded wife at about midnight this started further bleeding, including arterial spurting onto his clothing as he bent over her. If the blood on his clothing was clotted blood in part, then that blood must have got there well after the assault because it takes time for the blood to clot. Ms Wonder claimed to identify clotting from the photos of the clothing. She identified dark black centres to many of the bloodstains which she said indicated clotting that would have taken at least an hour to form. Some stains she identified as arterial spurts.

The tiny spots on the trousers she explained as dots from blood bouncing off pools of blood. There were two occasions during Lindsay's handling of his wounded wife when this could easily have occurred but there was argument as to whether the spots could bounce as high as those on the trousers.

Ms Wonder concluded that the assailant was left-handed whereas Lindsay was right-handed. She had conducted elaborate experiments to prove her point. However, conflicting expert opinion left this point very much in doubt.

A Dr Allen from Queensland conducted experiments which supported his claim that the stains were consistent with Lindsay's story.

Dr Andrew Scott of Adelaide supported the evidence of Ms Wonder as to clotted blood. He pointed out that Mrs McLeod-Lindsay may well have coughed blood having regard to her mouth injuries. Dr Harding also from Adelaide supported the clotted blood theories. Both he and Dr Scott were leading forensic scientists.

I was new to this type of forensic evidence and decided to call in Tony Raymond who had been so useful, impartial and reliable in the Chamberlain case. He was still with the Australian Forensic Science Laboratory of Victoria. He consulted Dr Byron Collins, a forensic doctor, who stressed that to survive with her injuries Mrs McLeod-Lindsay would have had to cough through her broken bones and teeth to clear her airways, otherwise she probably would have choked to death.

Tony Raymond took blood from his own body, lay in the probable position of the victim with the blood in his mouth while Dr Collins leant over him wearing a white gown, in the position Lindsay had claimed he was in when trying to assist his wife. To my mind the stains produced on Dr Collins' white gown, when Tony Raymond coughed, bore a striking resemblance to those said to be impact spatter on the windjacket. This was a crucial point, taken up by other witnesses.

Raymond also carried out experiments on blood spotting for the trousers, and clotting for the windjacket. As to the former, the spots did suggest proximity to the assault because they were so high up the trousers, but this could be explained innocently by dropping blood into a pool of other blood if the wearer was on his haunches. Expiration drops through coughing was a possible explanation.

The Crown relied on experts from the trial, but their main

witness was Professor Herbert Leon Macdonell. He was the author of the leading textbook on bloodstain dynamics, and was the pioneer of that study. He supported the proposition that the wearer of the jacket and the trousers was the assailant. He queried the clotting appearance in the photographs. He did, however, agree that there were at least some clots on the jacket in answer to one of my questions. He conceded the possibility that the trouser spots could be explained consistent with Lindsay's innocence.

Forensic evidence is best tested by considering what ought to be there if the theory in question is correct. Thus the Crown demonstrated the wielding of the jackpick in front of Professor Macdonell, from which blood would be spattered all up the front of the assailant. I pointed out to the Professor that there was no blood at all on Lindsay's cummerbund and nothing below mid-chest to just above the knee. Macdonell said that area should have been spattered with impact spatter so he must have been wearing an apron. But it is clear that he was not wearing an apron so the theory of a frontal assault causing the bloodstains lost some of its force.

What with blood clotting, the expiration (coughing) experiment, and numerous other matters, it was clear that the forensic evidence could not by itself support a finding of guilt. But all the other evidence was supportive of innocence. So Justice Loveday, in a careful report in July 1991 – which should be referred to in any future case of disputed bloodstain dynamics – found there were substantial doubts as to Lindsay's guilt. He was pardoned and I understand that his claim for compensation was mediated and compromised by a reasonable settlement.

Tony Raymond's experiment with Dr Collins led to a substantial amendment to Professor Macdonell's book so as to allow for expiration spatter. The inquiry may well have avoided injustices not only in Australia but in America and England, where bloodstain dynamics is now an established aid to crime detection.

Tony Raymond is now the Director of the Forensic Services Group of the New South Wales Police Service, a group set up by former New South Wales Police Commissioner Peter Ryan. Hopefully this group will expand because forensic evidence is an enormous aid to crime detection.

Since the Lindsay case I have heard Tony Raymond lecture at the Australian Academy of Forensic Science on bloodstain dynamics, and he has given numerous examples of how it has helped to detect and convict criminals.

Justice Loveday recommended the speedy completion of the project to provide for a modern integrated forensic laboratory in New South Wales. This was in July 1991. From time to time we hear of the project, but New South Wales is still way behind Victoria in this regard, and still awaiting the new laboratory.

Lindsay's case is a tribute to our law in that ultimately a grave mistake was corrected for a man of humble means, whose cause was taken up by the Public Solicitor and who was represented by the Public Defender. He was compensated for the injustice suffered insofar as money can be any compensation in such a case.

Yet, it was really nobody's fault. The two decisions of guilt made were undoubtedly correct on the evidence. It was only later that scientific knowledge and experience could ultimately expose the errors in the Crown case.

It is, as I have said before with reference to Lindy Chamberlain, dangerous to convict for murder, or attempted murder where the guilt of the accused is denied and there is no motive. A conviction founded entirely on forensic evidence, where there is no motive may well be questioned, and this is very much so if it is founded on outdated science. The discoveries of today reveal the errors of yesterday.

One would expect Lindsay to be bitter. Certainly he endured a dreadful experience that took away some of the best years of his life. I found him, when I interviewed him before the inquiry, a man whose attention for years had been centred on the injustice he had suffered, but I found his protestations of innocence impressive. It is very hard to judge such a man on his demeanour but he did seem sincere. Certainly his persistence in maintaining his innocence over so many years does give force to what he was saying.

It was a dreadful tragedy for Lindsay and his badly injured wife. It was a shocking tragedy for their children.

# 21

# ICAC and Other Inquiries

I have reservations about special permanent inquiry bodies. Royal Commissions or Crimes Act inquiries have served useful purposes many times. For example, years ago in the 1940s Justice Davidson inquired into the coal industry and produced a famous report that resulted in the Coal Mines Regulation Act. Years later, Justice McClemens in a Royal Commission into Callan Park produced a report that resulted in many worthwhile reforms of mental hospitals. Mr Costigan QC inquiring into the Painters and Dockers Union and Mr Gyles QC (now Justice Gyles) inquiring into the building industry exposed many rackets and reforms resulted. The recent Wood Royal Commission into the New South Wales Police Service and into paedophilia must be classified as one of the great successes of this type of procedure.

However the inquisitorial procedure has its shortcomings. It is a gross intrusion into not only the privacy of citizens but the fundamental right against self-incrimination, the American constitutional right supplied by the Fifth Amendment. The temptation to take short cuts by abolishing fundamental rights is always there. Only rarely is the sacrifice worthwhile.

But apart from specific subject inquiries, both State and federal parliaments have set up permanent bodies with overriding powers that sacrifice individual rights in order to fight crime. At times these bodies are grave instruments of oppression.

I had a case involving the State Drug Commission, now the State Crime Commission. It was an early case for them and perhaps they had something to learn. They interfered in the defence of a criminal trial, then targeted one person, threatening and bullying him and asking him deceptive questions. They had all the relevant documents – he had none – and they suggested false answers to him and attacked him when he adopted their suggestions. He was told that he could tell no one that he had been and was being questioned. He did not dare to tell his wife and feared to tell me as his legal adviser. He was eventually charged with a criminal offence and he was acquitted, but his case was an example of the evils of the targeting of a citizen by an inquisitorial body.

To be fair, I subsequently appeared before the State Crime Commission on quite a few occasions when Clarrie Briese was the chairman, and its proceedings were immaculate.

I never appeared, so far as I can recall, before the National Crime Authority, but I advised it quite often and appeared for its members before a Senate Committee. The National Crime Authority was criticised by many lawyers, but I am not in a position to pass useful judgment on most of the criticisms. Both the State Crime Commission and the National Crime Authority, needed careful appointments to their membership. They had wide powers that were open to serious abuse. However, at least they usually sat in camera, so their witnesses were not exposed to damaging publicity. Certainly the National Crime Authority has achieved quite a deal in its time and they each did useful work in the field of criminal intelligence, but whether the expense of the organisations and the sacrifices of civil liberties involved were justified by the results achieved is something I simply do not know.

I believe there needs to be an audit on such bodies, assessing the results achieved against the costs, both in terms of money and loss of civil rights. The matters involved are highly secret usually and there can hardly be a public audit. We depend upon parliamentary committees, which may or may not comprehend the issues involved.

It is still an unfortunate fact that there is no real public confidence in the integrity of the police service, and there is thus a need for other investigatory bodies. Perhaps it would be better to use the money spent on these bodies for proper policing, including an up-to-date integrated forensic laboratory.

In March 1988 the Greiner Liberal-National New South Wales State government was elected after 12 years of Labor government. This government established the Independent Commission Against Corruption (ICAC) in an atmosphere of dissatisfaction with standards of probity in public bodies. I believe ICAC is novel and dangerous. It is founded on a Hong Kong model and aims to be a permanent body ever ready to expose corruption. Often it operates in a public arena so that its witnesses, and still more its targets, are publicly destroyed before any finding by the commission. There have been bad examples of public bullying by ICAC officers of persons who had no real power to answer back. This has not happened recently to my knowledge, but it was a common event some years ago.

Perhaps abuses in such a body are inevitable. All sorts of people may from time to time preside over commission hearings. Some may turn out to be quite unfitted to do so. Is that a risk that simply has to be taken?

Many public rackets have been exposed by ICAC. Much useful advice has been given to public bodies as to how to tighten their procedures. On the other hand, ICAC failed dismally in inquiring into the New South Wales Police Service. It is a very expensive organisation, and though it has quite a few runs on the board it has sometimes abused its powers. Probably it has a useful purpose to serve but it needs a very careful audit of its achievements, which are rarely confidential, and there needs to be a reconsideration of the terms of its governing statute, particularly bearing in mind civil liberties.

I suppose I have a jaundiced view of ICAC. My first close contact with it involved the defence of Tim Moore, then New South Wales Minister for the Environment, over the Terry Metherell affair.

In May 1991, the Greiner government suffered an electoral reverse, remaining in power only with the support of four independents in the Legislative Assembly. One was the independent member for Tamworth, Tony Windsor, who consistently supported the government. The other three independents demanded various concessions in return for their support, most if not all of which were in the public interest – for example, fixed terms of parliament. These concessions or reforms were extracted by John Hatton, Peter McDonald and Clover Moore, the said three independents, in a memorandum of understanding tabled in the Legislative Assembly on 31 October 1991.

In October 1991 Dr Terry Metherell resigned from the Liberal Party and thereafter became an independent, highly critical of the government. He was a very able man who had pushed through many reforms as Minister for Education in the previous parliament. Some of these reforms were no doubt good, some were controversial, but overall he was, through his manner of doing things, an unpopular, even if capable Minister. As an independent he was somewhat embittered and his talents were wasted.

Of the five independents, he was at times the most difficult to deal with. It was obviously in the interests of the government that he should resign from parliament. It was in his own interests, and those of the community, that his undoubted talents should be usefully employed. So a position was created in the Environment Protection Authority, the EPA, as head of a strategic planning unit, and Metherell was appointed to it. Obviously this had political advantages to the government in that Metherell resigned from parliament and was replaced in his safe Liberal seat by a Liberal member.

This caused a tremendous political row. I suppose Australians have always hated those who ratted on their political party after an election and Metherell was perceived as a bad case of this. His apparent reward for betraying his party (and those who elected him) went against the grain to say the least. The independents who stood for higher political standards were enraged. The Labor Party licked its lips and enjoyed Greiner's troubles.

On 28 April 1988 parliament referred the matter to ICAC. Ian Temby QC was the ICAC Commissioner at the time

There was a long hearing and then a report adverse to Greiner and Moore finding corruption (within the meaning of the ICAC Act) against them. That finding was later overruled by the Court of Appeal.

In my view, this whole case was pure politics and was hardly a matter for judgment by an ICAC Commissioner, even one as able as Ian Temby QC. There were plenty of precedents for such an appointment in past political history: for example, Senator Gair's appointment as Ambassador to Ireland in 1974 by the Whitlam government. Gough Whitlam was certainly an honest man, a man of integrity, but felt that political purposes justified the appointment. Judgment on such matters is for parliament and the electors. When the law intrudes into the field of pure politics it is bound to come to grief. Temby considered that only merit, being the best applicant, could justify a public-service appointment. Perhaps life is not so simple.

During the long hearing, politicians were cross-examined as to their adherence to a code of conduct only known in a make-believe world. Political decisions were examined in the light of old, totally inapplicable laws.

The definition of corruption in section 8 of the ICAC Act is very wide indeed but qualified and reduced to common sense by section 9. Corruption normally means payment for favours for departure from public or private duty in the wide definition in section 8. By section 9 the matter must involve a criminal offence, a disciplinary offence or a reasonable ground for dismissal of the services of a public official. Whatever Greiner or Moore did, it did not fall within section 9. Tim Moore was criticised because for him a factor in Metherell's appointment, and an important factor, was the desire that his friend should get out of his embittered rut as an independent betraying his previous political allegiance, and use his undoubted talents in a position for which he was eminently suited. This was corruption under the wide definition in section 8 since only suitability should influence the selection. It was hardly a dismissal matter under section 9, assuming anyone had the power to dismiss a Minister of the Crown.

When the report came out, Greiner and Moore wanted to resign immediately but they were advised not to because in the view of all the lawyers the findings of corrupt conduct were wrong and should be challenged. This challenge was commenced in the Court of Appeal without delay and Chief Justice Murray Gleeson fixed an early date a couple of weeks off for the hearing. I remember working a very long day preparing the necessary documents for the court.

That evening I heard that the three independents did not intend to await the court's decision. They served an ultimatum that Greiner and Moore had to resign or they would bring down the government. In the interests of their Liberal Party Greiner and Moore did so and the State lost a very fine and able Premier and a dedicated Minister for the Environment whose achievements were quite remarkable.

That was ICAC's great achievement, but to be fair, Ian Temby left, as he had to, the ultimate decision to parliament, and the three independents decided the matter.

A couple of weeks later the matter came before the Court of Appeal. It reserved its decision, then found in favour of both Greiner and Moore. In those proceedings I appeared for Moore as I had appeared for him before ICAC. There was some satisfaction in the ultimate result. The Court of Appeal re-established the reputations of both Greiner and Moore, but the community had lost two loyal and dedicated servants who could hardly be spared. There are few Labor politicians, I believe, who would deny that these two Liberal politicians were way above the usual standards of ability and integrity in State parliament. Their fate served no real purpose other than to discourage good people from entering and taking part in politics. Party membership these days is very low indeed, in all parties.

Such was the triumph of ICAC. Was it worth it?

The court's decision was in August 1992. Nearly a year later in

June 1993 I appeared for Ron Woodham, a senior custodial officer of the Department of Corrective Services, in an appeal to the Supreme Court against an ICAC finding made against him by Ian Temby QC. It had been said that a reference he gave for a prisoner for special good conduct should have been qualified by the adverse background of the prisoner, a background that was well known anyhow. On 25 June 1993 Justice Grove upheld the appeal. He held that the standard of conduct applied was wrong in law and there was no objective basis upon which the conduct of Mr Woodham could be categorised as improper. Ron Woodham later became head of the Department of Corrective Services, the first custodial officer to do so. He was a self-made man, with many years of service to the State, and ICAC nearly ruined his career.

Perhaps it is because I appeared in the two main challenges to ICAC that I have a jaundiced opinion. It is a pity that both challenges were against findings by Ian Temby QC, who was a courteous and capable commissioner. These characteristics did not apply to all the assistant commissioners, of whom there have been many. Some were good, some not so good.

I appeared for one person charged with serious offences on the strength of admissions made by him at an ICAC inquiry. On the face of the transcript the proceedings appeared to be reasonably fair, although some of the questions were a bit fierce. The evidence had been sound-recorded so I insisted that the record be played. When this happened, the tone of voice and the bullying comments and questions were so bad that the judge had no alternative but to exclude the evidence as unfairly and oppressively obtained. My client was acquitted.

ICAC was a mighty weapon, open to abuse.

What should happen about ICAC now? In recent years it has been much more careful in its proceedings and has produced some good results. It may well be that it has useful functions to perform, provided that it is subject to careful supervision. At present, the courts only have power to check ICAC if it acts beyond its jurisdiction, which is the only real ground of appeal against its finding. There is also a parliamentary committee that supervises it.

It is easy to jeer at a victim of ICAC. Yet it is surprisingly easy to become a victim, even if ultimately you are shown to be innocent.

There is no doubt that the law these days is much more anxious to investigate improper activities than it was 50 years ago. Is this because, with the apparent decline of religion as a social force, we are more evil than we were before, or is it because we insist on higher standards of conduct? I think the latter is the case. The corruption of police and others by the drug trade tends to make us think that evil is more widespread in society than it is.

In addition, I think higher expectations from life make people insist on much higher standards of honesty. Furthermore, this generation is not prepared to pretend that all is well as used to be the case 50 years ago. Thus, despite its many shortcomings, our society is constantly trying to improve standards of honesty and behaviour generally. People are restless for reform, yet worried by the constant changes in society.

It is little wonder therefore that there is a constant demand for more and more inquiries. Sometimes the demand is purely political for political advantage, but often the call is for improvement in standards of honesty and conduct generally.

Already inquiries are active into various company disasters, both here and in America. We are going to see many more inquiries into business enterprises, and we are going to find that what was deemed honest enough years ago may well result in a severe prison sentence tomorrow.

When I was a little boy there was the Great Depression. People fought to eat enough, to dress decently. Then there was the struggle for sexual happiness or liberty or licence, depending on one's point of view. Now, for the most part, we have a well-fed, well-educated generation which expects a lot from life, and from its fellow citizens. Among them are many fine idealists, and many sensible, solid individuals who may in the future turn idealism into reality. These people will insist on many inquiries in the future; they will not be prepared to hide evil, or pretend that all is well.

So we will have to be careful lest the desire to expose and uproot evil endangers our fundamental rights as citizens. Striking the balance between the advantages of the inquisitorial bodies and the dangers to civil liberties will always be difficult.

I should add that such bodies tend to grow and expand their borders. The power given to the inquirer can very easily be abused.

Of course, the position is now complicated by international terrorism. It may be that the inquisitorial crime investigation bodies might be safer to deal with this problem than giving vast powers to ASIO and the police.

I can only say that all inquisitorial bodies are a real danger to our civil liberties, and restrict our rights. They should only be permitted to do so under strict supervision, upon proof of real public benefit.

# 22

# Matters of Sex

During my legal career, there has been a revolution in the law's attitude to sex.

For years, Australian law, like English law, provided divorce-law copy for the sensational journals, particularly the Sunday newspapers. Big adultery cases were tried in public and many a person's life was ruined because of a public finding of adultery against him or her. These cases occurred for years after I came to the bar in 1948. Now adultery is no longer a matrimonial offence, still less a cause for social disgrace. When matrimonial offences were finally abolished in the late 1970s and no-fault divorce became the rule, many thought that the law would cease intruding into bedrooms.

My working life covered these periods of considerable change. I appeared in many divorce and maintenance cases where the issue was proof of adultery. Usually this was done by confessions or circumstantial evidence, but in the later years modern technology was employed to obtain direct photographs of people engaging in sexual intercourse. The reason for these rather ridiculous photographs was that some judges would not accept anything but the most overwhelming evidence of adultery. So, unknown to the person under investigation, private inquiry agents broke into premises, then arranged equipment to hear from outside what was going on inside. They also arranged an easy method of re-entry into the premises. Then, when they heard unmistakable noises of sexual activity they burst in with their flashlight cameras. This degrading procedure was a powerful argument for no-fault divorce.

One of the aspects of adultery that frequently concerned me was the cruel deception involved. The victim's partner was told that he or she was imagining the adultery, was obsessed, or insanely jealous or mentally ill. They therefore suffered a great deal because of the uncertainty. The adultery raid often came as somewhat of a relief because it proved there had been no crazy imagination after all.

Of course, there are jealous spouses who suspect adultery without any real reason, but in my experience most of those whose suspicions were tested in court turned out to be right. They went through great stress before the truth was proved. Now, under no-fault divorce, many spouses never find out the truth.

I have been lucky myself in that I have been married happily for 50 years. In my practice I felt, at times quite deeply, the distress of divorce clients. Specialists in the field have to become coldly detached, otherwise they will find practice intolerable. Over the years I worked on many divorce cases, but never became a specialist. As a result I could express sympathy and many times I listened to the story of the marriage, not so much for the purpose of the case itself, but so as to permit my client to relieve wounded feelings by telling someone.

Adultery was humiliating to the victim in many cases, but denial of adultery by the offending party was cruel and cowardly. But there were no clear rules in marital attitudes. There were many spouses who knew but did not want to acknowledge that their partner was committing adultery. Some quite reasonable marriages were maintained in this way.

Whereas male homosexual conduct used to be a criminal offence frequently prosecuted, leading to quite a few suicides, modern enlightenment at last removed these offences from the statute book. Consenting adults could not be prosecuted for being gay, and, in fact, gay persons could take up prominent positions in the law, politics and society generally. During my working life, the reform of the laws against homosexuality have been a great success. For the stability of society and the perpetuation of the race it is obviously desirable that most people should be heterosexual. If the new laws encouraged people to be gay who were not inherently so, the reforms could be criticised on that basis, but I know of no real evidence to support such an argument.

Male gay persons suffered very much under the old laws. They were open to blackmail, and exposure in a criminal court led to social and often financial ruin. Perfectly honest people who happened to be gay were prevented from participating in various occupations on the grounds that they were not of good character. People who fell foul of the criminal law were often subjected to the misguided psychiatric torture of aversion therapy.

I did fight one pioneering case which helped the progress of reform. My client was a male homosexual with, as was often the case in those days, a number of convictions for offensive behaviour in public lavatories. He applied for an estate agent's licence, promised to get psychiatric aid and never offend again, but was refused a licence by the magistrate. I came into the case at that point and took what was then a novel approach. On the appeal I said he was homosexual (the word 'gay' was not used much then), that this was something probably beyond his control, and even if it was illegal or criminal (as it was then) his honesty and business integrity were unimpaired. The case came before Judge Peter Leslie, an enlightened man who was married to an actress. He was not shocked by homosexuality, nor did he find it necessary to pretend to be, as some judges did. He upheld my submissions and the case was reported in the law reports. It became a landmark decision and helped to foster the attitude of social tolerance that led to the legalisation of homosexuality.

The result of this reform of the law has been the abolition of much cruelty and persecution, and a much fuller contribution to the welfare of society by people who happen to be gay. It is good that they no longer need hide their sexual preference, nor do they have to apologise for it.

This is an enormous difference from what the law once was. I defended many gay males, and, looking back, I think now that the law wasted its time and was, more importantly, cruel and unfair.

Once divorce became no-fault and male homosexuality between consenting adults was no longer an offence it might be thought that the law would cease to worry about people's sex lives. It turned out very differently.

First there was an outbreak of complaints of sexual harassment in the workplace. These were, in many cases, allegations of minor indecent assaults, probably not sufficiently serious to warrant criminal proceedings, but in the nature of nasty bullying, usually by fellow employees, often supervisors. I was retained to defend one of the earliest of these, and also to defend an employer criminally charged by a female employee over an alleged minor assault.

Insofar as the anti-discrimination bodies sought to mediate and deal with these complaints privately by counselling and perhaps by facilitating apologies, they probably did some good. Where they sought to flex their legal muscles and publicly assert their powers, the results were not so good. Often there were two sides to the stories behind the complaints, and when there were public proceedings neither party gained much. The alleged offender was publicly humiliated and often penalised. The alleged victim was publicly branded a troublemaker, especially if his or her complaint was not established, but even if it was. (As a matter of common sense, once such a complaint has been made, whether by a male or female, whether justified or not, unless the alleged offender admits his or her fault, some people may not want to work with the complainant, fearing an unjustified complaint.)

It is a difficult area. Social customs are no longer clearly defined. What would have been grossly offensive sexual conduct in the 1950s may well have been the norm in the 1980s. Furthermore, the situation that forms the subject of the complaints is rarely clearly black or white; it is likely to be a confused grey. Mediation,

Michael and Lindy Chamberlain in Darwin in 1986 after Lindy was set free from prison. In April 1986 my junior, Bill Caldwell, and I were retained to assist the Royal Commission into the murder conviction of Lindy Chamberlain.

The inquiry's attention concentrated on Azaria's clothes found a week after her disappearance. To my mind, one clear fact emerged: there was simply no real evidence that Lindy killed her baby.

Early in the inquiry the Victorian Forensic Science Laboratory was appointed to assist us. After thorough forensic testing of the Chamberlains' car, the spray under the dash previously thought to be foetal blood consistent with the baby's throat having been cut while held on the front seat, was found to be sound deadener.

Former millionaire Sydney hotelier Andrew Kalajzich and his wife Megan in happier days. It is astonishing to think that a man of Andrew's intelligence should murder his wife in such a foolish way as to make it absolutely certain that he would be immediately suspected. He still claims that he is innocent.

Andrew Kalajzich with me at Glebe Coroners Court in 1986. It was a very difficult trial. Kalajzich had a great deal of evidence against him. I could not help but pity a man for whom life had been going so well until it turned into this nightmare.

A portrait of me by Phillip Player, Andrew Kalajzich's one-time cellmate. Player was also my client.

Patrick Cummins/Sydney Morning Herald

I have a jaundiced view of ICAC. My first close encounter of it involved the defence of Tim Moore, then New South Wales Minister for the Environment, over the Terry Metherell affair. The result of that inquiry was the loss to politics of two good men who could hardly be spared, Premier Nick Greiner (pictured) and my client Tim Moore.

News Ltd

Leaving the ICAC hearing into Nick Greiner. In my opinion, this whole case was pure politics and hardly a matter for judgment by an ICAC Commissioner, even one as able as Ian Temby QC.

Harry 'The Hat' Blackburn in 1989, arriving at the New South Wales Supreme Court for the start of the Blackburn Royal Commission in which I appeared as counsel assisting.

Alexander (McLeod) Lindsay. His murder charges were dropped after 29 years. Ultimately a grave mistake was corrected for a man of humble means whose cause was taken up by the Public Solicitor and who was represented by the Public Defender.

Justice James Wood at the New South Wales Police Royal Commission. Even after the Wood Royal Commission report and the many successful reforms that resulted, corruption on a large scale has been revealed again.

Frank McAlary QC, Tom Hughes QC and I shared celebrations of each of our 50-year anniversaries of being admitted to the bar. A special Bar Association dinner was held for us. Left to right: Ian Harrison SC, Tony Bellanto QC, myself, Frank McAlary QC, Tom Hughes QC, Judge McGuire.

Left to right: Michael Slattery QC, myself, Kirby J, Slattery J.

My fellow barristers on the 12th floor of Selborne chambers commissioned a painting of myself by Graeme Inson (pictured left) to mark my 50 years at the bar. On the back it is inscribed with the words by John Bunyan: *Who so beset him round / with dismal stories do but themselves confound. / His strength the more is. / No foe shall stay his might / though he with giants fight.*

Frank McAlary QC and I have known each other since we were at university together. Back when we were students, in celebrations marking the end of WWII his dance down a Sydney street made Australian cinema history.

Frank McAlary QC, Tom Hughes QC and myself (l–r) in 1999 after 50 years at the bar.

At the end of 57 years in the law, 52 as a barrister, it was time to hang up my wig in June 2000. At last I was able to sit back and look at the law. In 2001 the National Library of Australia recorded an oral history of my life for their collection and presented me with this picture as a memento.

conciliation and counselling can often be very useful indeed. Public litigation should be a last resort.

I have defended employees in industrial tribunals against disciplinary proceedings and I have appeared for employers. In one case it was clear that loose discipline had contributed to probable workplace misconduct, but the complaint against a foreman who was opposing some industrial demands was union-encouraged. In that context, the complaint could easily have been concocted. The tribunal reached a compromise result.

It is well to have some remedies for workplace persecution. Sexual harassment is only one aspect of a much bigger picture. It is a fact that many people go sadly to work each day knowing that a superior dislikes or even hates them, and a large part of their lives is made miserable accordingly. I have seen a competent man forced into invalid retirement by systematic persecution. The industrial tribunal failed to save him. He was the victim of a superior who disliked him. It is unfortunately a common story. There are many bullies at school, at work and in the armed forces. Given power, they love to make the lives of others miserable. It is a social problem of enormous importance. We are only just beginning to appreciate its magnitude.

Bullies are often popular. They are often convincing witnesses and the heroes of the crowd. It is rare for a bully to lack witnesses in support of his or her story. Dealing with school bullies is hard enough. Dealing with adult bullies is very much more difficult. By and large I fear that most victims of adult bullies either put up with it or change their jobs.

However, where the bullying amounts to sexual harassment I think there is much more chance of intervention by the employer. Anti-discrimination bodies are people best avoided. But I stress that workplace sexual harassment is only a small part of a much bigger problem.

There have always been cases of sexual assault, or indecent assault and rape. For centuries these cases were restricted by common law rules which, in effect, required that the evidence of sexual complainants be corroborated. Some years ago these rules were substantially abolished. For quite a few years now it has been possible, even likely, for an accused person to be convicted on the sole evidence of a complainant, sometimes a young child. I shall deal with paedophilia in the next chapter.

The old justification for the need for corroboration in accusations of sexual assault was that these complaints were easy to make and difficult to rebut. The need for corroboration undoubtedly saved many innocent men (those accused were nearly always men) but it also permitted many guilty men to escape justice. Since most accusations were female against male, the rule seemed to be sexually biased against females.

In former times, a woman was expected to fight for her virtue. In my early days at the bar I secured the acquittal of a young man charged with rape, largely because the woman and the man had a smoke together afterwards. She was uninjured, but a complete stranger to the man who had in effect 'jumped' her on a lonely footpath late at night. The old law books contain many cases setting out the substantial injuries to be expected on a rape victim. I think it was during the war that women were advised to submit to rape, rather than suffer injuries and by and large substantial injuries are not so common in rape cases today because women tend to follow this advice.

Of course there are various types of rape. The serial rapist who seems to derive great pleasure from assaulting and humiliating women is usually very violent both to the female (and her male companion, if there is one). He operates alone. One serial rapist I remember in a case had been terrifying, smashing car windows with an axe during his attack. Usually the only issue in serial-rapist cases is identification of the offender.

Another type of rape that has not infrequently led to murder is pack rape. There is nothing new about such cases. One famous pack-rape case, the Mount Rennie rape case, occurred nearly 100 years ago in Sydney. In these cases the usual issues are identification and consent. That a female would consent to intercourse with three, four or five strangers in succession is, to say the least, unlikely, but sexual ways are at times strange these days, and the defence of consent has succeeded in pack-rape cases.

In pack-rape cases there would often be as many counsel for defence as there were accused and the unfortunate victim would be cross-examined in relays over days. The accused would then avoid the witness box but make statements from the dock, being a version of the events stated by them to the jury, not on oath, and not subject to cross-examination. This was manifestly unfair. I do think that if someone is going to say that a victim consented to pack rape he should have to do so from the witness box, and that is now the law. Statements from the dock have now been abolished in all cases.

Serial rapists and pack rapists aside, the usual issue in rape is consent. This can be so in indecent assault, although there the issue may well be denial of indecency. Sometimes, in indecent-assault cases, the accuser can be malicious, sometimes genuinely mistaken.

Where the issue is consent, the parties usually know each other and the alleged rape is often called date rape. Under the new laws the victim does not have to be corroborated, nor can the victim's past sex life be used in cross-examination except in very limited circumstances. Furthermore, if the victim was late in making the complaint (a serious matter in the old days) the jury is advised that there may well be good reasons for the delay in making the complaint. Many cases of rape, attempted rape or indecent assault are brought today which would not have got to trial some years ago. I think it is fair to say that women are encouraged to make these complaints, but it must be stressed that they are not compelled to do so. They have a choice.

The abandonment of nearly all the old safeguards of corroboration has undoubtedly increased the number of charges for sexual offences on women.

The real safeguard of the law is that guilt must be proved beyond reasonable doubt. Where the charge involves two adults, it is, by and large, word against word. This often involves very difficult problems. These days it is not unknown for consensual sex to occur between adults on their first 'date'. A jilted person may make a false accusation. Often parties who have had quite a lengthy and intimate relationship quarrel and false accusations are made.

Close examination of the surrounding circumstances will often lead to a correct result in these cases. However it is dangerous in the extreme to rely upon the demeanour of witnesses. As I've said before, in my opinion good liars often have much better demeanours than careful tellers of the truth. In such cases an innocent person could easily be convicted. I do not think it happens very often because in my experience juries are very careful of sexual accusations between adults. Female jurors are just as careful as male jurors, probably more so.

Where the problem of sexually-related accusations often leads to grave injustice is where such accusations are made before professional or industrial tribunals where the charge does not have to be proved beyond reasonable doubt, but only to the comfortable satisfaction of the tribunal. An unfavourable finding can deprive employees of their jobs, or a professional person of the right to practice.

In the good old days when I was a boy, a male doctor (they were all males) had a chaperone present when a female patient disrobed. In fact, in one of my cases years ago, when acting for the Medical Board, the fact that a doctor had no chaperone was taken as some support for the female patient's claim of indecent touching. But chaperones cost money so many doctors took the risk of unjustified complaints, and I have no doubt that quite a few innocent doctors have lost the right to practice because of unjustified complaints by female patients.

These days there can be complaints by male patients, but they are unusual. I did once successfully defend a male doctor who was the subject of complaints by a gay male patient.

Complaints against doctors come before the Medical Tribunal, which can find a doctor guilty of professional misconduct, despite a reasonable doubt as to his guilt. It only has to be comfortably satisfied on the balance of probabilities, which is a big difference where the case may depend entirely on a doctor's word against a patient's word. There have been several cases where the doctor was acquitted by a jury, then tried again on the same charge before the tribunal, found guilty and then removed from the medical register.

This is where the law is in real danger of injustice to doctors. They are peculiarly vulnerable to complaints by patients who may be neurotic or just plain spiteful. In many cases the patient may be simply mistaken as to the significance of what the doctor did. In one case a patient was mentally abnormal and claimed a sexual assault by her doctor doing an internal examination. I appeared for the doctor and at his criminal trial the jury of its own motion stopped the trial before counsel addressed them and found the doctor not guilty. He denied even performing an internal examination. By the time the case reached the Medical Tribunal there was undisputed evidence that the patient was neurotic and inclined to make false allegations. This was obvious to the jury without the psychiatric evidence before the Medical Tribunal. Nevertheless the Medical Tribunal found the offence proved, preferring to believe the complainant because she stuck to her story in the witness box. One may ask what such complainant does not stick to her story? Only in Perry Mason films do complainants back down and admit they are wrong.

This last case is, I hope, not typical of the Medical Tribunal, but it shows what can happen when people imagine that they can tell if someone is telling the truth simply by watching him or her in the witness box. This somewhat conceited belief is responsible for most of the injustices in the law.

The doctors once had an appeal to the Court of Appeal from the Medical Tribunal on questions of fact. At their request, the Medical Practice Act was amended to abolish this right. All other professions still have such an appeal to either the Court of Appeal or the District Court.

I have appeared before the criminal courts and the Medical Tribunal for doctors charged with sexual offences with patients. Perhaps some may have been guilty, but most were acquitted by the criminal courts. Before the Medical Tribunal they were in much greater peril. Much depended upon the personnel of the particular Medical Tribunal. Fundamentally, these cases were the doctor's word against that of the patient. Only sometimes did the surrounding circumstances give some real guidance as to the true facts.

When it was word against word and nothing more to indicate the truth, the fact that the doctor was of Asian or Middle Eastern extraction and did not think on his feet well in English was a real handicap. There is also, at times, a tendency to believe attractive young women in preference to not-so-attractive middle-aged men.

I believe internal examinations of women are less frequently conducted now by male general practitioners than used to be the case. Often they are referred to specialists or women doctors.

I had several cases where Chinese doctors were so slow and careful in performing internal examinations that the patients believed they were being indecently assaulted. All the doctors in these cases were acquitted but they suffered a lot before that happened. In one case the patient concerned reconsidered her position after I cross-examined her in the committal proceedings before the magistrate. The doctor was committed for trial, but the prosecution was withdrawn. The patient seemed to me to be a very reasonable person and I think my questions may have persuaded her that she was mistaken. In this area a patient can easily make a mistake and believe the worst. The same mistake can be made if the doctor's examination of a patient's breast differs substantially from another examination made by another doctor.

But many complaints against doctors are certainly not mistakes. Either the patient or the doctor is lying. Although sometimes the surrounding circumstances or the evidence of other witnesses may make it clear where the truth lies, in other cases it is simply word against word. I am quite sure that in those situations quite a few innocent doctors have suffered the ruin of their careers.

There are many social workers and doctors who claim to be experts in the field of sexual assault. When I have cross-examined these so-called experts I have found, without exception, that none have done any research into the area of false complaints. They assume, almost without question, that all complainants are truthful. Research overseas in the United States and France in particular does not make the assumption of truthful complainants, but we have had little benefit from such research in Australia.

The perils doctors face in this area are shared by dentists, nurses, physiotherapists and other paramedics. They too can be falsely or mistakenly accused of misconduct with dire consequences, but they have extensive rights of appeal which doctors lack. Furthermore, although it is technically possible for all professions, only the medical profession, in my experience, will lodge a professional charge, on the same facts, against a doctor who was acquitted on a criminal charge.

In the medical profession sexual intimacy with a patient is a very serious professional offence. The obvious reason for this is the vulnerable position of the patient. The rule is particularly important in the field of psychiatry, but it applies even to the general practitioner who treats an ingrowing toenail. The consent of the patient is no defence for the doctor if he is charged professionally.

This is not the case in other professions. A lawyer acting for a client in a very private matter such as divorce may well have consensual sexual relations without suffering any professional charge. This has certainly been the position for many years, but I wonder whether it is not due for change.

The old safeguards against false allegations have been thrown away at a time when social customs have completely changed. The law at one time only approved of sexual relations within marriage. Now it imposes penalties on those who discriminate against people who indulge in sex outside of marriage.

Recreational sex is commonplace and permanent sexual relationships are not considered necessary by many.

Into this relaxed and easygoing social world in which there seems to be fewer and fewer rules of sexual morality, the law makes intrusions which are often sudden and unexpected to many people. The merry alcoholic party can result in charges of indecent assault or even rape. The husband over-anxious for sex can be accused by his wife of rape and even convicted, whereas until recent years such an offence was impossible between husband and wife. Soames Forsyte today would be charged by Irene with rape. The foreman in a rough workshop where there is much swearing and lewd joking may find himself charged with sexual harassment, or at least permitting it. The employer who touches a pretty employee may find himself charged with indecent assault.

The law has tried to keep up with the revolution in social customs, and in particular to protect victims of sexual misconduct.

The problem is that it has created a situation in which false accusations can easily result in the conviction of the innocent.

But the real perils lie where young children are involved. That is the subject of the next chapter.

# 23

# Paedophilia

Paedophilia is a great social problem. It seems to be widespread and the consequences to child victims can be very serious. At the same time it is easy for an innocent person to be accused and convicted of paedophilia. This can also have terrible consequences for the rest of the alleged perpetrator's life.

Sexual offences involving young children are naturally detested by most people. In fact, quite an atmosphere of hysteria has built up over recent years, and this is understandable having regard to the extraordinary public revelations which have occurred, particularly in church circles. In such an atmosphere the conviction of an innocent man (women are very rarely charged) is not only possible, but is certain to occur from time to time.

When the rules requiring corroboration for sexual complainants were abolished, the same happened with regard to the evidence of child complainants. So it can happen that a previously morally up-right citizen can be convicted on the sole evidence of a child.

Unfortunately, in this area people tend to take extreme views. When the crusade against paedophiles commenced not so many years ago, so-called experts, social workers and psychiatrists seriously maintained that children making allegations of sexual misconduct never lied. Now it is said that they very rarely lie.

Any parent of young children knows that they do lie, probably more than adults, although very young children often confuse dreams or fantasy with reality. Why they should invariably tell the truth in one particular situation, but not in others, is completely unexplained. In fact children do lie in the area of sexual abuse, sometimes prompted by adults, sometimes of their own accord.

I have acted in a case where a young girl made a telephone complaint of serious sexual assault to the police against her father. It was later discovered that she was reading from a paper written out by her mother. There were family-law proceedings happening at the same time.

In another case of mine a girl of about 14 years of age accused her father of full intercourse every night for a year. Medical evidence seemed to confirm her story, referring to scarring of her genital area suggestive of repeated brutal sexual assaults. The girl was referred to a specialist who in a simple operation removed the 'scarring' which was in fact found to be a congenital defect. This defect made any penetration, as alleged by the girl, physically and completely impossible. The first medical report which had incorrectly referred to this congenital defect as scarring, supposing it to be from a brutal sexual assault, was typical of the enthusiastic support given to child complainants by so-called experts in sexual assaults.

In fact, having appeared in many paedophile cases, all the medical reports by the first examining doctors said that the examination was consistent with the child's story. Cross-examination would then ascertain that there were often no features whatever confirming the story. In two cases in which, according to the girl, full intercourse occurred, she was *virgo intacta*. Her hymen was intact but nevertheless this was said to be consistent with her story.

Since children are said to never or very rarely lie about sexual assaults, in Australia there is little or no local expertise as to why some do lie. On the contrary there is quite an industry on this in America where experts will purport to demonstrate that a child is lying.

For a while there was an absolute rash of allegations against fathers in the Family Court, and as a result many fathers were deprived of access to their children. Now I understand that such allegations are less common. Special court rules were introduced to deal with these matters, to avoid a situation where they became far too common a feature of parental feuding.

I was involved in quite a few cases where accusations concerned events that occurred over 20 years before, and I just recently read of such accusations concerning events that happened over 50 years before. The ordinary criminal law in New South Wales requires no limitation for charges for serious offences. Minor summary offences must be charged within six months and some special offences such as company offences have special periods, but charges for stealing, assault, rape, murder and indecent assault can be brought at any time. In this respect our laws differ markedly from the United States and the Code Napoleon in Europe.

Yet it is a fact that many of these very old charges were soundly based. Often the accused pleaded guilty. It is a feature of paedophilia that the victim may in fact say nothing for many years, and this has next to nothing to do with the truth of his or her complaint.

If a complaint is made promptly, the person accused may be able to prove an alibi or perhaps call witnesses who were in the vicinity. When the complaint is made years later, the accused person can do little but deny it. Effective defence is almost impossible. Sometimes children accuse their fathers after many years, and there have been cases where the father was in his eighties when accused.

I have said enough so far, I hope, to show that it is very easy for an innocent man to be convicted of paedophilia. Whereas for sexual accusations involving adults, juries are very careful, if not suspicious, in the case of children there is a readiness to believe the worst and convict on slight evidence. Who wants to put a paedophile back on the street? It is always quite likely that the jury will contain someone with extreme views about child abuse, unwilling or unable to grant that an accused might be innocent.

In such cases the accused can only hope for a hung jury. Such a fanatic will rarely join in a unanimous – as it must be – verdict of not guilty.

The frequent crusades against paedophilia can have dangerous consequences. It may be they bring to the surface matters which should not be hidden, and this is certainly a good thing, but they also put in mischievous minds ideas for fearful revenge against enemies, they encourage fantasies, and of course they prompt recovered memories.

There is an idea, still prevalent, that under hypnosis memory can be enhanced or recovered. In fact, hypnosis only produces confabulation. I know of no case where hypnosis actually produced a reliable new memory. Some years ago, quite a few police detectives did hypnosis courses and hypnotised witnesses for that extra forgotten memory. This occurred in Blackburn's case. Many a witness under hypnosis was asked to remember a car-registration number. I believe no hypnotised witness ever did come up with an accurate memory of a car-registration number.

However there have been numerous cases where psychologists used hypnosis for enhanced memory and then the subject came up with a memory of sexual molestation that happened years ago, often by a close relative, often by numerous close relatives. The entire recovered memory might involve factors such as witchcraft, blood, child abuse, baby murder, etc. There have been many recovered memories under hypnosis but I know of none that have been proved to be accurate. Most, I believe, were the result of conscious or subconscious suggestion.

The courts, here and overseas, have started to come down heavily on accusations based on recovered memories after hypnosis, or even after EMDR (Eye Movement Desensitisation and Reprocessing), a milder form of hypnosis based on eye movements. Now care has to be taken lest a witness's evidence becomes inadmissible because his or her mind has been muddled by questions under hypnosis.

Lost memories can be recovered through other means and the recovered memory may be true. I have seen this happen in court where a witness under cross-examination recovered, through the questions asked, a memory lost by hysteric amnesia years before. (Apparently some things happen which are too dreadful to remember and are therefore forgotten, and often they are never remembered. There was a woman who hit a cyclist in her car and could not recall it, even when charged with a serious offence. She never did recover her memory. This is referred to as hysteric amnesia.) Hypnosis in these cases is only likely to turn up a false memory by confabulation. Memory lost through concussion, traumatic amnesia, by and large seems to be irrecoverable.

In my opinion, paedophilia is an area where cranks abound, well-meaning people who snatch children away from perfectly innocent and respectable parents. There have been many instances of this. In New South Wales not so many years ago the Department of Community Services (DOCS) seized many children whose parents were members of the Children of God Sect. Ultimately the children had to be returned and compensation claims had to be dealt with. In England there have been quite a few cases of mass seizures of children by well-meaning public servants. Perhaps the most famous is the Cleveland Case resulting in the report of Lord Justice Elizabeth Butler-Sloss in June 1987.

According to this report one of the doctors concerned in a gigantic medical blunder regarding child sexual assault was a woman who seemed to become quite obsessed with the idea that children were being sexually abused, and she diagnosed many children as having been so abused. Another doctor supported her, relying upon what turned out to be an unreliable test based on anal dilatation. As a result, numerous children were diagnosed as having been abused anally. Place of safety orders were then made separating the children from their parents. In a period of five months, but mainly in May and June 1987, the two doctors diagnosed sexual abuse in 121 children from 57 families. These children were taken from their parents by one means or another, mostly by place of safety orders. Eventually nearly all the children were returned to their parents.

This and other similar cases illustrate how much harm can occur due to mistakes or fanatical accusers in this area. However, there is undoubtedly a considerable number of paedophiles in the community and their activities must be eliminated. On the one hand there are children at risk; on the other there are innocent adults who will be sent to gaol for lengthy periods as pariahs, not allowed to be visited by their own children, perhaps delayed parole because they refuse to admit guilt, then on release placed on a list of paedophiles available to various government bodies, a list liable to be leaked in the same way as most confidential government documents.

Any schoolteacher is at risk of a false accusation by a pupil, or more deadly, by a group of pupils. The risk may be quite considerable if the teacher has disciplined pupils. This is why teachers are advised not to touch pupils, not even to help them if they fall over. They are advised not to be alone with pupils. The same advice is given to choirmasters and scoutmasters.

Years ago, in 1942, I was doing an oral French exam for the Leaving Certificate Examination. As the dictation commenced I realised my fountain pen was dry so I could not write. Very distressed, I signalled a supervisor at this public exam; he was certainly a teacher, probably from a State school. He filled my pen and squeezed my arm in a friendly way to reassure me. I managed to catch up because his kindness in that friendly physical contact saved me from panic. I can still remember vividly that friendly man. Could he touch me like that today? He would be advised not to.

I appeared for quite a few teachers charged with indecent assault. Some were innocent, the victims of malice; some were foolish and their physical indications of affection for pupils had been given a sinister connotation; some were guilty, one terribly so, but he admitted it. I doubt whether many of my clients who were innocent were found to be guilty, but one cannot be sure. The evidence by which guilt could be found was by no means overwhelming. I secured quite a few acquittals and, by and large, I would say that innocent teachers would rarely be convicted if they had not been foolish – but that is hardly a satisfactory position.

Looked at from the other point of view, the activities of serial teacher paedophiles have been covered up and concealed, to the grave detriment of students in Catholic, Protestant and State schools. Some of the cases were horrific. I'd like to think that the headmasters and others who hid these offences for the sake of the school's reputation did not appreciate how bad and extensive the offences were. There have been suicides, quite a few, not merely of the offenders but of those who concealed what occurred. The consequences of paedophilia reveal many sad stories for everybody concerned.

I acted for many priests charged as paedophiles, and I was very successful in my appearances. I am not a Catholic myself but I am rather an Anglo-Catholic in my beliefs, and I sympathised with Mother Church in the crisis she had to face. Recognition of the crisis came slowly. There were priests who seemed to have been a bit foolish, rather stupid, who were thought to need psychiatric care after inappropriate sexual behaviour to children, but who offended again and turned out to be serial paedophiles. These days such persons would not have been treated so mercifully and foolishly as they had been then by the church hierarchy, but it is unfair to judge past actions with present knowledge.

Some priests – quite a lot of them – were falsely accused and were certainly innocent. In one case I acted in, the child involved was encouraged to misconstrue innocent events by malicious anti-Catholics. That priest was acquitted and I was relieved. He was undoubtedly innocent, but had indulged in perfectly innocent physical contact that today would be regarded as not merely unwise but extremely foolish. That this is so is a criticism not of the priest, but of the times.

Another was acquitted, who, in my opinion, was the victim of a desire to jump on the bandwagon and accuse priests (and claim compensation) when such accusations were fashionable.

There were several who may well have been the targets of revenge for the cruel canings that not so long ago were common in Catholic and Protestant Church schools alike. I think some ex-pupils realised that no one cared if they had been cruelly caned (unless they were incapacitated and could claim damages). However if a teacher – priest or otherwise – was accused of paedophilia, even if it were 20 or 30 years before, he would be arrested and charged, simply on an ex-pupil's word, without any corroboration.

Greg Walsh, a very enthusiastic and hard-working solicitor, instructed me in many of the cases I worked on involving Catholic priests. He was realistic but determined to see that no client would be wrongly convicted in the wave of prejudice against such clients. In this, he and his counsel were remarkably successful. Greg practised at Chester Hill in western Sydney, but his clients came from all over New South Wales. He is a dedicated man and he richly deserved the OAM he received in June 2002 for service to the law as a member of the Council of the Law Society, and a solicitor who ably acted for many and varied clients, mainly once-only defendants in criminal cases.

The person who makes a false accusation of paedophilia and gives evidence accordingly takes no real risk. There have been many false accusations and many acquittals, but, so far as I have been able to ascertain, no one in New South Wales has been charged for making a false accusation or giving false evidence in such a case. In Victoria, two girls were convicted of falsely accusing their father of sexual assault in order to help their mother in a matrimonial feud. They were girls in their late teens. They went to gaol, but, so far as I know, that case is unique.

If a teacher is accused of sexual indecency or assault by more than one pupil his position is very serious indeed. Yet it would be so easy for two girls, or boys, to decide to get their own back on a teacher for some grievance. In such a case the pupils would probably not appreciate the enormity or the consequences of what they were doing.

Children often behave strangely. It is, I think, a mistake to regard their evidence as completely reliable, or as reliable as the evidence of adults. Very young children can confuse imagination with reality. It is said children cannot have criminal intent under eight or 10 years of age. This is common sense. In older children who are still under 14, criminal intent, or the appreciation of wrongdoing, has to be proved. Yet evidence to ruin a man's life is often given by a girl younger than 10 years of age, and, even more deadly, by a mature girl of say 16 years of age as to what allegedly happened when she was eight years of age.

I recall a young girl of about 12 or 14 who was attending the school sports of a private school. She went to the toilet and claimed that a man was there and interfered with her. Police were called and a search made that went on for some time. Finally, as the girl was being questioned again, she broke down and said she made the story up. But why did she do this? The obvious answer is that she was attention-seeking, but who really knows the workings of an immature mind?

In years gone by, corroboration was essential to support a child's allegations, but this is not so now. Hence, some guilty men escaped the consequences of their actions in the past but now we take the risk of convicting the innocent.

For the guilty, the old need for corroboration was not an enormous safeguard. It was simply necessary to produce a witness who saw some suspicious movements and the accused was very likely to be convicted, particularly by an all-male jury whose members competed with each other to express their abhorrence of such conduct.

I had the experience of being defence counsel in such a case soon after women were as likely to be jurors as men, and on this particular jury they were either six or seven out of 12. I was impressed by the questions asked by the women jurors. It was obvious that they fully appreciated the presumption of innocence, and did not have to trumpet their horror of the alleged offence. Instead, they pursued systematically and intelligently the task they had, and I could tell this by their note-taking and their questions. They were a long time considering their verdict and the result was not guilty, not I believe because the innocence of the accused was obvious, but because in a difficult conflict of evidence there was a reasonable doubt.

This case taught me a lot, and thereafter I always hoped for an approximate equality of sexes on juries, particularly in sex cases. The simple fact is that the combined wisdom of both sexes is much better than the limited wisdom of either sex on its own. This is a lesson that I hope we are learning throughout the community, in politics, in companies and in the law.

I incline to the view that it was only because of women on juries that the abolition of the old safeguards in sex cases has worked out as well as it has. Women are less prone to accept without question the evidence of a child because she is pretty or because she cries in the witness box. Women do not have to reassure the world that they disapprove of the conduct alleged.

Of course, women themselves are not completely immune from allegations of sexual misconduct with minors. During my career I only struck one such case myself, and it came to nothing. The usual case is a woman having sexual relations with a boy under 16, the woman being often a schoolteacher. In most of the cases I have read about, the woman was acquitted, although I must say in at least one case she was lucky.

In England, a teacher who helped a young boy who had wet himself was accused of indecency. This is a reflection of the public hysteria about paedophilia. I think women teachers are wise to follow the same no-touching, no-being-alone-with-a-pupil rules that apply to male teachers. Complaints by boys are unlikely but are possible, and girls might accuse a well-meaning teacher of lesbian assault. However, complaints against women teachers do seem to have been much more common overseas than in Australia.

It does appear that the priests and brothers of the Catholic Church have comprised a surprising number of serious serial offenders here, in Ireland, in Canada and particularly in the United States. I wonder whether this has always been so but in the past has been successfully concealed. I rather doubt this. Perhaps the sexual liberty of modern times has tempted people with criminal desires to act them out, rather than control them. After all, both heterosexuals and homosexuals are now legally and socially permitted pretty close to full licence to do what they like. They can have sex on a first meeting, spouses can commit adultery, anyone can have multiple partners. Anyone who objects to sexual licence had best take care lest he or she infringes anti-discrimination legislation. Is it any wonder that those inclined to paedophilia no longer maintain the restraints of past years?

Certainly, although the Catholic Church has come out from the anti-paedophilia crusades looking bad, the Anglican Church is not in a position to throw too many stones, and I doubt whether the other churches have done very well either. The Catholics run many boarding schools and offences are more likely to occur in those circumstances. But there have been many, many offences by State-school teachers in State schools. I doubt whether the vows of celibacy taken by priests and brothers have been the causes of paedophilia to any great extent, if at all, as some people suggest.

However I do think that the prevalence and causes of paedophilia in schools are subjects desperately in need of careful unemotional research.

Domestic paedophilia with young children by family members or friends is a difficult area. No one familiar with the Family Court's history could doubt that many false claims have been made by mothers against fathers as part of the matrimonial feud and in order to deny the father custody or access. The charge does not have to be proved beyond reasonable doubt or even on the balance of probabilities. It is sufficient to prove that the child is at real or substantial risk. These allegations rarely result in criminal charges, but they have often had devastating effects in custody cases.

In one case with which I was familiar, and which received a deal of publicity, a father lost all access to his three children. Then as each was abandoned or rejected by the mother, they all came back to the father repudiating the allegations they had made, which they said had been made under pressure from the mother.

DOCS workers were apt to accept a child's allegations against a father despite the parents' denials, and required the mother to leave the father or lose her child, or even all her children. In one such case it ultimately turned out that the offender was not the father, but the daughter's sibling, protected by the daughter's lies.

If a child suggests he or she is being sexually abused to a doctor, social worker or schoolteacher, these professionals are then obliged to report it to DOCS. In my experience such reports usually lead to drastic action without sufficient inquiry. Certainly, many children have been removed from their family without anyone in authority even interviewing the allegedly guilty father. For that matter, the police, if they are called in — which usually happens after a report to DOCS — frequently arrest the allegedly guilty father without hearing his version at all. Of course, children need protection but the whole issue is affected by the basic belief by social workers and police that children never, or very rarely, lie about these matters. Once a child has made a complaint, even a suggestion, there is a tendency to press the panic button rather than to make a calm investigation.

No doubt many reports or complaints are well founded. Some are the result of suggestions made to young children by hostile spouses or sometimes well-meaning fanatics. I appeared in proceedings to reopen a case of a de facto husband convicted of indecent assault on his partner's young daughter (who was about 10 years of age at the time). The child had been excessively corporally punished by someone and was taken to a hospital by a relative for welts from the beating. A doctor believed that such cases normally also involved sexual assault (a doubtful proposition to say the least) and the child was eventually persuaded (despite her initial denials), to accuse her stepfather. Later she reversed her story, then before the trial she returned to her accusation and rather surprisingly the accused was convicted. This story of a child being persuaded, even compelled, to make such an accusation is far from rare. After the accused became a prisoner in gaol, the child was persuaded perhaps, or at least did, withdraw her accusation. On the appeal she came back to her accusation. There was obviously a reasonable doubt and the conviction was set aside and the prisoner released. But the court did remark that the zeal to pursue a sexual charge had meant that the person who had apparently flogged the child escaped his or her just deserts.

The much-publicised case of Frank Button, an Aborigine convicted of raping a 13-year-old girl in an Aboriginal community, also illustrates the point. The victim did not know who was the culprit. She accused Button as the result of suggestions made to her by various people. She was quite wrong, as DNA evidence later proved on appeal.

These two cases are both cases when decisions on questions of fact were reversed on appeal because of new evidence put before the Court of Criminal Appeal. It is easier to do this in criminal cases than in civil cases but generally such new evidence will only be considered if it was not available at the trial and could not have been found for the trial by reasonable diligence. In criminal cases decisive evidence clearly proving innocence will be admitted and considered in any event.

It may be noted that in Frank Button's case the identification, mistaken as it was by the child, was of someone she knew well, but it was dark. There is always the tendency by police and others to push an identifying witness into certainty rather than probability. Any adult is vulnerable to suggestion, but a child witness is especially so.

In 2001 Ian McEwan published his brilliant novel *Atonement* in which it is explained with great skill and perspicacity how a child's evidence, deadly in its effect, could convict an innocent man of rape. The child purported to identify, ultimately with dogmatic certainty, a person she knew well, but the glimpse was fleeting and in the dark. She was mistaken. The child was not the victim so there was no need for corroboration of her evidence.

An adult witness, doing his or her best, may well be inaccurate or completely wrong. A child would probably be less reliable than a mature adult, and this is more so if the child is young.

DNA evidence does provide certainty in rape cases as to the identity of the offender if any body substance can be found. Serial rapists have been known to use condoms to avoid detection by DNA evidence. Otherwise forensic evidence is rarely of decisive effect in paedophilia cases, especially as it is often the result of examination by a doctor who believes that all accusations of sexual offences are reliable.

If the decision in the case ultimately comes down to the child's word against that of the accused, the accused is in a perilous situation. As I have already said, there is a real chance that one member of the jury will fanatically support the child over the accused, whatever the evidence and, unlike in the United States, we have no procedure for examination of prospective juries. A normal jury is more likely to convict on the word of a child than on that of an adult making the same accusation, because no-one wants to put a paedophile back on the street. If the accused person is ugly, or has a naturally sinister appearance, and the child – male or female – is intelligent and presents well, then these circumstances may result in a conviction. A silly slip in words when answering a question could result in a conviction.

There is another type of paedophile. He usually preys on young boys rather than girls, but not necessarily so. He has studied the art of seducing children and maintaining their silence, so that he is rarely detected. His victims are often children of not so well-to-do families, and in simple terms he buys the child's affections to such an extent that the child will not give evidence against him. When the child grows up the man remains friends with him or her, but seeks another young victim. Often he is a member of a paedophile ring and sometimes discovery of the activities of one member of the ring leads to the exposure of others. When this occurs suicides are not uncommon because members of the ring are often well-respected members of the community. Some of these cases were exposed by the Wood Police Royal Commission.

Long before that Commission I had come across such a case in my practice. The police had carefully investigated the case, which was unusual. Apparently they had received some information, not from the boy's parents, and they did some observation work before the boy was brought in for questioning. After much pressure the boy made a full statement as to the offence committed on him by the offender, who was then arrested. The accused was granted bail on strict terms of no contact with the boy. Some time later the boy went back on his statement and refused to give evidence. The observations made by the police would have been strong corroboration of the boy's statement to them, but without his evidence the case collapsed. The alleged offender went free.

It is difficult to say how many of these paedophile rings still exist. In recent years quite a few have been more or less destroyed.

It might be noted that whereas one can lawfully buy and possess adult pornography, the possession of child pornography – 'kiddie porn' – is a serious criminal offence. This is so even if the pornography consists of images on a computer.

The Police Royal Commission advanced public knowledge of paedophilia considerably, but it is an area where research is quite desperately required, hopefully to assist in suppressing paedophilia, at the same time reducing the chances of convicting the innocent.

As to punishing the guilty, there are many who call for more and more draconian sentences. Some serial offenders have in fact been sentenced as severely as if they had been guilty of murder. A severe sentence does have the advantage of keeping a potential re-offender off the street, but severe sentences are limited in their deterrent effect.

When the death sentence applied to many offences, including simple theft and poaching, this hardly affected the level of crime. As Professor Radzinowicz pointed out back in the 1940s, the real deterrent is the likelihood of detection. A severe penalty hardly deters a person who believes he or she will never be caught. An increased rate of detection is much more likely to reduce paedophilia.

It must be appreciated that there are gradations and variations in paedophile offenders. There are brutal and violent paedophiles who may murder their victim to avoid detection. These are fortunately rare. There are serial offenders. There are rapists. Then there are those whose offences are mild in comparison with the others, some of whom are once-only offenders who were foolish. The courts are careful to differentiate and make the sentence, so far as possible, consistent with the offence and the circumstances. However, some politicians, looking for votes from the ignorant, advocate mandatory sentences of great severity. This is politics on a very low level.

I have appeared in many child-abuse cases. Quite a few were assaults, even manslaughter, without any sexual elements. Many were allegations of rape and indecent assault. Some were on boys, some on girls. Most involved cross-examination of children which is a very difficult art.

It is foolish to shout at or bully a child witness. The gentler the questioning the more effective are useful answers. But the position is very difficult for the cross-examiner. Inconsistencies and contradictions that would destroy the evidence of an adult are readily excused in the case of a child. A tearful little girl is a formidable accuser, even if her evidence is full of contradictions, even if her story seems highly unlikely.

I remember a little girl whom I cross-examined in a case where she was accusing her father of very serious sexual assault. She and her little friend, each about 12 years of age, were laughing and joking outside the court before they came in to give evidence that was to ruin a man's life. The judge thought this was not significant, having regard to the ages of the children. He was a good judge, but I disagreed with him on this matter.

In another case I cross-examined a child of about 15 or 16 years of age. Whenever I was getting anywhere she said she wanted a rest, which was always granted. While in the witness box she hugged a teddy bear. When the adjournment occurred, which was for about a quarter of an hour, she dashed outside and tossed the teddy bear to a policewoman while a DOCS social worker lit a cigarette for her.

The siren on the street, made up and wearing adult clothes, has been known to give evidence without make-up and dressed in school uniform.

These cases are hard to conduct for the defence. It is very easy to attract sympathy for a lying child by unwise or severe cross-examination. It is said that it is a great ordeal for a child to give evidence in such a case, and this is obviously true, whether the child is a witness of truth or otherwise. Every effort will be made by the judge or magistrate to put children at their ease and protect them from bullying or unfairness. This is only right and proper but in many cases the child witness is for these reasons more deadly and more invulnerable than an adult witness.

A magistrate can only hear the committal proceedings in these cases. A jury has to decide the case.

In my opinion, in many sex cases involving children it is simply impossible to say with real certainty where the truth lies. In such cases juries should acquit on the basis of reasonable doubt, and normally would if the complainant were adult. If the complainant is a child the position is much more uncertain.

Paedophilia is an important social problem requiring calm, unemotional research. Where there is a criminal accusation there should be thorough and careful investigation by the police, not to target a prospect, but to ascertain the truth.

There are terrible consequences for children who suffer as

victims of paedophiles, and there are terrible consequences for innocent adults who are subject to false or misguided accusations. Not least of the consequences of the crusade against paedophilia is the fact that physical contact with children by relatives, family friends, teachers, pastors and priests has been restrained and inhibited. It is a sad day when adults may fear to cuddle a child.

# 24

# Disaster on the Roads

Every year literally thousands of people are killed or shockingly injured by road accidents. Every barrister who practises in the area of common-law damages appears and advises in many tragic cases. I acted in many cases of persons whose lives were substantially ruined by a driver's mistake or stupidity.

Probably the greatest reduction of road deaths in Australia was produced by the introduction of random breath-testing and a legal blood-alcohol limit. Historically, police powers to test drivers who had had an accident or were driving erratically were only partially effective and drivers were, in many cases, prepared to rely on their supposed good driving and ability to hold their liquor if they chose to drink and drive. However when random breath-testing came in, the chance of being caught for PCA (prescribed content of alcohol), was quite high on the law of averages, so that many drivers simply did not drink too much before driving. The death toll on the roads came down quite dramatically.

This was a good example of the principle that the greatest deterrent is not a severe penalty, but the certainty or probability of detection. After random breath-testing commenced, any person who regularly drank over the prescribed limit and then drove was quite likely to get arrested and charged, even if he or she was involved in no accident, and drove competently. This caused most sensible people to be careful of drinking and driving.

At first the limit was 0.08 grammes of alcohol in 100 millilitres of blood, but it soon became 0.05 in Australia, although some American States still prescribe 0.08. The Australian limit rarely seems to encompass a person drinking moderately with a meal. In my experience it is very rare indeed that a person doing this would be 0.05 or over. Drinking sessions in clubs, pubs or at parties are the usual reasons for exceeding the limit.

There are still drivers who take the risk of substantial drinking followed by driving. If offenders are lucky they get home without being tested. Once they enter their own premises they cannot be breath-tested. This is the defence of 'home and dry'. If offenders are less lucky, they are breath-tested and fail the test. Offenders are then arrested, taken to a police station and tested on the breath-alyser machine. If they fail the test by being over the limit then they are guilty of the offence of driving with the prescribed content of alcohol. Depending upon the amount of alcohol in their blood offenders will be fined and suffer a suspension of driving licence. The procedure usually involves arrest and custody for some time before bail is granted by the station sergeant.

Once alleged offenders have been tested on the machine and failed, there are hardly any defences available to them. These cases involve pleas of guilty and the main object is to save the driver's licence, or at least keep to a minimum the period of suspension. If offenders are very unlucky, they will severely injure or kill someone in an accident. The consequence of that these days is very likely to be a gaol sentence, and often for a substantial period.

The point is that these drivers are equally guilty, whether they are caught or not and whether they are involved in an accident or not. The unlucky ones who have serious accidents go to gaol. In this area of the law, the punishment depends upon the consequences, rather than the guilt of the offender. (This is not the only part of the criminal law where the penalty depends on the result rather than the degree of guilt. A pub brawl can result in a fine if there are no serious injuries, but not infrequently there are unintended consequences. Sometimes a brawler may die and the assailant is charged with the offence of manslaughter. I have appeared in a number of these cases.) The guilt is equal usually, whether the injuries are trifling or tragic, but the criminal punishment tends to increase with the consequences, not the guilt.

For some years there has been a movement for alternatives to prison. These include binding over to be of good behaviour, community service, and weekend detention (periodic detention). The last-mentioned in particular can be a very severe punishment extending for as long as three years; that is, in effect, no weekends off, every weekend doing community work under disciplined conditions. One might think that these punishments should cover the most serious driving offences, particularly where the offender is otherwise of good character, as is usually the case. Surely the dreadful humiliation of gaol, which marks a person for life, should be avoided if at all possible.

However, parliament in its law-and-order exhibitions, the Director of Public Prosecutions and the Court of Criminal Appeal have succeeded in ensuring that where death results from the actions of intoxicated drivers the accused almost invariably goes to full-time prison for a period of two years or over. Five-year sentences are common. Such sentencing has been achieved despite the efforts of merciful, but also experienced District Court judges who well appreciate the devastating effects of gaol upon people who are otherwise of good character.

I appeared in many such cases. Often the accused was affected by traumatic amnesia resulting from the crash so that the punishment of a gaol term was inflicted on a person who had no memory of what had happened. In my experience a person who suffered a substantial head injury in a car crash usually remembered nothing between leaving the club, hotel or party, and waking up in hospital. There was no memory at all of driving the vehicle. This never seemed to worry those who imposed heavy sentences, but to me there is something horrific about a person of excellent character serving time in gaol, without having any memory of the events for which he or she now has to suffer for a period of years.

My PCA clients were often young men, sometimes with a promising life before them. But they were by no means all young men. I can recall successful professional men and businessmen. I acted for a great number of men. In this area women offenders were not so common and I can not recall acting for one.

One client I particularly remember was a very well-respected and highly successful businessman, a family man, who employed a substantial number of people in a large business. He made it his business to provide work for unemployed people. His last memory was of leaving a club, his next waking up in hospital and then finding out that he had had a head-on collision on the wrong side of the road. His blood test showed that he was well over the prescribed limit, in fact twice over 0.05.

I came into the matter for the purpose of conducting what we all knew would be a hopeless appeal. The appellant received some sympathy but his appeal was dismissed and his quite lengthy gaol term remained to be served. As a direct consequence his business collapsed and his many employees lost their jobs under circumstances where they were unlikely to find other employment. So was it worth it? Very few intelligent people would seriously maintain that a lengthy gaol sentence as against the loss of licence plus periodic detention would be a greater deterrent to potential offenders.

The ideas behind criminal punishment are that it acts as deterrence to others, it reforms the offender and provides retribution, sometimes called deserved punishment (who among us would like to receive what we deserve?). However, in actuality, criminal punishment is often becoming a case of revenge for the victim. We have reached the stage in recent years where the media – talkback radio, television and newspapers – seek out some relative of the dead victim to find out their opinion as to whether the sentence was punishment enough. Not unnaturally, it never is. The politicians think there are votes in clamouring for vengeance. It would be wishful thinking to believe that courts are never affected by this media and political outcry. There is no doubt that the punishments for death and injury on the road increased enormously over, say, the 1980s and 1990s, without in any way reducing the incidence of such offences.

Revenge is contrary to Christian teachings and, I believe, the teachings of many other religions. Yet now we encourage the victims – injured persons or the relatives of the dead – to clamour for barbaric sentences in order to find the dubious comfort of retribution. In truth the first exhilaration of revenge is usually followed by depression.

In the particular case I have been discussing, the offender was known as a person of moderate and sober habits. The intoxication of this one night was completely at odds with the way he normally lived. He was tired that night but it would have been completely out of character for him to drink to excess. Did someone spike his drink? There are plenty of idiots prepared to do this. In fact, it was done to me when I was a young man, and it could easily have led to tragedy in my case.

I could prove nothing for my client. He had no memory beyond leaving the club after some drinks with people whom he could not remember. Of those who were drinking with him no one came forward. I was helpless to prevent what may have been a terrible injustice. I never met him again.

That, I often found, was the regrettable part of a barrister's life. He or she learns a small but important part of the client's life and usually never hears of that person again. In many cases I have wondered what more I could have done. Successes pass by; failures haunt me.

Jack Thom, a famous solicitor, used to say that lawyers should be like doctors: 'Wheel out that corpse, send in the next patient.' I know that most doctors are affected by the deaths of their patients and I think most lawyers worry about their failures.

It is not simply a matter of learning from one's mistakes. Often cases went badly wrong without there being any mistake on the part of the barrister. Some causes were hopeless from the start. Some became so. However, when one has acted for a person, often a good, friendly person, and then sees him go off to gaol for one foolish but dreadful lapse as a driver, sleepless nights follow for the barrister. It was so in my case.

If an otherwise worthy citizen has to be punished severely for one act of unintentional selfishness or stupidity, surely in most cases periodic detention will suffice. After all, the offender's remorse will be a terrible punishment in itself. I have seen such cases often. In the case of several young offenders the remorse was quite overwhelming and required medical treatment.

If there has to be a gaol sentence, a full-time prison sentence, surely one year is more than enough punishment. Two years or more will almost certainly destroy the offender's marriage.

If a traffic offender has to go to gaol he or she should be confined in a special prison for traffic offenders. He or she should not, as is the case now, be vulnerable to rape and/or brutal assault by fellow prisoners. When embittered by the sentence, this type of prisoner should not be pushed into the company of dedicated criminals.

The politicians and many judges have no real idea what imprisonment involves. The desire on the part of those who mould public opinion for retribution intrudes into those cases where momentary inattention results in tragedy, but the courts are not so anxious – yet – to send these unlucky drivers to gaol. There is a clear distinction made between deliberate wrongdoing such as drinking or driving very fast, and momentary inattention.

I appeared for a petrol-tanker driver with an immaculate record sustained over many years who, it was alleged, went through a red light when returning to his depot at the end of his shift. There was a collision with a taxi in which two people died. An independent witness swore my client went through against a red light whereas he swore that the green light was with him and the taxi must have gone against the red light.

The jury obviously believed the independent witness beyond reasonable doubt and found my client guilty. The judge was merciful and my client received a bond. Of course, he lost his licence and his job. There was no appeal by the Crown. There was no public agitation on behalf of the victims, but this was quite a few years ago.

The jury's verdict was to be anticipated. Normally where there is a dispute as to what happened in a traffic accident, the evidence of an independent witness will be accepted to decide the dispute.

It would be rare for such a witness to lie, but he or she is as likely to be mistaken as anyone else. When one suddenly sees a giant tanker crash into a taxi with devastating consequences, one is subconsciously apt to believe that the tanker was to blame. In the confusion of a dreadful accident, one's recollection of the state of the traffic lights may well be wrong. The judge remarked, when imposing sentence, that my client certainly believed that he had gone through on a green light. I know the jury did its best and the conduct of the trial was immaculate, but there is the possibility that my client was right. An accident is sudden and in this case was horrifying. To say afterwards what happened may not always be easy. In fact, it rarely is.

Accidents – fatal accidents – can happen as the result of simple misfortune. I know of at least two cases of people being killed by drivers suffering a heart attack. In the law books the classic example is a swarm of bees attacking the driver, but I have never struck such a case. I have encountered, more than once, cases of epileptic drivers suffering a fit at the wheel, with dire consequences to others.

One of my last cases before I retired was for a driver who was driving at a moderate speed early in the morning. There was no possible suggestion of alcohol but she had a cold. She coughed and her car went across onto the wrong side of the road and struck two cyclists. One was killed, the other badly injured.

My client was acquitted on the basis that she suffered temporary loss of consciousness due to cough syncope, an unusual but known consequence of coughing. Usually the result of such an occurrence would be at worst a minor accident. On this occasion the result was tragedy. My client, to my knowledge never drove again after the accident.

The Crown pressed the case with some enthusiasm before the jury. However, it seemed to me that this enthusiasm was misconceived. No one suggested that there was anything reckless about the way she had been driving. The Crown disputed that she had lost consciousness. Even if that were so it was obvious that something made her lose control, and that was apparently the coughing. Was that dangerous driving for which she was to blame?

Many accidents have occurred because the driver has fallen asleep. If he or she knows that drowsiness is occurring, if the driving has proceeded for a long while without a rest, criminal consequences may follow from falling asleep at the wheel. However, the Crown rarely has much idea as to whether the driver had any warning of pending sleep, and convictions are unusual when this defence is raised.

Long car trips involve a real risk that is best avoided. Taking rests or meals on the way and rotating drivers are sensible measures but I have had a case of a dreadful accident occurring nevertheless. Husband and wife rotated the driving and rested while they took breakfast at a café. Soon after breakfast the husband went onto the wrong side of the road, killed two persons, injured himself and blinded his wife. Obviously he fell asleep, and the consequences were horrific. Yet, really in no way was he to blame. There must not always be a culprit for tragedy.

Alcohol or drugs, and excessive speed are probably the leading causes of serious accidents. Another cause which may well not be known to the police investigator is mental distress. For example, it is not at all uncommon for a spouse to leave home in a furious temper and drive away in the family car. Upset and distracted, such a driver is much more likely to have an accident. I had a case of a woman who left home in a fury after an intense row with her husband and collided with quite a number of cars not long after she left home. She was charged with numerous offences, principally with being under the influence of a drug while driving. This charge I successfully defended and she pleaded guilty to negligent driving and was fined.

There is a great deal of luck in these matters. This woman merely damaged other cars so did not bring the full wrath of the law upon herself. Yet she might well have killed somebody, even a young child, and been sent to gaol. Mental distress, such as that caused by domestic battles, and driving do not mix well.

People get surprisingly and stupidly angry when driving cars. I appeared in my first road-rage case back in 1952, led by the famous Jack Shand KC.

Our client had apparently offended some driver in the Burwood district and thereafter was pursued at high speed all around the district by a screaming maniac. Not unnaturally, when this had gone on for a very long time the victim, having failed to get away by increasing his speed, suddenly applied his brakes so that the other car crashed into his rear and became disabled. He then drove away. After quite a fight, on appeal the offence was found proved but, in the circumstances, no conviction was recorded. A conviction would have automatically suspended his licence to drive.

Much worse was a case from the Wollongong area in which I acted. There was the initial cause for offence which was, as is usual in these cases, obscure. Then an enraged middle-aged man indulged in a long, long process of provocation, mainly consisting of driving in front, slowing down to almost nothing, but swerving over to stop my client passing him. All the while insults were being shouted. Eventually the two cars stopped and the other driver rushed over to my client – who was a young man – and threw a punch at him. Naturally my client dodged and threw a punch back which connected.

The result was tragic. As I have known to happen before, the person punched lost his balance and fell backwards, hitting the back of his head on the road, and he died. My client was charged with manslaughter. Since most of these facts were verified by independent witnesses, the prosecution was eventually withdrawn.

The worst example of crazy road rage I encountered was my one-time client Neddy Smith who was in a vehicle with another man when the car behind flashed his lights, which was regarded as insulting. Neddy then, so the Crown alleged, attacked the light-flashing driver with a knife and killed him. He was convicted of murder. (I knew Neddy quite well at one time, when I pursued a legal point through the courts to the High Court and he was released from gaol in the late 1970s. He seemed a quite intelligent and reasonable man to me and he was polite and pleasant. Apparently he went crazy when intoxicated, as depicted in the television mini-series 'Blue Murder' although it is possible that he did not commit the murder but took the blame for someone else.)

Road rage seems to be getting more frequent these days. I was recently overtaken by a young girl on P-plates who was screaming with rage at me. I have no idea why. I said and did nothing in reply, which is a course I recommend in such circumstances. As I've said, I acted in many cases of persons whose lives were substantially ruined by stupidity.

# 25

# Of Police and Police Evidence

Few people would have had as much contact with police and the Police Department as I had over 57 years, first as an articled clerk and then as a barrister. I have acted for many policemen; I have acted for the Police Department; I have prosecuted and I have defended. I know many policemen; I have been friends with quite a few. I have seen the worst and the best. I have been involved with the New South Wales Police, the Australian Federal Police, the Northern Territory Police and the Australian Capital Territory Police. This chapter mainly concerns the New South Wales Police Service.

Sometimes one feels disgusted, and rightly so, with members of the police, and at other times one comes across acts of kindness and unselfish bravery. There have been some very fine police in New South Wales. I was privileged to meet Joe Ramus, one of our finest detectives in the 1930s and 1940s, whose careful and intelligent work made him quite famous. In 1951 it was my task to go through his immaculate police diaries, written in his wonderfully neat writing, a reflection of his careful mind. These were diaries for

1936 and were studied for the purpose of the McDermott Royal Commission.

In my early years at the bar I frequently appeared against police prosecutors, most of whom were friendly and courteous. I particularly remember Sergeant Don Goode, one of the ablest Police Court advocates ever, and a decent and fair opponent. He was a very tall man with an excellent court voice which carried easily to the far corners of the old Central Police Courts.

In those days, and until comparatively recently, police prosecutors did all the prosecution advocacy in the New South Wales Courts of Petty Sessions. Police prosecutors in training acted as court ushers. Gradually the feeling grew politically that police should not dominate the Courts of Petty Sessions, then known as the Police Courts. First the Police Court staff and the prosecutors discarded their police uniforms in favour of civilian clothes. Next the ushers were replaced by sheriff's officers, and then the Director of Public Prosecutions took over all committal proceedings for serious crimes. This was all the more desirable since committal procedural laws had become quite technical. Police prosecutors still act in summary matters decided by magistrates but they no longer dominate the Local Courts.

The police prosecutors varied in character and ability, but in my experience their standards were high in legal knowledge, in advocacy skills and in courtesy. There were exceptions but generally they were a credit to the force. When I was a very young barrister I received courtesy and friendship from many police prosecutors. I remember them as good friends. When I became a QC I think I went out of my way to be courteous and friendly to police prosecutors, particularly the young men. It was a debt I owed to my friends of years before.

The ordinary, general-duties uniformed police officer is likely to be a polite and helpful person to someone in trouble. By and large, the standard of courage of ordinary constables has been remarkable. But the police service and corrective services departments also have an attraction, beyond other occupations, for bullies and people who throw their weight around. There have been some nasty cases of police revenge bashing, where officers have been hurt, and there have been some cases of simple bullying. This has been very much the result of poor supervision by higher ranked officers. It must be appreciated that people are mixtures. A policeman who is a noted bully might be a hero in facing a criminal or in rescuing a civilian.

In my early days at the bar, police boys clubs encouraged good boxers to join the force, and in what were then the rougher suburbs of Sydney, such as Redfern, Newtown and Glebe (in which Police Courts I often appeared), young constables often had to earn respect with their fists on the street. There were plenty of lads ready to try them on. When 21 Division — a special squad made up of hefty policemen from all over the city — was formed to stop street bashing soon after the Second World War it was filled with the toughest of the tough. In no time the streets of Sydney were safe again, after comparatively few arrests and a lot of physical persuasion.

There used to be a police remedy for louts known as the 'Manly bond'. It consisted of a mild belting from the police, but no charges, no paperwork, and for the lout, no criminal charge and no conviction to haunt him in later life.

These types of police assaults and fisticuffs were tolerated, if not approved, in the 1940s and 1950s. The police themselves sometimes suffered casualties. I remember appearing for two ladies who had mauled the police very severely indeed with their fingernails in the back of a police car. When I saw the police wounds before court I advised my clients to plead guilty. They were not imprisoned. The police and the magistrate seemed to accept such assaults as part of the police job.

It was generally believed that most of the police bashings, as they were called, were more or less deserved by the louts and criminals, but sometimes there were bad examples of bullying and brutality. The community became very intolerant of things it might have overlooked before. Even the magistrates began to wonder about badly bruised defendants.

I remember seeing the photos of one man who had been given a tremendous bashing, with fearful bruises and welts the result, as evidenced clearly even in black–and–white photos. Yet the magistrate in that case accepted the police evidence that he had tripped and fallen against his cell door. So long as magistrates made decisions like that, police brutality would continue and increase. However colour photography became popular in such cases and police brutality became much rarer as a result; colour photographs of a badly beaten man are unanswerable. At the same time the standards of the magistrates were improving rapidly, resulting in better decisions that assisted in decreasing the incidence of police brutality.

21 Division soon lost its reputation for keeping the streets safe and acquired a name for inexcusable violence. Victims of police bashings, who at one time would have put up with it, brought actions before juries for assault. The community, which at first was content with only louts and criminals being bashed, gradually refused to accept any police bashings at all. After some delay most magistrates refused to make ridiculous findings to protect the police. Soon the police were being hounded by complaints that were not always rejected.

I remember a case I acted in that involved going through a very lengthy police file created after a most unattractive and provocative lout indulged in an orgy of provocation at a police station. It was difficult to say whether he had been the subject of a minor assault or not. Certainly he deserved it if he was hit, and I could not help feeling that the expensive investigation was a waste of public money, not to mention an unfair strain on a policeman who may have been provoked beyond endurance.

In cross-examination I was often in the position of attacking police. I was also often in the position of defending police against complaints. Then, and still, the complaint could be anonymous, whereas in most professions any complaint has to be in writing and signed. The complainant who does not have to disclose his identity should, in my opinion, not be heard. I believe he or she is not infrequently an enemy from within the police service. A police officer's lot is hard enough without having to endure anonymous complaints. I realise some might be justified but the evil of such complaints outweighs the advantages of investigating them.

When the police are vulnerable they, not unnaturally, stick

together. It is, of course, wrong for them to lie to protect their mates, but it is understandable.

For many years complaints against police were substantially futile and they got away with much too much. Now I think the pendulum may have swung too far in the other direction. For earnest young persons, as many police are, to have an unjustified complaint hanging over their heads for months or longer, is a big strain in a job that already has too many strains.

The New South Wales Police Internal Affairs Division has not distinguished itself. Rather, in many cases it has taken an inordinate time in order to reach dubious decisions.

In New South Wales there used to be an Internal Police Security Unit (IPSU), quite independent of Internal Affairs, whose main business appeared to be investigating alleged police corruption. Numerous officers were prosecuted on the word of criminal drug dealers, and many of these prosecutions came to grief after much distress to the police concerned. Since detectives were believed (perhaps with some reason) to be subject to corruption, IPSU was recruited from other police with little or no experience of criminal investigation. I acted in a number of cases involving IPSU. Their methods left much to be desired and their incompetence was notable. The unit was eventually disbanded 'unwept, unhonoured and unsung'. Their activities had done little good and much harm, but I give credit to those who formed them. They were genuinely trying to fight corruption, even if they were unsuccessful.

Corruption afflicts most police forces to a greater or lesser degree. Not so long before the British left Hong Kong the police force there was almost totally corrupt, and the New South Wales Independent Commission Against Corruption is partly copied from the Hong Kong Anti-Corruption Commission that tried to clean up the mess. American police corruption is notorious. New York's finest is a sarcastic name for the New York Police Department. The London Metropolitan Police and famed Scotland Yard have had their share of corruption. There have always been police in New South Wales who gave in to temptation in matters of soft crime such as gambling, prostitution and sly grogging. In these areas I doubt whether any police force in the world succeeded in maintaining integrity for a prolonged period.

By and large it is hard to maintain unpopular laws. Sometimes the local attitude to the particular law makes enforcement impossible: for example, trying to stamp out year-round two up in Broken Hill. For that matter, Thommo's Two-up School at Surry Hills was hardly opposed by the police.

I knew one lad who was there one night. The game was interrupted by the manager saying, 'There is going to be a raid so just wait out in the street; it will not be long. Anyone who wants to earn two quid by being arrested stay here.' My friend decided to earn the money. Soon the police arrived and the first words the sergeant uttered were, 'There are only 22, and you promised me 25.'

The manager replied, 'I'm sorry, you didn't give me enough time.' The sergeant proceeded with the arrests saying, 'Give your names, and make them short ones. We haven't got all night.' The prisoners then went off in the paddy-wagon and the manager followed in the police car with a bag of money to bail them all out. No one turned up next day at court and the bail was forfeited.

One of my clients was a Starting Price (SP) bookmaker before Starting Price became a government monopoly. (SP bookmakers lost most of their business when the government per the TAB took over the business.) He operated in a local suburban pub and had his usual station every Saturday afternoon. Off-duty police drank there and on one occasion he asked them to move away a bit because they were known to be cops and they were putting off the customers. Police protection served the SP bookie in two ways. He was not raided but any rival bookie was.

The gaming laws have always been rather farcical, an unholy compromise between placating the wowser vote, and seizing the gambling revenue for the State. In recent years the latter has prevailed over the former.

Since there has always been little public support for gaming laws, police toleration for, and unofficial regulation of, illegal betting did not provoke community protests. The same applied to prostitution and liquor laws.

Soft-crime corruption, in my opinion, afflicts all police forces to some degree, and I doubt very much whether New South Wales was any worse than other States and countries. Then came drugs.

The amount of money made by drug importers and dealers is quite colossal, tens of millions of dollars. Cocaine has been in Sydney off and on since the razor gangs of the 1930s and even before that. The main drugs of later years were at first heroin and cannabis, then amphetamines, ecstasy and large quantities of cocaine. The money available to bribe police became enormous. Furthermore, a successful raid on a dealer was likely to reveal large amounts of cash, very large amounts, and each such raid was a test of the honesty of the police officers who confiscated the money.

Long before the Wood Police Royal Commission of 1996–97 clients on drug charges complained to lawyers that a much higher sum of money had been seized than that revealed to the court. Worse still, the amount of drug seized was very frequently less than the defence client said he'd had. Soon it became fairly obvious that some corrupt police were selling back on the street not only the drugs not revealed to the court, but also the drugs exhibited in the case, which were not destroyed as required. I personally acted in a case where the drugs when first seized were mainly heroin, but cut with glucodin. Much later, after the committal hearing for the trial, a second examination was necessary because the analyst who had originally examined the exhibit was overseas. The ratio had become mainly glucodin with much less heroin.

I was amazed at how careless police were in the custody of dangerous drugs. At one time, when I was prosecuting, I found myself having custody of 35 grams of heroin in the form of pink rocks, when there were no police in court. One could see bags of cannabis in court, almost available for anyone to take a handful.

The corruption of the police over heroin soon led to corruption over other hard crimes such as armed hold-ups. Of course, there always were pockets of bent police. At one time it was in the company squad, at another it was in the motor squad. These were both revealed before the drug trade had become the enormous problem it is today.

Corruption has mainly occurred among plain-clothes police. The uniformed police have generally not had the same temptations as detectives. Occasionally a uniformed police officer has taken a bribe to overlook a traffic offence, even such as driving under the influence, but this was not, in my experience, very common. Several times I struck cases where police giving evidence with regard to traffic offences, even very serious ones, were 'fixed', but it was exceptional.

On one occasion I defended a detective charged with perverting the course of justice by interfering with the court papers so that a driver's bad traffic record was concealed and his misdemeanours were reduced in the statement of facts. The policeman was convicted and it is noteworthy that he was reported by the safety patrol officer who originally arrested the driver.

By and large I found that traffic officers were quite dedicated and incorruptible. They saw horrible sights after serious accidents and became crusaders against dangerous driving. One client of mine, a young man who may have done better in court than he deserved, killed a young woman. Shocked as he was after the terrible accident he was taken by a police officer to look at the consequences. I do not condone that officer's conduct but I can readily understand it. I also know of a number of instances of great kindness and compassion shown by police and fire-brigade rescuers at the scenes of accidents. I experienced this myself in my own car accident.

The strain on police officers dealing with dreadful accidents is very severe. From what I have heard they do not always get used to it. Nervous breakdowns occur from time to time.

I was saddened, but not very surprised, by the revelations in the 1996–97 Wood Police Royal Commission. Some of the officers were just rotten. Others I knew were, for the most part, decent, capable, and at times very brave men who succumbed to the temptations of the drug trade.

There were some cases in which I was concerned where men who were not corrupt were accused of corruption, because the so-called 'police culture' prevented them from exposing their bent workmates or colleagues. Many sacrificed their careers by lying to protect bad men.

I did find it surprising that even after the Wood Police Royal

Commission, the Police Integrity Commission has exposed so much corruption in Manly and other areas of Sydney's northern beaches. I suppose to some evil minds, easy money was irresistible, and their mates went along with it. I blame the superior officers. Any good supervisor of detectives should know what they are doing, and should have his or her ear to the 'grapevine'. Isolated acts of corruption are difficult to pick up, but serial corruption should be obvious enough.

As for the newer, younger detectives, I am saddened for their sake by what has occurred. The corruption concerning drugs has been so extensive that anyone who was ever involved in drug law enforcement might be suspect. However, I think fair-minded observers should note that detectives now are younger, less experienced, but probably better than some of the old hands who let down the service. It is not fair to blacken ordinary police officers with the disgrace that has befallen many detectives. There are many fair-minded, decent people doing a good job in the city and the country. The new regime has achieved some good results in investigating current crimes and some old ones.

As for the old detectives, they were able and solved many crimes. Some were corrupt. Many were foolish in protecting corrupt colleagues, but it is unfair to condemn all the old detectives. There were some very fine men among them.

I blame the magistrates and judges for many of the troubles in the police force, not so much those on the bench now, but rather those who sat in the past. At least one magistrate and one District Court judge in the past at their respective farewell ceremonies said that in a long career on the bench they had never known a policeman to give false evidence. Such statements reveal the stupidity of the speakers and the prejudice in favour of the police then common among many magistrates and not a few judges.

Promotion to the bench is a boost to the dignity of certain people in the legal community, and their enhanced dignities sometimes make them solid protectors of law and order. They notice with pleasure that the police treat them as superior beings, and in return they try to believe everything the police say in court. Furthermore, there are a few judges who regard defence counsel as persons paid to secure injustice because all persons before them are probably (or certainly) guilty. So the judge's duty is to obstruct the defence by coming to the rescue of Crown witnesses under cross-examination and by making various comments about the unfair methods of defence counsel.

Such judges are hopefully the exception, but they certainly have existed and still exist. Johnny Mortimer's judges in the *Rumpole of the Bailey* books were not fictitious. They were the product of bitter experience at the bar.

My experiences of anti-defence judges improved when I became a senior counsel, but I still came across them. However I must say that in recent years such experiences have been the rare exception. I have never struck these characteristics in a female judge. In the many cases I have had before women judges I was impressed by their impartiality and their efficiency.

I have noted before how magistrates have improved enormously with regard to their attitudes to police evidence, but for many years it was almost headline news for a magistrate to reject police evidence, let alone find that one was lying.

Thus it was that until very recent years convictions were often the result of a concocted confession. Sometimes the victim was in truth guilty. For instance, 'Chow' Hayes admitted his guilt for the Ziegfield Club murder at the end of his life, but only a naive person would believe (as the third jury did) that he would confess this to Inspector Ray Kelly, now long dead, and often referred to with contempt in the media today.

I knew Ray Kelly. He was a brave, capable and ruthless man. He knew that Chow Hayes was guilty. He had shot a man in full view of many not-so-respectable people in the Ziegfield Club. None of them dared to give evidence against the Chow. So Ray Kelly and his mates, according to Sammy Isaacs QC (later Mr Justice Isaacs) 'verballed' Chow Hayes with a fictitious oral confession. Today such a confession would not be admissible in evidence. Today a confession must be made on an electronic recording of the interview with a suspected person (ERISP).

Strangely, although the practice is old enough, I never heard the word 'verbal' used in connection with police confessions until

Sammy Isaacs QC used it in the Chow Hayes trials. Two juries disagreed. The third convicted.

Suspects were often persuaded to confess by police trickery or threats of violence. I heard of one foolish suspect who confessed to breaking and entering to steal because he was told that his fingerprints were found on a rusty barbed-wire fence. I had many a client in the old days who said that he had been bashed into signing a confession. For one such client I obtained leniency on the ground that he had readily confessed. The police could hardly say otherwise.

As I've just mentioned, photographs taken after release on bail, particularly colour photographs of substantial injuries, made it very difficult to bash a prisoner into confessing and then claim the signed statement was voluntary. There was need for something new. So there came into being quite a while ago now but well after the Chow Hayes trial, the record of interview. Verballing now became a skilled science practised very extensively by the Criminal Investiga-tion Bureau (CIB) and later detectives (as many have now admitted) right up until the ERISP law just about eliminated the practice.

The idea of a record of interview was that the exact words of questions and answers during an interview would be recorded on a typewriter as the interview proceeded. The suspect would then sign the record of interview and there would be an unanswerable record of what was said. However, since typing is laborious, compared to shorthand, it often occurred that the record left out asides and sometimes consisted of summary sentences rather than every word spoken. There were times when the record deliberately departed from the words used by the suspect and substituted incriminating words. Any police threats or persuasions would never appear in the record.

The suspect was supposed to sign but if he refused there was the record of what he was alleged to have said. Sometimes suspects did not sign, although admitting later that the record was correct. I found quite a few instances of this. More likely the unsigned record was a sophisticated 'verbal' containing either a bogus confession, or if not that, tying the suspect to a ridiculous story which made his defence almost impossible.

I have often heard the story from clients and others of how the police typed the false record in front of the accused, laughing as they put alleged words into his mouth. It was a very long time, however, before judges realised that seemingly fine upstanding policemen could do this. Now the practice has been admitted by many disgraced detectives but few, if any, have been prosecuted for the conspiracies, perjuries and perversions of justice involved.

Long before the Police Royal Commission I was told by an ex-detective how he was ordered by his superior officer to arrest a suspect and verbal him for murder.

The practice of verballing was the cause of slapdash careless investigations. Instead of doing the careful work required by a proper investigation it was easier to find out from a 'fizzgig', (an informer) who was supposed to have committed the crime, then verbal him. No doubt many of those verballed were believed to be guilty by the verballers, but, in my opinion, usually it does not take much to make a detective believe that someone is guilty. There was at least one case before the Police Royal Commission where the police were alleged to have verballed a person, knowing him to be innocent. No doubt there have been many others.

It cannot be stressed too much that the line between convicting the guilty on bad or insufficient evidence and convicting the innocent is very vague and indistinct.

Now the reforms of the ERISP law and Peter Ryan's reforms as to protecting crime scenes, collecting forensic evidence and generally carefully investigating have changed the picture completely. No longer do police stub their cigarettes on crime scenes. The said scenes are carefully preserved and examined. There is a Forensic Services Group in New South Wales presided over by Dr Tony Raymond, formerly of the Victorian Forensic Science Laboratory. The standard of detective work has improved enormously.

I should stress that verballing was mostly limited to detectives, in particular the armed-hold-up squad, the breaking squad and the drug squad. Company investigators of white-collar crime never verballed in my experience, nor did the Child Protection Agency detectives dealing with paedophile crimes.

Uniformed police rarely verballed. Traffic police used to write the defendant's words in a notebook at the scene of an accident and the defendant signed. For minor offences this procedure suffices under the new law. A breach report statement of the facts always contained what the defendant had said. In my experience these reports were fair and accurate.

Uniformed police usually gave accurate evidence. Deliberate lying on their part was unusual. In fact, country uniformed police, in particular, were almost painfully honest.

I believe that the post-Peter Ryan New South Wales Police Service is vastly improved from how it was before, in both honesty and efficiency. It was, however, a mistake to close small police stations. Friendly and frequent contact between the public and police is crucial to good policing. People should not be remote from the police. They should know them and want to help them.

Zero crime tolerance is bad policy. Tormenting people for minor offences only makes them hostile to the police, who should be regarded as friends. Setting quotas for traffic police so that traffic patrols become revenue collections is very bad for public relations and honest policing.

The new New South Wales Police Service has great potential. The old police force, despite recent revelations, did contain many, many fine people. Only a small minority deserve the shame of being branded corrupt.

The full picture of the service reveals much public service, and not a little heroism. I am optimistic as to the future, but a great deal depends upon the commissioned officers. In the past these officers have let the service down.

There are numerous prescribed inspections and supervision exercises conducted in police stations by inspectors and superintendents, but in my experience these tend to be formalities. This was revealed in the Blackburn Royal Commission.

There used to be a procedure – there probably still is – whereby inspectors went from station to station inspecting. Each inspection was noted. In the not-infrequent cases where a prisoner alleged he was bashed, or a prisoner died, the inspector's visit was noted in the record, but according to the records nothing undue had been observed.

For many years promotion was strictly on seniority, subject to passing the sergeant's exams. Then it became a merit system, but it seems there have been some weird promotions of those who were in favour. Inspector Thornthwaite in the Blackburn case had been promoted twice on the same day. Some very experienced and able detectives never passed the rank of sergeant.

These days the very high ranks have done courses in such things as management and personnel, but so far as I can see they are still blind to what is going on at the coalface. The Manly and northern beaches police scandal illustrates this.

I often noticed how there was a constant stream of instructions and directions, not to mention regulations, flowing into the police stations that were duly put up on the noticeboard and sometimes, perhaps often, completely ignored. I certainly noticed a top-heavy administration in which numerous officers had to see and initial documents, but no one seemed to do anything. A file from Internal Affairs is a revelation of bureaucracy gone mad.

I suppose there have been many business-efficiency inquiries into the police service but without much success. The Blackburn case showed how everyone could see, supervise and initial, yet no one knew what was going on. That seems to have been the story in Sydney in the case of the police of Manly and the northern beaches.

Good reform usually proceeds from the top. In this regard there has been a lot of shuffling chairs in recent years but, as the problems at Manly, the northern beaches and Cabramatta showed, those at the top of the police service still do not know what is going on.

# 26

# Deciding the Facts

Some cases involve only questions of law. Others involve both questions of fact and law. However the vast majority of cases are decided solely on the facts, with no dispute as to the law applicable.

It is not only in criminal cases that so much depends on questions of fact. Even in giant commercial cases there are invariably disputes as to the facts, in particular what was said by those involved.

Photostat machines and computer printers used in modern legal practice generate enormous volumes of pages, some of which contain information that is truly relevant to a commercial dispute, some of which is conceivably relevant and most of which is superficial. All of it is wheeled into court in big folders on numerous trolleys. It is unusual for the parties not to expend much time and money on discovery proceedings aimed at producing still more paper. The result is that only very large purses can withstand the ravages of commercial litigation. An ordinary individual or a small company has little chance of justice against a mega-company. They will be financially ruined by the interlocutory preliminaries, long before there is a hearing on the merits.

Of course, big companies do not complain about a situation where they can bully small companies and individuals in court proceedings. Even so, when the mega-companies quarrel with each other they very often go to mediation to avoid the enormous expense of commercial litigation.

The judges who sit in commercial cases tend to be the one-time geniuses of the bar who earned large fortunes being briefed by mega-firms of solicitors retained by the mega-companies. In much of the commercial litigation in which I appeared I was instructed by the State so I was not particularly concerned about costs mounting absurdly. If I appeared for a small litigant I usually managed to settle. However I was often left with the nasty impression of a court for the wealthy and manned by the wealthy in which the little persons were completely out of their depths. I sometimes wondered whether the judges had appeared much for the smaller players when they were at the bar.

Let me illustrate. I was appearing for a woman who should have been a wealthy widow but the estate was tied up by litigation and by the demands of the State for death duty. As a result, the woman was literally almost penniless. When I pointed this out to the presiding judge he simply replied that the executor had his executor's year to make arrangements. By law no one can sue the executor until he or she has had a year to sort things out. It was useless to point out that this trite comment on obvious law did not put food into the widow's mouth. In the equity and commercial courts the ghost of *Jarndyce v Jarndyce*, the never-ending suit in Dickens' *Bleak House*, still lurks along the corridors.

Meanwhile, trolley after trolley of dubiously relevant documents are wheeled into court, lengthy affidavits are argued ad infinitum as to admissibility of evidence, applications for discovery and production of yet more documents proceed drearily from day to day, interspersed with lengthy written submissions by counsel. Eventually the case resolves itself into numerous issues and proceeds from week to week in cross-examination, legal objections, and so on. That costs per party can run into the millions is not surprising.

Even in that sort of litigation the case is as often as not decided on who is believed as to the conversations between the parties. It is, in fact, surprising how enormously important a few words can be between senior company officials. I can remember one quite recent case where tens of millions of dollars depended on a telephone conversation.

How does one decide the true facts in such a case? The persons speaking may or may not have made notes soon after. Contemporary notes are valuable, but often record the conversation as desired by the speaker, rather than as it actually occurred. This does not mean the notes are dishonest, but merely that people often have very faulty immediate recollections of what was said and tend to believe what they want to believe.

Of course there are the not-so-honest witnesses who doctor their notes or diaries. In one case I was faced with a business diary recording conversations very different from the account in my instructions. Normally such a diary would win the case for the opposition, but I was able to point to significant indications of concoction, and we won. It is actually quite difficult to concoct a business document in a foolproof fashion. I remember one client of mine whose takings book for a shop had been concocted using the wrong year's calendar!

However, the normal conflict in a business conversation is between reasonably honest people who quite genuinely only recall a version that favours their side of a dispute. How then does a judge decide who is giving an accurate account of what was said? Sometimes there are documents that record what was allegedly said. Often there are documents and events that provide a context for the disputed conversation. The judge (there is no jury) has to decide on the probabilities.

Courts of Appeal and the High Court of Australia frequently talk about the inestimable advantage of the trial judge in that he or she observes the witnesses in the witness box. If that were so, one would expect quick judgments based on the impression formed by the judge of the recently heard and observed witnesses. However, in big litigation almost invariably judgment is reserved and the transcript of the evidence is obtained and pored over by the judge in chambers. After a few weeks, any impression gained by seeing and hearing the witnesses tends to fade away. Yet cases are usually reserved for some weeks, not unusually months.

As I have probably made clear already I do not believe that seeing and hearing a witness is of as much assistance in assessing his or her evidence as is claimed by the Superior Courts of Appeal. The demeanour of a witness, if carefully studied, is often more likely to lead to error than enlightenment.

Some witnesses are nervous. They look very unimpressive in the witness box. But the witness who appears to have 'something to hide' is likely to be a perfectly honest person as nervous of a court as of a dentist's chair, and probably with good reason.

Some witnesses are confident. This is particularly so with witnesses with much previous experience of business litigation who know just how to impress a judge. They give the evidence in direct speech purporting to state the exact words spoken in a conversation, and they watch the judge's writing hand so that they do not go too fast for the judicial notes. They exude respectability, decency and reliability. In fact, they are exact replicas of good confidence tricksters and are usually quite indistinguishable from such criminals. In 52 years of experience at the bar the best witness of conversations I ever saw and heard was a crooked developer. He was even better than the police verballers of the bad old days.

Some witnesses are inarticulate or at least careless with words. They may be perfectly honest and have accurate recall, but they make silly verbal 'slips' in the witness box, and for that reason are often disbelieved.

Some witnesses are maddeningly slow to come to the point and can drive a busy judge to distraction. Yet ultimately they are honest and accurate.

Some witnesses, particularly expert witnesses, are conceited, often to a most irritating extent. Yet they are correct in their views. It is by no means unusual to find that the geniuses of this world are by no means pleasant or amiable.

Numerous experts earn good livings in the courts by giving their evidence pleasantly and simply so that everyone can understand it and believe it, even if it is wrong. Many years ago a collision between ships on Sydney Harbour resulted in a wrong judicial decision (in the famous case of the *Greycliffe* and the *Tahiti* in the 1920s), largely because the experts for one side were difficult and conceited.

The study of a witness's demeanour in the witness box is often a cause of error because the judge comes to dislike the person. From dislike to disbelief can be a short step indeed. If we are honest with ourselves we realise that some people appeal and some repel, and often there is no reasonable or logical explanation for the differences.

The demeanour of a witness can reveal bias, anger, sorrow, even love. In particular, a careful, experienced judge may detect feigning of mood or feelings. Yet the judge must exercise great care lest the witness be misjudged because he or she is unattractive in person or manner, or otherwise does not appeal as a person to the judge. In the case of the ordinary witness, study of demeanour may be useful, sometimes very useful, but it is well to appreciate that reliance on demeanour is as likely as not to lead to error. It is wise to remember the words of Lord Justice Atkin, a notable English judge: 'An ounce of intrinsic merit or demerit in the evidence, that is to say the value of the comparison of evidence with known facts, is worth pounds of demeanour.' In the case of expert witnesses, except in the case of a deliberate liar, study of demeanour is probably a useless distraction more than likely to lead to error. A witness should be judged as a witness. It may be necessary to assess the witness as a person in order to form a judgment as to his or her reliability or veracity but the process of witness assessment by demeanour is much more difficult than many people think, and very likely to lead to error.

Demeanour is an untrustworthy guide in courts and in ordinary life. I know of a judge with great faith in his ability to perceive demeanour who in his non-judicial life fell for a confidence trickster, much to his cost. Confidence tricksters make excellent witnesses. They usually have perfect demeanours.

Assuming, however, that demeanour may indicate whether the witness is honest, so what? Most witnesses are. The real problems are the subconscious bias of the witness, the ability of the witness to recall events accurately, and the ability of the witness to translate his or her memory into accurate language in the witness box.

The study of the witness speaking in the witness box will rarely give as good an aid to the judge as the quiet study, in chambers, of the printed transcript of evidence.

Discovering a judge's likes and dislikes is often not very hard, even on one's first appearance before him or her. Evidence can then be slanted; for example, the fact that the witness is a keen rugby union player sometimes intrudes into the story of a business conversation being recounted in evidence. For years after the Second World War, the wearing of an RSL badge was considered to be a witness asset.

Frequently witnesses are accused of lying, in my opinion too frequently. The differences between the recollections of honest witnesses can be very great. It happens every day in the courts. Only rarely is the witness giving evidence of something that he or she took pains to note and remember accurately at the time.

However, the simple fact is that most witnesses are biased. The parties want to win and their witnesses tend to join the cause. When one wants a party to win, one's memory is affected. This is not a question of dishonesty at all; one's memory just tends to be swayed by one's loyalty.

Take the typical case. Good old Bill leaves the club with his mates after being there some hours and he has a motor accident. These days his blood-alcohol level will be measured with some accuracy. But before such scientific aids Bill's sobriety was decided by the evidence of witnesses. Those in his car would say, 'He'd had one or two but he was quite sober'; 'He only had two drinks all night'; 'I would not have been his passenger if he had been at all affected'. Those in the other car would say he was 'staggering, slurring his words and reeking of alcohol'; 'blind drunk'. All would believe he or she was telling the truth.

Of course a total abstainer who believes alcohol is the work of the devil is likely to draw more extreme conclusions from the situation than one of Bill's drinking mates.

We have an adversarial system in our courts, as distinct from the inquisitorial system in France and in Europe generally. The latter purports to inquire into what is the truth. The former simply balances the evidence on behalf of one party against that on behalf of the other, even in criminal cases. Thus it is that in the adversarial system the parties choose who are to be witnesses and each side's witnesses tend to be part of that party's team or cause. A party, with rare exceptions, cannot cross-examine his or her own witnesses.

In Royal Commissions we more or less copy inquisitorial procedures, and there is no doubt that a Royal Commission gets much closer to the real truth than an ordinary court case following adversarial procedures. But inquisitorial procedures are very expensive, at least in our experience with inquiries. Just how well they work in Europe is a matter of some controversy.

The simple fact is that witnesses on controversial parts of the evidence are very likely to be biased on behalf of the party calling them to give evidence. I doubt whether many judges, and the witnesses themselves, realise this. Most bias is subconscious.

I have had the experience of giving disputed evidence several times. I found myself mentally on the defensive with myself. Was I trying to push my cause, or the cause I was supporting, or was I telling the plain unvarnished truth? When one is attacked in cross-examination one naturally goes on the defensive. Is the truth completely unaffected?

My advice to witnesses was to understand the question and answer it correctly. Do not try to do more. It is good advice but hard to follow.

Peter Cabban in the second *Voyager* Royal Commission answered questions by imagining in his mind that the events were happening again, and answering the questions from what he was mentally re-enacting. This is a good model for a witness to follow.

However it is very difficult to eliminate bias from evidence because it is largely subconscious. Quite apart from bias, memory is a faulty faculty of the mind. Numerous tests have shown that if a scene – for example, a fight – is enacted specially before an audience of intelligent students who know that their recall is to be tested, there are still vast differences between the witnesses. How much more is this so when a person suddenly confronts a situation and then is asked to recall what happened; for example, how fast one car was going, what colour that car was, whether or not it braked, and the same for the other car. I have been driving for over

50 years and have had occasional accidents, all but one minor. I have tried to reconstruct the events for an insurance claim form with very great difficulty, and not the desired accuracy.

Car accidents are often the source of litigation that is frequently decided by the evidence of an independent witness. I remember one case I had where I thought I was on a winner with the right-hand rule clearly in my client's favour. Yet unknown to me there was an independent witness working on a church roof at the intersection and he said my client was driving much too fast. He was a volunteer church worker, obviously honest, with a bird's-eye view of the accident. We lost, probably rightly so.

Yet many an independent witness is very unreliable. Most accidents happen in a flash and it is easy to get a false impression. Furthermore, it is human nature to garnish the story when one is the crucial witness who is going to decide the case.

Most judges grab for the independent witness as a means of solving their problems. But that witness may easily be a bent reed.

Some witnesses are just difficult. Doctors earn big money from accidents, but often resent being called to give evidence for injured plaintiffs. I learned long ago not to ask such a witness whether the plaintiff had suffered much pain. The answer would be that appropriate drugs had dealt with that problem. No, the proper course was to leave it to the defendant's counsel to suggest that the analgesics had substantially eliminated the pain. The doctor would vigorously reject the proposition and say that the plaintiff suffered a great deal of pain. The witness had to contradict someone. So let it be counsel for the other side.

Quite a few witnesses try to be smart. What lawyer has not been bored witless at some social event by the layman who gave evidence in a case (only one, thank goodness) and confounded cross-examining counsel? Being smart is usually a path to disaster against good counsel. As an advocate, I quite frequently let such witnesses take charge of proceedings and dominate me. In no time they would say something extraordinarily stupid and they were able to destroy their own evidence.

To return to demeanour, how does demeanour help in deciding beween an ugly man and a pretty girl? I lost faith in the accuracy of legal fact-finders years ago and one case which helped to clear my thoughts was between my client, a very ugly man, and a pretty socialite woman for whom he had done some contract work in her luxury home. The contract was verbal. The case depended on who was believed as to the terms of a conversation. It was obvious that my client had no chance, none whatsoever, not because he was a liar or a fool, but because he was ugly and spoke with a thick accent and his opponent was a pretty socialite woman.

Some time later I appeared again before another judge in a motor accident case. He was noted for always finding for the plaintiff, but this time he found for my client, the defendant, a pretty girl from a leading socialite family. It was not due to any skill on my part.

Cross-examination is both negative and positive. Negative cross-examination is aimed at destroying the effect of the witness's evidence. Positive cross-examination seeks evidence from the opposing witness in support of the cross-examiner's case. In one commercial case I acted in I had worked back the night before an appearance with my junior, Rodney Parker (now QC), planning a positive cross-examination of the defendant's managing director. Next day I took the witness gently, even deferentially, for he was, after all, a great man. In half an hour he had built our case up to an impregnable edifice and destroyed his own. He probably still thinks how clever he was to have told the story his way.

For negative cross-examination the most important thing for cross-examining counsel is to watch for the unusual, or for the inconsistency. It is surprising how often it is there, if one has the necessary experience to recognise it.

Identification witnesses are in a class by themselves. They have been, and continue to be, the cause of many injustices. To recognise a person again, when he or she was a stranger and seen only for a short time under conditions of stress, is hard enough. To be sure that one is right is harder still.

These witnesses are honest. In all my experience I have never heard of a dishonest identification witness. However, those useful to a prosecution case are almost invariably biased. They see themselves as important members of the Crown team, as key witnesses, and they put their best foot forward. To concede the slightest doubt as to their identification of the accused would be to let the side down. Furthermore, it would let the witness down because no one likes to be wrong.

The police build on this. They take a witness gently, then flatter him or her, congratulate the key Crown witness on whom everyone depends to put a dangerous criminal away, and in no time hesitation gives way to certainty, and nothing will shake the witness.

I particularly remember a bank clerk who was absolutely, completely and unshakeably certain that the defendant was the malefactor. He was conclusively proved to be wrong.

How does one assess the reliability of an identification witness? His or her demeanour might indicate that the witness is dogmatic, short-tempered or nervous, but none of these things help much in judging the accuracy of an identification.

The old Criminal Investigation Bureau (CIB) of the 1950s (and earlier) trained detectives to recognise faces and build and describe them so that others could make an identification by description. Every morning there was a prisoner parade at Central Police Station so that detectives would be able to recognise known criminals. Detectives with this knowledge were very useful at race meetings and public gatherings. They had a skill way beyond that of most laymen. The ordinary witness usually finds it very hard to describe the characteristics of some person he has seen. This is a good illustration of the difficulty a witness may find in translating an accurate recollection into words.

It is an interesting mental exercise to try to describe in words the appearance of someone you know very well, such as a spouse, a parent or a sibling. The usual words depicting colour are often quite inadequate to describe hair or complexion. In fact, we tend to recognise people by the expressions on their faces, and these expressions are extremely difficult to describe.

A sensible, reasonable person would rarely give a positive identification of a stranger seen only for a short time. Such a witness would at the most say that the person seen resembled the accused, or even that he or she was probably the accused. The police and the judges want more than that. They want a positive identification and it may well be that only a foolish person would make a positive identification in the circumstances. A line-up identification is not all that convincing since it is unlikely that anyone else in the line-up resembles the accused. Furthermore, sometimes the witness has seen a photo of the accused before the line-up, and in such a case he is really only identifying the person in the photo.

Yet the witness may well be right after all. On 4 June 1962 James Hanratty was hanged in England for murder. A bad case of rape followed the murder of the victim's boyfriend and the conviction of Hanratty was founded to a considerable extent on the unshakeable identification made by the victim. Hanratty's family long after his death pressed for the reopening of the case and many people assisted in acquiring information likely to set aside the conviction in the Court of Criminal Appeal. Advances in DNA profiling enabled the Crown to prove that the vaginal swab from the victim had the same DNA as James Hanratty, whose body was exhumed to make the comparison. His guilt was conclusively proved after all.

Yet in the Blackburn case at least one victim made a mistaken identification in similar circumstances, although her friend was not killed.

DNA profiling has brought a lot of rapists to justice, and it has exonerated men who were suspected in error.

Another category of witnesses is those who observe brawls or assaults, often in pubs. Pub brawls can lead to serious charges, even murder as in one case of mine. For too many people, consumption of alcohol means no control of temper.

With the best will in the world it is hard to say who started a pub brawl and whether a blow was in self-defence or in attack. These things can happen so suddenly: one moment there is laughter and goodwill, the next there are angry voices and blows.

Any witness of a pub brawl may well be affected by alcohol, be a friend of one of the participants, or be a person with poor powers of observation. If a friend of one of the participants, the witness is certain to exonerate the friend and blame the other party. This is not lying. In a confused situation people believe what they want to believe.

The fact that many witnesses blame one person may mean that the person was in fact the aggressor, or it may mean that he was drinking with people who were friends of his opponent. Often the witnesses side in equal numbers with each participant of the brawl, and the truth is almost impossible to ascertain.

I remember many years ago appearing before a very good and acute magistrate, Mr Cocks SM. I was appearing for a bar manager accused of hitting a customer. There was no doubt that the customer was aggressive and nasty under the influence of alcohol. He had been barred several times from the same hotel. There were plenty of witnesses from nearby who said that the customer slipped and fell when trying to attack my client. One of these witnesses was the local licensing sergeant of police. I seemed to have a strong case.

However there was one drinker who from some distance away saw my client hit the customer. 'It was a little beauty of a punch; it only moved less than a foot.' To knock down someone with a fist that only moved less than a foot was some feat, even if the victim was drunk. The witness was obviously favourably impressed. He was quite impartial, in fact admiring my client's pugilistic skill. He was believed over many other witnesses and I have no doubt that Mr Cocks was, as usual, correct in his finding of guilt.

I very much doubt whether the other witnesses, apart from my client, were lying. They liked the manager and detested the victim who was a noted troublemaker, but they did not lie on my client's behalf; they missed seeing what they were not meant to see.

Provocation is not a defence to a charge of assault, even though it may reduce a charge of murder to manslaughter. That was the case in one pub brawl case in which I appeared. The insulter was attacked by my client (according to the jury's finding) in circumstances of extreme provocation. Although the blows were only struck with fists, the victim, as too often happens, fell against furniture and suffered fatal injuries. My client was convicted of manslaughter. Everyone involved was well under the influence of alcohol. It was a typical pub brawl which resulted in unintended tragedy.

From time to time some judge decides to bestow the epithet of 'deliberate liar' on a witness. No doubt this should be done at times but great caution should be exercised. Very often the witness is simply foolish or careless. Sometimes he or she is actually telling the truth.

I think the public flatters the courts and the courts flatter themselves as to their ability to discern the truth. I remember one Court of Appeal judgment (reversed in the High Court) where a judge saw no particular difficulty in a jury deciding between a father of good character and a young daughter who accused him of sexual assault. In fact, the first step in reaching a correct decision in such a case is to appreciate the difficulty of the task. Judges who imagine that they have an intuitive sense as to who is telling the truth flatter themselves and are often wrong. It is surprising how often the intuition is in favour of the Crown in criminal cases.

In some of the worst past cases of untrue Crown evidence – for example, the IRA cases – it is worth remembering that the presiding judges urged the juries to convict. The position is not that different in various false-evidence cases recently exposed in New South Wales.

For myself I am horrified by the ease with which some courts can rush into error in deciding disputes as to the facts. Good judges know this and proceed with care and caution.

It is to be hoped that in many cases forensic evidence may provide a sounder basis for decisions as to facts than judicial intuition. DNA and other less spectacular inventions of recent years have served to reveal many past errors, and hopefully will assist in much more accurate fact-finding in the future.

The Royal Commission into the Police Service as well as the Police Integrity Commission have exposed numerous 'verballings' and 'loadings' by police witnesses. We should remember that in nearly all of these cases the police were believed 'beyond reasonable doubt'. The law has no magic means of detecting clever liars.

In criminal cases the truth at times emerges later, sometimes long after the hearing. In civil cases this happens much more rarely. In fact it is very difficult to reopen a civil case. One wonders how many litigants suffer grave injustice because of mistakes made in deciding the facts. I know that the number is not small.

Some progress has been made recently in establishing rules which provide some safeguards in the case of expert forensic evidence. Ample notice must be given of the expert's report which must set out the facts on which the opinions were formed and the reasons for the opinions. The National Institute of Forensic Science (NIFS) has done much to improve standards in government laboratories.

However, the fact remains that many mistakes are made in finding the facts in both civil and criminal cases. This is well illustrated by the wrongful convictions recently discovered in the United States of persons on death row (over 100).

Our Appeal Courts have done very well indeed in deciding questions of law, but the mechanisms for correcting errors in deciding questions of fact in civil and criminal cases are few and inadequate. Our great lawyers tend to become hopelessly involved in abstruse and difficult questions of law. They tend to regard questions of fact as unworthy of their attention. One superior English Court of Appeal actually said as much, but many years ago.

The process of fact-finding in the courts is not well understood, under-researched and calling for improvement. Hopefully new, fresh minds in the law, perhaps those of women in particular, will effect substantial improvements.

# 27

# Expert Evidence

Where a person has special knowledge or skill beyond that of ordinary members of the community, he or she may be permitted to express expert opinions as to matters arising in litigation. The usual examples of people called as expert witnesses are doctors, dentists, engineers, surveyors, scientists, accountants and other professional men and women who acquire their special knowledge in universities and in professional practice. Some branches of expertise may be self-taught, as for example Mr Bruner in the Chamberlain Royal Commission who had made a special study of animal hairs and was able to identify an animal from the hairs that it had shed. In the particular case of the Chamberlain Royal Commission he identified dog hairs in the Chamberlains' tent.

Ballistics and handwriting evidence are often given in criminal cases. Particular skills in these areas are acquired by special training and experience, usually in the police force, but there is a modern tendency for both skills to be acquired by qualified scientists.

In recent times, a great deal of attention has been paid to expert evidence in criminal cases in both Australia and England. There have been too many miscarriages of justice because of the unreliability of such evidence.

In England there were the IRA cases, namely those of Judith Ward (1974), the Guildford Four (1975), the Birmingham Six (1974) and the Maguire Seven (1974). These cases involved, inter alia, the Skuse Test or the Griess method, supposed to detect nitroglycerine on the hands. Eventually the particular chemical involved was also shown to react to soap, playing cards and cigarette packets so the forensic tests were found to be unreliable. There was also the pathetic case of Jacqueline Fletcher, convicted of murdering her baby by drowning when it was actually a case of Sudden Infant Death Syndrome (SIDS). In evidence, a pathologist described the baby's lungs as 'water-logged' when the fluid was in fact oedema, a bodily secretion.

In Australia, prominent miscarriage-of-justice cases included the conviction of Lindy Chamberlain in 1982, Edward Charles Splatt convicted in 1978 and Douglas Rendell convicted in 1980 on misleading ballistics evidence. All these convictions were set aside and the first two cases prompted considerable reforms in forensic evidence. The Chamberlain case triggered the formation of the National Institute of Forensic Science (NIFS) which has worked at raising standards in the various State and federal forensic-science laboratories.

One of the great dangers of police investigations is the practice of targeting. A suspicion is formed, a target is identified and the inquiry ceases to be a search for the truth and becomes a search for evidence against the target. If this 'Yoicks tally-ho' fox-hunting approach infects the expert witnesses, one gets the forensic evidence fiasco revealed in the Chamberlain case.

In my opinion, and I share this opinion with many, it is absolutely essential that government forensic laboratories be available to assist the defence as well as the Crown. These institutions should aim to ascertain the truth, not to secure convictions. This philosophy exists in the Victorian Forensic Science Laboratory and the New South Wales Institute of Forensic Medicine. However, the

New South Wales Analytic and Biological Laboratories at Lidcombe were only available to the Crown.

In contrast, Professor John Hilton for years has made the Institute of Forensic Medicine (dealing mainly with postmortem pathology) available to assist both the Crown and the defence. This saves court time and reduces the chances of injustice.

What is needed in New South Wales, and wherever there is a government forensic-science laboratory, is a properly integrated forensic-science laboratory with the following features:

1. Adequate equipment to deal with all relevant inquiries. Thus there should be a microscope to examine suspected blood sprays and equipment to analyse the material present. The tragic farce of the sound deadener identified as a foetal blood spray in the Chamberlain case would thus be avoided. Long after the Chamberlain trial, microscopic examination showed duco on the alleged spray.

2. Properly qualified staff. A modern laboratory needs scientists and experts in numerous spheres of knowledge; for example, biology, chemistry, mechanics, etc.

3. Impartial staff. It is essential that scientists in a government laboratory seek only the truth. They should not be infected by targeting.

4. Careful staff. The Chamberlain case revealed that the standards of care in laboratory staff fell far short of the standards required for papers in scientific journals. I believe NIFS has produced improvements in this area.

5. The services of the laboratory must be available to both Crown and defence. The laboratory should exist to secure justice, not convictions.

In America in particular, but also in England, a practice has grown up of friendly (or not-so-friendly) battles between government experts and independent experts hired by the defence teams. We experienced this in the last McLeod-Lindsay inquiry.

I have been quite horrified by the attitudes of some overseas forensic experts who seemed to be prepared to say almost anything in support of a legal side. That innocent persons might go to gaol (or guilty ones escape justice) did not seem to worry these forensic experts. In one case the expert suggested that a Crown prosecutor write out what he wanted the expert to say and he, the expert, would swear to it. This offer was naturally refused. Forensic evidence should not be a game between experts, especially in criminal cases where liberty is at stake.

It is idle to imagine that incorrect expert conclusions will be exposed by cross-examination. It is rare for the defence team in a criminal matter to have the means to check government expert opinion using other experts. Almost all the expert conclusions from government laboratories go unchallenged. In the rare cases where they are challenged (as in the IRA miscarriage-of-justice cases), the Crown prosecutor and often the presiding judge will tell the jury that the government laboratory scientist does these tests every day whereas the defence expert is a university academic who may know the theory but lacks the everyday expertise.

It is essential that government laboratories reach only correct conclusions. Fundamentally, if they make a mistake there is little chance the mistake will be corrected.

Reliable forensic evidence is invaluable in crime detection. This is why fingerprint evidence is only put before courts if clear imprints are available for unmistakable comparison. For years it has been appreciated that if a fingerprint blunder occurs, the reliability of fingerprint evidence will be jeopardised. There is now also need for great care with DNA evidence. Such evidence can be quite conclusive as to guilt or innocence and if it is ever discredited, the damage to successful crime detection will be enormous. Fingerprint evidence has been challenged recently in England both by suggestion of police manipulation and incorrect interpretation. Such challenges are rare indeed in Australia.

What has to be very carefully appreciated by police and lawyers is that DNA evidence is ideal for manipulation. It is hard (but by no means impossible) to place the accused's fingerprints at the crime scene when he or she was never near the place. For example, a drinking glass used by the accused can be 'found' at the crime scene. I am not entirely convinced that a fingerprint can be convincingly transferred by means of Sellotape, as has been claimed.

Potential for DNA framing of suspects exists. It is not hard to find hairs of the accused and place them to be 'found' at the crime scene. It is essential that police be trained to realise that such actions strike a deadly blow against the use of crucial forensic evidence. Apparently in the O.J. Simpson case in the United States, the jury did not believe that a glove had been found where stated by police.

In New South Wales, and Australia generally, the public's faith in the honesty of detectives has taken a very heavy battering. It is essential to restore public confidence in police honesty, and this can only occur when there is a transformation in the attitude of the detectives. 'Loading' suspects with drugs and firearms is a practice that has now been revealed and exposed. The wickedness of the past has created great problems for the future. This was revealed in recent Police Integrity Commission hearings. There was nothing surprising about this to any experienced criminal lawyer. 'Rod planting' was rife when I started in practice in 1948. I appeared for the State of New South Wales in the Supreme Court in the reported Sergeant Benson case – *Marshall v Benson* – when he was found to be in possession of a number of pistols taken from persons arrested, but not handed over as prescribed to ballistics for destruction. The sergeant retired from the police force, but the lesson was not learned by the police administration.

If judges and magistrates had not been so ready to believe police evidence we would not have the unhappy position we are in now, where all denied police evidence of finding items is more than suspect. The police had a free kick for many years and now the community pays the price.

As the former New South Wales Commissioner of Police Peter Ryan understood, the need for crime-scene examination has to be beyond reproach. He set up the Police Forensic Services Group (FSG) under Dr Tony Raymond. These FSG employees collect specimens under strict conditions aimed at avoiding manipulation or contamination.

The necessity for collection of specimens under strict conditions is illustrated by the 1996 case of Nick Lisoff. The accused denied being one of a number of brutal assailants who savagely assaulted the victim whose blood was splashed around. The Crown claimed that blood spots on the knees of the accused's trousers matched the DNA profile of the victim, so that there was only a one in 10 billion chance of it being anyone else. An independent examiner of the specimens, Dr Brian McDonald, found bands of another person's DNA on the sample taken by the police from the victim in the hospital after he had had a blood transfusion. These bands appeared also on the trousers, but not on a recent blood sample of the victim. It was argued that the extra bands came from the blood transfusion made as a result of and after the assault, and would only appear on the trousers if the blood came from the blood sample taken from the victim at the hospital. The accused was acquitted by a judge sitting without a jury on the grounds that there was a reasonable doubt. The lesson from this was that the police blood sample was unsealed at the relevant time and was available to be used to stain the trousers of the accused. There was no evidence that any particular person had done this. Procedures now in place should reduce the chances of such possible manipulation.

Comparatively new procedures known as Preliminary Chain Reaction (PCR) enable tiny bodily specimens to be multiplied and then identified. This means that it is essential to prevent contamination of specimens by careless handling. In other words, a suspect identified by a DNA profile could say that the identification had come about by contaminating the specimen with his DNA. This allegation was made in the English case of James Hanratty, in which his clothing and that of the victim had been together in exhibit bags during the 1962 trial. The Crown successfully met this allegation by pointing to the fact that only one DNA profile of a male was revealed in the female victim's underwear. The DNA examinations occurred many years after 1962.

Nevertheless, the possibility of contamination by careless handling of exhibits, as distinct from deliberate manipulation, remains. The FSG protocols are aimed at avoiding this.

Sometimes DNA profiles are open to more than one interpretation in cases where there is very little specimen. This occurred in the bank-robbery case of Marc Renton, where the John Tonge Centre's interpretation of DNA evidence in 1996 was later challenged by Professor Barry Boettcher (who was a witness years before for Lindy Chamberlain). It is interesting to note that the John Tonge Centre, the government laboratory in Queensland, made a mistake in the trial of Frank Button for rape and failed to find a DNA profile in the victim's vaginal contents or the sheets. The latter were not examined at all. After Button's conviction at Kingaroy in August 2000 the John Tonge Centre, to its credit, at the request of the defence lawyers, did the test of the vaginal contents again and the sheets for the first time. A male DNA profile was found that was not that of Frank Button and he was freed after some time in gaol.

In New South Wales there is no government laboratory available to the accused, apart from the Institute of Forensic Medicine, as is the case in Victoria, South Australia and apparently Queensland.

DNA is very strong evidence against an accused. The only rebutting arguments for DNA evidence are:

1. an identical twin
2. contamination
3. manipulation
4. incorrect interpretation.

The identical-twin rebuttal hardly ever arises and incorrect interpretation should be rare. The chance of contamination can be reduced by careful FSG management. It is up to the police to prevent manipulation that is only likely to occur through police misconduct.

Usually DNA profiling will result in dropped prosecutions or pleas of guilty. It is quite conclusive evidence. However, I do not like the situation where DNA may profile a suspect who denies guilt and has no motive, and against whom there is no other evidence. McLeod-Lindsay was confronted with apparently unanswerable bloodstain dynamics evidence. Many years later, after he had served his sentence, there turned out to be a very strong answer to that forensic evidence.

DNA evidence should be conclusive, but this may not always be so. The importance of DNA makes the establishment of a New South Wales integrated government forensic laboratory as efficient and as independent as that in Victoria very urgent indeed. It has been advocated for years.

Forensic evidence, and particularly DNA evidence, is far more important than savage sentences. Money to be spent on prisons would be better spent on an up-to-date integrated forensic-science laboratory. Deterrence by likely detection is far more likely than punishment to prevent crime.

In criminal cases most, if not all, of the forensic evidence will come from the government laboratory. That is why it is so essential for it to be as far as possible perfect.

Other forensic evidence may not be so accurate. In my practice I had at least one client who may have been the victim of a thoughtless doctor. Physical examination showed he was perfectly sober, yet a blood test showed a high alcohol content. Did the doctor sterilise the needle taking the sample with alcohol, the standard antiseptic? This mistake has been suspected more than once, but of course it will not be admitted and can never be proved.

Sometimes experts are called in by the police for skills outside the facilities of the government laboratory. Thus, botanical residues can be identified (as happened in the Chamberlain case) or the date of death can be estimated from an old body by insect infestation. Most of this evidence is excellent, but in some cases there is a danger of 'targeting'. An outside expert, feeling important as a vital witness, looks to incriminate the suspect, rather than to find the truth. After Chamberlain, most government forensic scientists realise that they must be unswayed by anything but a search for objective truth. A first-time expert witness may be in danger of failing to appreciate this. I have also come across a case where the outside expert in a serious criminal case was quite careless, regarding a criminal charge as a triviality. Fortunately this is rare.

New expert skills are being developed all the time. One of recent years is a machine that can examine a written document and reproduce the writing from the previous page imprinted on that document. This has been important in some English cases involving doctored police notebooks.

Bloodstain dynamics is a fairly new science which has solved quite a few crimes. Although it initially led to a probably erroneous conclusion in the McLeod–Lindsay case it has, to my knowledge, been successful in a number of cases. Like many other forensic aids, it is very useful to confirm or supplement other evidence. It is risky to rely upon it as the only evidence against a suspect.

An important problem which arose in the Chamberlain case was when to 'call' a scientific result. If a result is dubious but nevertheless indicates the guilt of the accused, should it be called? A good example is a smudged fingerprint. Fingerprint experts by and large only 'call' a print if they can be certain, otherwise they do not call it. The same caution does not apply in other forensic areas. However NIFS and other bodies are working on this problem.

One of the expert skills that fascinated me as an advocate was tracking by Aborigines at Ayers Rock. Their evidence was powerfully in favour of Lindy Chamberlain. I have also encountered police dog-tracking evidence where the dog handler gives evidence of the dog's reactions. There is an argument about whether this evidence is admissible. On the other hand, 'sniffer-dog' evidence may be admitted. Usually it leads to other evidence.

Much of the Chamberlain case concerned dog wounds and bites. In that case there was only a matinee jacket, jumpsuit and clothing to examine. There was no body. It is interesting to note that, long after the Chamberlains were exonerated, in 1989 a mother Debbie Loveless and her de facto husband, John Miller, were convicted in Emory, Texas, U.S.A. of the murder of Debbie's four-year-old daughter. After four years in prison the couple were released. Careful examination of photos of the body proved that the child was killed by a hybrid wolf-dog. These photos should have saved the suspects in the first place.

How does one test forensic evidence? Firstly one may ask whether the conclusion is theoretical or whether actual experimental work has been done. Thus in the Chamberlain case it was assumed that canine teeth could only tear, not cut – an assumption which proved to be incorrect when experimental work was done.

One must also beware of gadgetry. In the Chamberlain case Professor Cameron produced a gadget whereby when one looked at the jumpsuit one could distinguish the finger imprints of a little hand. The High Court was unimpressed by this gadget and it ultimately turned out that the alleged imprints were largely red desert sand.

When an expert talks in technical language he or she should be asked to translate into simple English. Sometimes the results are surprising, particularly in the case of psychiatrists.

Special care should also be paid to the phrase 'consistent with' which is often used by biased Crown witnesses. In their evidence almost anything is consistent with the guilt of the accused, and so it is. The landing of an American astronaut on the moon was quite consistent with the guilt of Ned Kelly but it was not in any way proof of that guilt. But as the expression is given in evidence it sounds like evidence of guilt. The medical examination of a sexual-assault complainant is always, in my experience, consistent with her complaint, but only rarely does it in any way confirm her story. All 'consistent with' really means is that the expert finding is not inconsistent with the complainant's story.

One should ponder whether the research on a particular area of expertise has gone far enough to produce confidence in the experts' findings. In the McLeod–Lindsay case the Crown experts honestly believed that the bloodstains on the defendant's clothing conclusively proved guilt. Years later, further experimental work proved them quite wrong. In that case the bloodstains were only consistent with guilt, but they did not prove guilt.

In our time, the dogmatic statements of yesterday – for example, that DDT is perfectly safe – have become the proved errors of today. Passive smoking was once thought to be harmless.

Sometimes expert evidence wrongly asserts something is impossible. I had one case of alleged homicide of a very young child who died of head injuries. The child was proved to have been in the habit of bashing her head against walls. A paediatric psychiatrist had been consulted who was very much on side with the accused, who denied striking the child. Other paediatricians said that it was impossible for the child to have inflicted such injuries on herself. Nevertheless the accused was acquitted.

In the case of Arthur Peden, who in 1921 was convicted and sentenced to death for allegedly cutting his wife's throat, the conviction was based on medical evidence from a number of leading practitioners that she could not have cut her own throat in the way it was done, even though she was deranged and suicidal. Fortunately, the trial judge and others were concerned about this evidence and there was a Royal Commission into Peden's conviction. Luckily for him there was a very similar case of undoubted suicide with a razor, almost identical to that of Mrs Peden, that occurred not long before the Royal Commission. It was clear that the experts at the trial were wrong and Peden was freed. (The cut-throat razor of yesterday was often used for suicide. In such cases, suicide was often detected because of the presence of 'tentative cuts', being other lesser wounds as well as the fatal wound. These cuts were made by the suicide plucking up the determination to make the fatal wound. (During the Great Depression wounds such as amputated fingers were sometimes self-inflicted. The same test of tentative cuts often defeated these desperate efforts to obtain workers' compensation payments.)

The more I saw of and studied cases of homicide, the more I appreciated how few things were impossible. However, this was not so in the case of R v Price in which the defendant was convicted of murdering her husband who died from a .22 bullet wound to his head, fired from his own rifle in his bedroom. She is now free having served her sentence. I only appeared for Mrs Price in the appeal which set aside her conviction in her first trial, but she was convicted in her second trial, and that conviction stood, despite a subsequent inquiry into her guilt. The obvious defence was suicide but the powder burns showed that the rifle was not fired very close to his head, which meant that he could not have fired it himself. The rifle could not be held out and fired a few feet from his head. Mrs Price always maintained her innocence, and eventually placed the blame on someone else, but she was not believed in a subsequent inquiry into her conviction.

If a rifle is fired at white paper from various distances one gets a pattern of powder burns from which it can be deduced how far from the wound the rifle was. Unfortunately for Mrs Price, the margin for error was nowhere near sufficient to make suicide possible.

The expert's notes should be inspected in all cases where it is questionable and in particular one should inquire as to whether there were proper controls for the tests. For example, if testing for human blood, it is usual to have a control, say rabbit blood. If the test shows positive for both human blood and rabbit blood, the result is defective.

One may also ask whether the methods used by the experts in a case are well established. For example, the tests for foetal blood in the Chamberlain case were pioneering so should not have been given so much weight.

Where a result arises from the efforts of a number of experts one may ask whether each is prepared to endorse the final result. For example, the famous under-dash spray of foetal blood which was the most deadly evidence against Lindy Chamberlain turned out to be sound deadener. A number of experts deposed to parts of the Crown case on this aspect. As the fiasco was revealed no one was anxious to accept overall blame for one of the worst blunders in our forensic-science history.

It is interesting to see whether the expert makes reasonable concessions or whether he or she is a stubborn advocate for a cause.

Under numerous new reforms of expert evidence in civil cases the expert is required to state his or her qualifications, the facts on which the conclusions were formed, and the methods used to reach the conclusions. There is a move, in some courts, towards reducing expert evidence to one witness; for example, for valuing a home in the Family Court. Considerable improvements in the accuracy and expense of expert evidence may be expected from reforms in the civil area.

However, one problem of civil cases involves targeting. This occurs where the expert is sought to prove a point, usually to blame someone, not to ascertain the truth. Thus in obstetrics and neurosurgery, there are babies and patients who turn out to be grossly disabled and damages are sought for negligence. Experts are sought, not to ascertain what happened but rather to find a way to blame the doctor and recover massive damages. The plaintiff with gross disablement is an object of pity and if a doctor can be found here, or often from overseas, to place the blame on the treating doctor, then that unfortunate defendant is at risk of paying massive monetary damages not to mention suffering damage to their reputation and practice, even if many top-ranking specialists say that he or she was not to blame. The medical insurer may well settle for big figures in such a case, even though the defendant was clearly not negligent. After all, a remote chance of obtaining damages of 10 million dollars is well worth a settlement figure of two million dollars.

The remedy may be that in some cases, such as obstetrics and neurosurgery, all mishaps should be examined by an expert panel, not to place blame but to ascertain what happened. If the panel finds the doctor was or was not to blame, that finding would be conclusive. Assuming a careful selection of experts of the highest repute for the various expert panels, this course would reduce the damages payable by medical insurers to those cases where the doctor really was at fault. This type of procedure is being used already in the field of workers' compensation to assess disability. It is, in my opinion, a desirable step towards securing justice for both the medical profession and its patients. I think that the expert panels would, in such a fair system from the doctors' viewpoint and that of their patients, be relied upon to make accurate findings.

It can be seen that what I am arguing for are methods to achieve correct expert evidence, just as I seek a government forensic laboratory that will reach correct conclusions. It will rarely be possible to rebut expert forensic evidence and, in the case of contradictory medical opinions, court procedures will reach a correct result more by good luck than by efficient methods. The main object should be to try to ensure that expert evidence is correct. If it is not, the courts will be lucky if the errors are revealed.

In the Chamberlain case, the New South Wales laboratory had destroyed the samples, the plates of biological examinations. This was quite outrageous, but as the result of an excellent report by the then Ombudsman, George Masterman QC, this destruction of exhibit samples is unlikely to occur again.

Government laboratories should seek justice, not convictions. They should be open to all parties and they should get their results right. The consequences of government laboratory errors are likely to be serious injustices.

I should conclude by mentioning demeanour. By majority, the New South Wales Court of Appeal has held that the demeanour of expert witnesses is observed by the trial judge and his or her impression of their demeanour is a very substantial obstacle in the way of upsetting on appeal any findings of fact made at first instance. This is an invitation to error, and unappealable error at that. Scientific experts are noted for undesirable demeanour. Geniuses tend to be arrogant, irascible and annoying, but none of these matters has any relevance at all to the correctness of their conclusions.

On the other hand, experts who attend court frequently soon learn to kowtow to judge and jury, to adopt a pleasant and likeable demeanour and to sacrifice, if desirable, accuracy for simplicity. The presiding judge is very likely to be attracted by these smooth-talking professional witnesses and the jury will be directed that whereas the professor called for the accused may have a brilliant academic background, the government scientist does these tests every day. Peruse the records of the IRA cases and the judgment of the Full Federal Court in the Chamberlain case and you will find this argument. In the latter case it was said that Lindy Chamberlain's experts at the trial demonstrated an unbecoming arrogance. If that were true, what is the relevance to accuracy except to show that demeanour study of experts leads to error?

The great advances of my life in the progress of mankind have been technical and scientific. Technology and science have an enormous contribution to make to the very difficult pursuit of truth in legal fact-finding. It is of vital importance that the courts should make full use of expertise, yet avoid the errors of false science.

I am happy to say that much has been learned from past errors. Let me conclude with some warnings:

1. Simplicity and attractive presentation are no substitutes for accuracy.
2. Complicated use of technical language is often a disguise for nonsense.
3. Theory without experimental proof is no better than unproved theory.
4. The expert who performs the tests every day may well have fallen into bad habits.
5. The expert who performs the tests for the first time is likely to be more careful and check the results obtained more thoroughly than the technician who performs the tests every day.
6. History shows that the greatest experts were by no means always pleasant people. An expert's results should be judged on their merits, not on the expert's appearance as a witness.
7. Often, but by no means always, a real expert can explain his or her work in simple language.
8. An impartial witness will be prepared to make concessions. An expert who is an advocate fights against making any concessions.
9. Expert evidence should be considered carefully in the light of the known facts.

As to point 9 it should never be forgotten that Lindy Chamberlain was mentally normal, proved by many witnesses to be a loving mother, and her evidence of the presence of dingoes at the camp site that night was verified by impeccable witnesses. Furthermore, no secretly buried baby's body was ever found. There was no blood on her clothing. There was blood in the tent. All of these matters and more should have been considered before they were overwhelmed by evidence of an alleged arterial blood-spray and a car allegedly swimming with blood.

In other words, if the expert evidence points to a conclusion contrary to the known facts a court will be wise to think again.

# 28

# Improving the Law

As a colony of England New South Wales inherited the English law, the common law made by the judges over the centuries, equity made by the judges more recently, and many English statutes. To this inheritance over the course of more than 200 years we have added many federal and State statutes from the Commonwealth parliament and New South Wales parliaments respectively and our common law has branched off from what we inherited.

Since I started in the law as a student in 1943 during the war and went to the bar in 1948 there have been numerous statutory reforms and most of them have been substantial improvements. Besides these, the judge-made law has developed and improved, both in common law and equity.

The improvements have been notable in legislation to protect workers from industrial accidents, and to protect consumers and others from unfair contracts and practices. Children born out of wedlock and their mothers no longer suffer the injustices of the past, homosexuals are no longer persecuted, and much hypocrisy has been removed from family law.

Historically, the common law – it was said by one judge in olden days – did not try to protect fools from their folly. I acted for many victims of dishonest tricksters in business. They were working people trying to better themselves, very often by starting a small business. There seemed to be a mass of smart crooks waiting to deceive them and trick them out of their money. There were fine-print contracts that they signed without understanding the stringent provisions that would ruin them. There were 'guarantees' printed with articles sold which in fact mainly served to exclude such common-law rights as the purchasers had. I and other young barristers fought hard but often in vain to protect the victims of smart deception.

How much easier it is for the consumer now with the Trade Practices Act, the Fair Trading Act and the Contracts Review Act.

I was privileged to be a barrister during many years of continuous law reform, most of it good and effective. In particular I saw many improvements in criminal trials, which are now much more careful and less liable to error. But the law still needs reforming, as no doubt it always will.

By statute, an accused person may now elect to be tried by a judge alone, but only if the Crown consents. I see no reason why the Crown, through the Director of Public Prosecutions, should have this right of veto, which in practice is quite frequently exercised. Some cases are unsuitable for juries. I have obtained trial by judge alone in a case with much documentary evidence, and in another where the defence involved admitting that the accused was once in prison. This is a useful right of the accused to trial by judge alone and should not be subject to a Crown veto for which there seems to be no substantial justification.

In America, jury persons are questioned and can be challenged for cause; that is, it can be requested that a prospective juror be dismissed because there is a specific and forceful reason to believe the person cannot be fair, unbiased or capable of serving as a juror. We have not adopted this procedure because it is expensive and time-consuming and it is doubtful whether it produces better juries. Apart from challenges for cause, which are very rare indeed, we have only three challenges without cause each for Crown and defence. The challenges are based on a study of the appearance of the jury persons in waiting and as each is called to be sworn. This procedure is important, tending to eliminate bad-tempered, prejudiced individuals. However three challenges are not enough. It used to be eight, and 20 in murder cases. Now it is only three, even in murder cases, to select a jury of 12.

The law with regard to jury challenges was changed at the end of a year just before Christmas without warning, and before the obvious protests could be made. No doubt the reason for the change was simply to save money. It is a poor economy if it lowers the quality of justice. I think that there should be at least five challenges without cause permitted to both the Crown and the defence.

The big problem of the criminal courts is how to do justice in what we called one-on-one cases; that is, where there is only one witness against the accused. This happens frequently, often in situations where the surrounding circumstances give little guide as to who is telling the truth. The problem has always been there: for example, a person claiming that the accused in a denied conversation deceived him or her by a false pretence through which he or she lost money, or a person who claims that the accused assaulted him or her. Who really struck the first blow? The problem reaches its extreme form when a child accuses an adult of sexual abuse.

A necessary reform is the better investigation of these offences. Police and doctors should not simply presume guilt. They should make a detailed inquiry as to where the truth lies. In my experience as a barrister this did not occur. In particular, police arrested people without even asking them to reply to the charges against them. If they had carefully investigated the statements of the accused some cases would never have proceeded. In others the court would have a much better background of surrounding facts in which to decide between the accuser and the accused if they had carefully questioned the accused and investigated the case more thoroughly.

Under existing law the judge directing the jury in such a case should direct the jury that where the Crown case depends on one witness, the evidence of that witness should be scrutinised with care. That is only common sense but does not draw the jury's attention to the fact that where the Crown case depends on one witness only, who is not corroborated by other evidence, then there is a real danger of miscarriage of justice unless very special care and scrutiny are exercised by the jury.

The fact is that numerous sexual-assault cases, and for that matter other one-on-one criminal cases, involve a special danger of jury error. If we are honest with ourselves, we have to admit that many jury errors occur in all types of criminal cases. In holding that the death penalty involved an 'undue risk of executing innocent people' (*Sydney Morning Herald*, 3 July 2002) Judge Rakoff in the US District Court for New York said, 'What DNA testing has proved, beyond cavil, is the remarkable degree of fallibility in the basic fact-finding processes on which we rely in criminal cases.' United States death-row convictions investigations have already revealed over 100 wrongful convictions.

We flatter ourselves if we think our courts do that much better in this regard than those in the United States.

How can we improve this? The best reform is of police practice. At present the police find a suspect and then target him or her. If they could be persuaded to search for the truth rather than evidence against the target, many injustices would be avoided. Not only would fewer innocent people be convicted, but if the defences of suspects were impartially investigated before trial and preferably before arrest, false defences would be more likely to fail.

Many times juries retire to consider their verdicts when the decision could go either way. How often are they wrong? For years this has worried me. I have been quite unable to assume, as some judges do, that accused persons are almost always guilty. I know that there must be many innocent people who are convicted. How many, it is hard to say. In one-on-one accusations of sexual assault there must be many errors, since we do not have anything like a reliable system of fact-finding.

The fact-finding side of the law needs much more research and study. In the past the great minds of the law have concerned themselves with esoteric points of law. The law journals have rarely dealt with fact-finding, and the appeal courts usually avoided it by saying that the trial judge had the 'inestimable advantage' of seeing and hearing the witnesses. But I believe things are changing.

It is obviously desirable that there should be public confidence in the courts. However, maintaining public confidence should not result in pretending that problems do not exist.

The problems of fact-finding also exist in the civil courts. Often the presence of documents guides the decision but there are many cases of one-on-one witnesses with little else to assist the court. In these cases, proof only has to be on the balance of probabilities so that a defendant can incur heavy damages on slight evidence.

The problem about being a busy practitioner is that one has little time for thought about the wider problems of the law. I found that as a barrister my thoughts were preoccupied by the problems of my clients. Now that I have retired I appreciate more and more that the real problems are not the law itself, but the ways in which the law is enforced.

Quite frequently I read about how misconduct, even criminal conduct, is not exposed because those who know the truth fear being sued for libel. This particularly occurs in company affairs. Sometimes in practice I had to advise auditors who feared to do their duty by making appropriate criticisms lest they be sued. It was not a foolish fear. Being sued for defamation can ruin an ordinary person and can result in the loss of his or her home to pay damages and costs, particularly the latter. The threat by a wealthy man to sue an ordinary person is no empty one. It is a brave person who defies that threat.

Defamation has become technical. It was always expensive; now it is much more so. The purse of an ordinary person will be emptied long before the case comes on for hearing. This will be the result of endless interlocutory (or preliminary) proceedings which seem to grow up like Hydra heads in defamation proceedings. Pleadings – that is, the filed statement of the case – will be challenged and argued over, further particulars will be sought and argued over, discovery of documents is quite likely, and so on.

When the case comes on at last, there are arguments and findings about what the allegedly defamatory words really mean, and then at last (in a different hearing) there will be an argument about defences.

The auditors doing their job will have a defence of qualified privilege because they were only doing their duty. However an auditor cannot act maliciously. Malice will destroy the privilege. But an angry exchange of words during the audit might be evidence of malice. Of course, truth will be a defence, but often what is well known and certainly true is hard to prove in a court of law.

If an auditor finds that a rich director has been dishonest, he has a duty to expose the director, but the auditor may well be at risk.

In local government, a mayor or councillor who has been involved in shady deals may well intimidate the other councillors by threats to sue for defamation. Such stories are not infrequent in local papers.

I am sure that the Watergate exposure of President Nixon would not have occurred in Australia because of our defamation laws. Reform is constantly advocated but difficult to achieve. The need to protect reputations is to be weighed against the need to expose evil. One partial answer is along the lines of American law which permits bona fide criticism and 'exposure' of public figures even if it is erroneous. In America, unlike Australia, public figures cannot easily recover big windfalls of damages if they are lucky enough to be defamed although recent Australian decisions have improved this situation.

The defamation problem is closely related to the general problem of expense in litigation. This is particularly apparent in commercial litigation. The smaller individual or company has no way of litigating against wealthy and ruthless companies and cartels.

The unfortunate fact is that court procedures are now very detailed, complicated and expensive, which obviously favours the wealthy. When I started at the bar procedures were much simpler. Interlocutory proceedings were short, if they occurred at all. Cases were also much shorter. Since everything had to be typed, if it was to be copied, only relevant documents were in the brief. One did not see trolleys full of binders of documents. One did not even see binders. The hearings were for days rather than weeks or months. There were no computers to dig up reports of cases which were probably best forgotten. Written submissions were almost unknown. Furthermore, in those days the State willingly provided courts to hear disputes, and court fees were cheap. After all, the courts were one of the fundamental functions of government.

It is not so today. Under the principle of user-pays, court fees are very expensive indeed. Today we have many more citizens, much more commerce and many more disputes. Judges have to work much harder in most jurisdictions. The courts have an endless battle against backlogs of cases waiting to be heard. They have succeeded in clearing the backlogs again and again, but they recur. Rules now exist exhorting counsel to explore mediation and settlement prospects in the hope of reducing the flood of litigation.

If one glances at the real-estate news in the daily papers it can be seen that not merely hundreds but thousands of people can afford to pay over a million dollars for a home. Some can pay 10 million dollars. There are many wealthy people and there are many wealthy companies; there are company officers receiving salaries of over a million dollars per annum. The affairs of these people can often lead to expensive court battles which they can probably afford. They aim for Rolls-Royce litigation with senior counsel and trolley-loads of binders full of documents. Over the years they have established a pattern of expensive commercial litigation in which the wealthy are likely to bully the not-so-wealthy.

It is said with some truth that only the wealthy and the poor can afford to litigate, the latter on legal aid. The middle class litigate at their peril. They are not wealthy enough to afford the battle; they have enough assets to be ruined if they lose. This is not new, but in recent years litigation has become much more expensive.

One remedy is greater flexibility in the awarding of costs. Ruinous costs should not be awarded against a small player in favour of a mega-company, where the small player has acted reasonably. I recall a fairly recent case where a small business operated with a name that resembled that of a mega-company. This was done in all innocence by the small business, in ignorance of the very existence of the mega-company. Probably the resemblance between the two names would not have been sufficient to obtain an injunction, particularly as they were entirely different businesses. The small player at first refused to alter its name, but as the costs piled higher, it yielded, and then its business folded under the further costs ordered against it.

Why should there be a bill of costs of enormous magnitude in order to decide whether the name of one business is too close to that of another business? Fundamentally, the question is one of impression which is unlikely to change despite hordes of witnesses and trolleys of binders.

Much of the expense in commercial cases is incurred by the numerous short and not-so-short interlocutory appearances which have grown very much over the years in the interests of court efficiency. The idea is to ensure proper revelation of evidence and documents including witness statements before trial. The result is an enormous expenditure of costs before the hearing even begins. No doubt court time is to some extent saved but the price paid is large indeed.

All of this is perhaps inevitable between wealthy litigants but it is a financial nightmare for a small business. The position seems to be little different in England and the United States, although in the latter there are not the same costs orders. In New South Wales, costs are almost inevitably awarded against the losing party. The threat of this is the big weapon of the litigant bully. Here at least there is room for reform.

One idea might be to give a party a right to seek a costs-ceiling order so that if that party loses, the winning party could only recover costs up to the ceiling figure. That way, the incentive for running up costs against a weaker party would be reduced.

However, there should be a general wide discretion as to awarding costs. The successful winner of unreasonably prolonged litigation should not necessarily obtain all or any of its costs. The rich litigant should not necessarily recover against a poor litigant, who has acted reasonably. An injured worker who reasonably sues for negligence seeking to recover damages should not necessarily have to pay an insurance company's costs if he or she loses.

One of the great reforms of Lionel Murphy's Family Law Act was that costs were only to be awarded in special circumstances. Otherwise each party would pay his or her own costs. This reform has worked well and might well be applied to other courts.

Commercial structures are very complicated today, largely for taxation reasons. When a wealthy man is respondent to a Family Court application for settlement orders, assessing the value of all his assets can be a very expensive process. Years ago I argued before the Full Family Court that it was not necessary to do an entire assessment, but I lost.

However, the Family Court has done a lot to streamline its procedures and has tried to reduce its costs. If both the parties are reasonable, the Family Court does provide facilities for a quick and not-too-expensive settlement. Doing justice in contested cases is extremely difficult but the results I have seen have left me favourably impressed.

The fundamental no-fault philosophy of the Family Court works well in most cases, but there are a substantial number of cases in which a party is manifestly at fault yet is entitled to a substantial share of the other party's means. In these cases, which are the exception, the party not at fault feels that the law is unjust, and he or she has to be right. Framing a law to meet such cases should not be all that difficult. If a party by his or her conduct has completely renounced the marriage obligations, then that should involve also renouncing its benefits.

Regard for marriage is declining. Many young and not-so-young people prefer to be partners rather than spouses. I think that the orders carving up a spouse's assets, made by the Family Court, have been a factor in this preference. De facto couples only experience this after three years of cohabitation and the orders are not so severe. I think that heavy orders in favour of manifestly misbehaving spouses deter people from marrying at all. Second marriages are now much less common, when people may be more safely partners.

Easy divorce is contrary to the religious convictions of a component of the Australian community. In British India the divorce laws followed the laws of the marriage religion chosen, whether it was Islam, Hinduism, Christianity or otherwise. Why should not Christian churches be empowered to bind parties married in the churches to a marriage that can only be dissolved for serious matrimonial fault by a spouse? Perhaps this would encourage a fuller commitment to marriage by many people.

Those who are happy as 'partners' with minimum commitment are missing the further happiness of a successful marriage, particularly in later life, and society misses the stability of permanent marriages. Too many children today have divided parents.

The breakdown of the family is one of the tragedies of modern life. It is a social problem of great magnitude that all political parties choose to overlook, because it seems to be too difficult. There are far more votes in urging higher sentences for criminals rather than focusing on family issues.

It is surprising how well many children of broken homes cope with their situations, but a glance at the pre-sentence reports in the criminal courts will show the proportion of such children who go badly astray compared to others. I think it is possible that such children will find it harder to form binding relationships themselves.

The other great problem in our society is the enormous and rapidly growing gap between rich and poor. Unfortunately riches only occasionally go to those who contribute most to society, and frequently go to financial manipulators.

We have a Trade Practices Act that does an enormous amount, together with the State Fair Trading Act, to protect consumers. We have a Corporations Act that in recent times has badly failed in protecting investors. This failure to protect investors is not necessarily due to substantial defects in the law of corporations, but rather is due to defects in the machinery to enforce the law. What with internet transactions and the speed of modern financial transactions, a prosperous company can be ruined overnight by dishonest persons. If auditors fail to do their duty, eventually the shareholders lose. There is no doubt that the supervision of companies must be much tighter and this involves spending money to provide better resources for the supervisors and investigators.

In taxation and corporate laws the complications would amaze the layperson, as they amaze me. Every reform seems to make the meaning of law even more impenetrable.

I have often thought that these complications are caused because the relevant laws have been drafted by specialists. Why should not ordinary lawyers try to draft a taxation law that the layperson has a good chance of understanding? This has never been tried.

Corporation or company law is by necessity complicated but the fairly recent federal laws are far too difficult for almost anyone but a specialist lawyer to follow. This is quite wrong if ordinary individuals are to carry on business under company structures. Much needs to be done to simplify these laws but I fear that again no one is trying.

One great reform I have seen in my time in the law has been the abolition of death duty, the State tax on deceased estates, and estate duty, the federal tax in such cases. The State death-duties authorities in New South Wales, in my experience, wielded their powers ruthlessly and inhumanely. For example, nothing could be spent, even on supporting the widow and children of the deceased person until death duty had been assessed and paid. In a complicated estate this might take years. In a simple estate it took months. Those who remember will never agree to such a tax again.

Estate duty was a charge on the estate and its imposition was administered with more common sense. However, both forms of duty were avoided by the wealthy, with the aid of clever lawyers. Middle- and lower-income families often suffered real hardship.

We are still left with the task of imposing fair taxation. The Income Tax Act is far from fair. The wealthy still avoid its provisions by highly skilled legal advice. The middle- and lower-income earners pay for the wealthy. This injustice has not been solved, partly because the problem is difficult but mainly because the wealthy wield great political power.

So a waiter who works two jobs and fails to declare one is likely to be caught and punished. The tycoon who avoids tax on millions of dollars has little to fear. The waiter evades tax because what he does is illegal. The tycoon avoids tax because thanks to the well-paid efforts of his lawyers, he is acting in some elaborate scheme that is within the law. Thus the great gap between rich and poor is aggravated even more. This gap is, in my opinion, one of the greatest problems of our age, and we ignore it at our peril.

However, we should appreciate that economic reforms did at least, at first, produce great wealth, spread throughout Australian society. If things seem to be in need of urgent reform now, it may be that the law will have to interfere, perhaps in new types of laws, which we have not seen before.

When I started in the law I was taught to admire the law rather uncritically. Then I started to see its faults only too clearly, and then I appreciated the problems.

I think that great progress has been made over the last half-century but we cannot be complacent. There are many more problems for the law to try to solve.

# 29

# Looking Back

I retired at the end of June 2000. I was then 74 years of age, and a little tired of being a daily gladiator in the courts.

I started off in the law as a very young man with all the enthusiasm and confidence of youth. I threw myself into politics, and local government. I was also on the local church council.

I was lucky enough to have an ideal marriage with Jean, and my daughters Dorothy, Mary and Josephine have been good children and have each achieved success in their respective chosen professions. Jean successfully pursued her career as a science teacher after our youngest daughter, Josie, could go to school by herself. All the girls went to Queenwood School where Jean taught, so my wife was a mother and a teacher almost simultaneously.

For myself, I did my best to allot my time between family and practice so that the former did not suffer. My interest in nature and the bush and birds and animals was shared by Jean and my children. My domestic life has been a happy one, despite the normal problems of growing children.

The fact that my own marriage was happy and that my children loved me, made me, I think, more sympathetic to clients with unhappy marriages and rebellious children. There were many such clients.

I became well familiar with how cruel members of a family could be to each other. For example, one of my clients did not know that his daughter, living in the same house, was being married. His wife went off with the bride to the church, and the father knew nothing until days later. One of my earliest big property cases was a son against his father and I never did become immune to the miseries of some family lives.

In my own family Jean and I preserved a rule that no quarrel would last overnight, whether between us or with a child. The old saying 'Let not the sun go down on thy wrath' is one of the most useful guides to a happy family life. We all had our ups and downs and this rule was frequently invoked.

I had overworked in the McDermott case before my marriage and paid a health penalty with my digestion for the rest of my life. However, this never incapacitated me or even handicapped me in many bouts of hard work and emotional court appearances. It did serve as a convenient brake to force me to rest if I pushed myself too hard.

I was lucky to have powers of intense concentration. This often enabled me to find simple answers to apparently difficult problems concealed in enormous files of papers. I also had some good secretaries, especially Lesley Wilson my last secretary.

My progress at the bar was quite slow, certainly in comparison to some of the high flyers. By the time I had my accident in 1983 my practice was quite a good QC's practice, but by no means all that outstanding. My time in hospital and recovering at home was the turning point in my life.

By that time my youngest daughter, Josie, was married. Mary was also married and a very good veterinary surgeon, the profession I might have practised myself if I had not become a lawyer. Dorothy had published several books of poetry and was well on her way to wider recognition. Both Mary and Josie had won university medals in veterinary studies and social work respectively. I was a proud father.

I had a lot of time to think and had quite a deal of pain and incapacity before I recovered from my injuries. It is strange how one's own suffering makes one understand the suffering of others. I had been in a wheelchair for weeks and on crutches for months. As I recovered I realised how lucky I was and how unlucky others were.

All this made me reluctant to prosecute cases and anxious to defend. There was one time when I appeared for the Crown before the Court of Criminal Appeal and had the respondent's sentence (for dealing in cannabis) substantially increased. As I came out of court I passed by weeping friends and relatives of the respondent and I felt rotten.

Of course, by the rules of the bar one must appear for whoever wants to brief you in the courts where you normally practise. I was lucky that Crown briefs fell away after my accident and I became a leading counsel for the defence. It was then 1985 and in March of that year I turned 59 years of age.

I suppose few professional men and women do not reach their peak until they are almost 60. I was 59 during the Foord case. I was 60 when I started the Chamberlain case. In my seventies I won some of my most difficult murder cases, and also victories in the Appeal Courts. I am a good example of the stupidity of retiring professional men and women when they turn 60.

When I was young I had to watch my temper in court. As I grew older I learned the golden rule that an advocate may appear to be angry, but one's temper must never be lost. One must always be in full control.

As a young man I thought I knew most of the answers, and I did in fact have some good ideas. The trouble with age and experience is that one loses faith in one's own ideas. It is so easy to become a person capable of knocking down everyone else's good ideas, and one's own as well. It is easy to find the negative, but hard to maintain the positive.

For over half of my career I was anxious to be a judge. I thought that I was reasonably balanced and impartial. For some years it was rumoured from time to time that I was about to be appointed. If there was anything in those rumours, someone was blocking me. This put me off the bench, and as I grew older I liked less and less the idea of judging my fellow man, until I positively recoiled against it. By that time I was too old to be appointed.

I am glad now that I never was a judge. Perhaps looking back I would have found it unbearable to preside over a trial if I thought the jury had convicted an innocent person. Perhaps at the end of my career I was too conscious of the law's shortcomings, despite the legal reforms over the years.

One interesting fact is that throughout my professional life I never made a formal complaint against anyone in the legal profession, even for not paying my fees. I had quite a few grievances over the years but I refrained from making any complaints to the authorities. I have no regrets that I did not.

On the other hand, I had to defend myself (successfully) against a professional complaint and I successfully defended many of my fellow barristers against such complaints.

These days professional complaints in all professions are much more frequent. Partly this is good because it deters misbehaviour. Partly this is bad because it encourages spiteful and petty complaints.

I have very much enjoyed the fellowship of the bar. I made a point of trying not to quarrel with my opponents. Sometimes this was not easy, but I was usually successful. Quarrels in court do not assist the court or the clients, and sometimes such quarrels can result in feuds that run for years. I was never involved in such a feud.

By and large I found the company and conversation of my fellow barristers exhilarating. I was in a good barristers' floor, firstly in the old Denman Chambers, then on the 12th floor of Selborne Chambers, and then the 12th floor merged with the 12th floor of Wentworth Chambers to become a large floor. Over the years I have had many good companions on my floor in chambers. Among many I particularly note my friend and former junior Brian Sully QC, now a Justice of the Supreme Court. He has the ideal temperament for a judge. My friend Rodney Parker QC was forced by health to retire soon after me and we still enjoy following the stories of the law.

When I took silk I was very serious about the old idea that a silk should always be ready to help a junior. If the junior was in trouble the silk should drop everything to help him. On many occasions I have interrupted important conferences to do just that. My solicitors and clients understood what I was doing.

In normal cases the junior, not necessarily from your floor in chambers, could at a convenient time obtain the silk's assistance in any problem he or she had. It was a compliment to the silk if he was chosen to help.

Of course, juniors and seniors discussed cases with each other and obtained assistance from time to time. I had a bad memory for case names but had made indexed notes of my legal researches over many years, and these were very useful to me and often to my colleagues.

I had a very happy relationship with my fellow barristers on the 12th floor of Selbourne Chambers and many counsel who had been my juniors. When I had been 50 years at the bar they commissioned a painting of myself by Graeme Inson which I have at home as a memento.

After I retired I was made an Honorary Life Member of the Bar Association, an honour which I value very much.

Now in my retirement as I look back on a career of many ups and downs, of victories and losses, I know that I enjoyed it.

I have had many good juniors, and quite a few are now judges. There was Bob Greenhill, now SC, a loyal, capable, hard worker; Peter Johnson SC, very learned in criminal law; Des Anderson QC; Stephen Stanton; Jock Dailly SC, a stringent cross-examiner; Judge Judith Gibson who is a good lawyer and a great discerner of the truth in conflicting fact questions; Bill Caldwell QC whose scientific work in the Chamberlain case was outstanding; Paul Byrne SC, a brilliant lawyer; Justice Brian Sully; Justice Greg James; Justice Peter Rose; Rodney Parker QC; and Bob Baker. There were many others, notably Peter Hastings (now QC), Peter Maiden, John Robson and Patricia Hanna. I hope they learned something from me.

There is marvellous teamwork in running a case. I was lucky to have some very good instructing solicitors. I particularly remember Gordon Beard, Tony McDonald, Greg Walsh and Warren Madgwick.

With a good solicitor and a good junior one could have very useful conferences before the case went to court. The law has a camaraderie among its practitioners which is one of its most attractive features.

Some of my friends have retired, some no longer survive in this life. I found at the end I was no longer 'young Chester'. Towards the end of my career the co-accused of one of my clients told his counsel 'Don't offend the old man', meaning me.

At the end of 57 years in the law, 52 as a barrister, it was time to hang up my wig in 2000. At last I was able to sit back and look at the law. When one is in one's late seventies, it is not so easy to see the answers to the many problems raised by the law – but it never was.

A great problem in legal practice is overwork. Those who consistently overwork can find themselves mentally punch-drunk. It is vital in court to have an alert mind, not a tired mind.

Activities outside the law are of great assistance in keeping one's mind fresh. I had my interest in and love of living things as my constant refuge from the law. I kept poultry and animals at home. I was always a great dog lover.

Jean and I were great bush walkers, not to cover distance, but to observe the life of the Australian bush, mammals, birds, reptiles and plants. We were both birdwatchers, but we were interested in anything living in nature.

Being even an amateur naturalist is a humbling experience. One may read, observe and study over a lifetime and at the end there is so much more to learn. The wonderful patterns of creation never cease to intrigue me, just as living things entrance me. Whenever I went to country towns to do law cases I took my field-glasses with me.

My mother was quite right to guide me into the law. But I was able to pursue my interest in birds and animals, nature and the bush as well. Now I have a little more time.